The Interior Sense of Scripture
The Sacred Hermeneutics of John W. Nevin

Cover. *Jesus with the Doctors* (Luke 2), a nineteenth-century woodcut
(by A. Bertrano) of an illustration by (Paul-) Gustave Doré (1832–1883).

1. *Reimagining America. A Theological Critique*
   of the American Mythos and Biblical Hermeneutics
        by Charles Mabee
2. *Norman Perrin's Interpretation of the New Testament.*
   From "Exegetical Method" to "Hermeneutical Process"
        by Calvin R. Mercer
3. *The Community of Interpreters. On the Hermeneutics of Nature*
   and the Bible in the American Philosophical Tradition
        by Robert S. Corrington
4. *The Poetics of Revelation. Recognition and the Narrative Tradition*
        by Diana Culbertson
5. *Faith and the Play of the Imagination.*
   On the Role of Imagination in Religion
        by David J. Bryant
6. *The Second Naiveté. Barth, Ricoeur, and the New Yale Theology*
        by Mark I. Wallace
7. *Reading Sacred Texts through American Eyes.*
   Biblical Interpretation as Cultural Critique
        by Charles Mabee
8. *Hermeneutics as Theological Prolegomena. A Canonical Approach*
        by Charles J. Scalise
9. *A Common Sense Theology. The Bible, Faith, and American Society*
        by Mark Ellingsen
10. *The Politics of Biblical Theology. A Postmodern Reading*
        by David Penchansky
11. *Making Sense of New Testament Theology.*
    "Modern" Problems and Prospects
        by A. K. M. Adam
12. *Theology as Cultural Critique. The Achievement of Julian Hartt*
        by Jonathan R. Wilson
13. *Beyond the Impasse. The Promise of a Process Hermeneutic*
        by Ronald L. Farmer
14. *The Interior Sense of Scripture.*
    The Sacred Hermeneutics of John W. Nevin
        by William DiPuccio

The Interior Sense of Scripture

The Sacred Hermeneutics of John W. Nevin

by
William DiPuccio

MERCER UNIVERSITY PRESS

ISBN 0-86554-568-5   MUP/P167

The Interior Sense of Scripture.
The Sacred Hermeneutics of John W. Nevin.
Copyright ©1998
Mercer University Press, Macon, Georgia 31210-3960 USA

Library of Congress Cataloging-in-Publication Data

DiPuccio, William, 1958–
The interior sense of scripture :
the sacred hermeneutics of John W. Nevin /
by William DiPuccio.
xii+228pp. 6x9" (15x23cm.) —
(Studies in American biblical hermeneutics ; 14)
Includes bibliographical references and indexes.
ISBN 0-86554-568-5 (pbk. : alk. paper).
1. Nevin, John Williamson, 1803–1886.
2. Reformed Church—United States—Doctrines—History
—19th century.   3. Mercersburg theology.
I. Title.   II. Series.
BX9593.N4D57   1998
230'.57'092—dc21   97-45763
                                            CIP

Contents

*To the memory of
John Williamson Nevin,
and all those who share his passion for Christ,
and his passion for truth.*

Editor's Preface

The soul of American biblical hermeneutics is prophetic. Why? Because at its core, American biblical hermeneutics is cultural critique. Those who labor at the intersection of the Bible and American culture are seeking an alternative vantage point from which to observe and address the vast panorama of the American experience. What American biblical scholar worth his or her salt has not found encouragement and inspiration in Amos, Isaiah, Jeremiah, or another of those strange men ancient Israel coughed up out of its soul to reflect back an imaginative image of itself? What American theologian has not lain awake the better part of at least one night wondering if God will not take the frail words that roll off her or his pen and turn them into a mighty sword that will slay the obstacles that keep America from achieving its true destiny—as those very same Israelite prophets of old attempted in their society? In that restricted sense it is not too far off the mark to speak of the grammar of American biblical hermeneutics as being rather "Hebraic," deeply anchored in the lifeblood of those who came before and inspired what we have come to know as the Western religious tradition.

The volume before us maps out the contours of the hermeneutical work of the Mercersburg theologian John W. Nevin—which this volume's author, Bill DiPuccio, terms in a word "transcendental" or "incarnational." If the source of the ancient prophetic tradition was in some sense transcendental, then it follows logically that it is important to preserve something of that same transcendental source for the modern world, lest we risk the loss of the authentic critical voice itself. Nevin provides us with a model of one way to do that.

One of the fundamental perceptions that DiPuccio plays Nevin's thought off against is Scottish Common Sense Realism, especially as it has generally been rethought in the American context. In an earlier volume in this series, *A Common Sense Theology* (StABH 9), Mark Ellingsen made his argument for a grassroots approach to American theology rooted in common sense. While certainly not intellectually congruent with the territory staked out in the present volume, the two works may be fruitfully approached as two poles of a spectrum. It may be the case that these two arguments *need* each other to be complete, especially if either or both are to blossom in American soil. It might well be that these two authors have grabbed the "American elephant" from opposite ends. I will not even attempt an answer to this question in the short space allotted this preface, but only suggest it as a possibility. Both approaches eagerly seek to confront a culture perceived to have gone seriously awry. Both have important things to say. May the readers of both texts decide between them—or for both of them!

This is an important issue for those of us trained in Eurocentric historical-criticism of the Bible (called by Nevin "grammatical-historical method"), and we will have our cages rattled yet one more time by this book. As all practitioners of Eurocentric historical-criticism may readily acknowledge, there is very little "transcendental" about it. Yet, it is important to hear this criticism from a fresh angle that is neither postmodern nor fundamentalistic. Here is a reasoned argument that is set against the background of a broad, rich understanding of the Western philosophical tradition. Nevin's primary concern was not to allow the collapse of faith into the merely human. In defending this approach DiPuccio does battle with many sacred cows of the late twentieth century, such as liberation theology, the social gospel, intellectual skepticism, and the like. Like Nevin before him, DiPuccio will not allow the dissolution of the Christian religion into ethical thought. He relentlessly follows this principle to the edges of the intellectual topography of the American experience. The key point, of course, is the transformation of society. The argument laid out here will finally be judged by its power to *transform*. That seems to be the question historical-criticism itself must ultimately face, and it is one which likewise must be faced by a transcendental hermeneutics.

This book is a clarion call to abandon the modern gods of subjectivism and perspectivalism. It seeks to reclaim ancient truths buried deep in the Christian psyche that have all but been covered up in an age when political correctness dominates our universities, and the established "mainstream" seminaries that derive much of their intellectual capital from them. The "struggle for the Bible" (that is, how we choose to interpret the Bible) is finally the open window on the soul of the American church. This book provides us with a paradigm for biblical study that is both old and stunning in its freshness. It is an alternative voice that perhaps needs to be heard today more than ever if we are to keep alive the hope for prophetic voices in our midst.

Ecumenical Theological Seminary, Detroit   *Charles Mabee*
15 February 1998

Acknowledgments

This book began as an M.A. thesis ten years ago under the guidance of Timothy Phillips and Mark Noll at Wheaton College. It was subsequently developed into a doctoral dissertation (tripling in size) at Marquette University. The historical, theological, philosophical, and stylistic direction provided by Patrick Carey helped to turn a protracted work into a highly focussed monograph. Publication became a reality when I contacted Edmon L. Rowell, Jr., senior editor at Mercer University Press, almost three years ago. Seeing the hermeneutical possibilities in my manuscript, Edd placed me in communication with Charles Mabee, the editor of Mercer's Studies in American Biblical Hermeneutics series. Charles's suggestions have helped me achieve a hermeneutical focus, reduce a bulky manuscript to publishable size, and smooth over some of the more difficult parts. Moreover, owing to Charles's recommendation, I have attempted to place Nevin's hermeneutics in dialogue with contemporary ideas where appropriate.

Special mention needs to be made of Mark Noll who has not only shown a special interest in my scholarly and professional development over the years, but was willing to recommend this work for publication. I am also grateful to Justin Miller, my *gespräch* partner, who, by providing invaluable feedback, has helped me develop many of my ideas and connections. Finally, and not to be forgotten, is the support of my wife Barbara and daughter Rebeccah who tarried many long hours as I was preparing the manuscript for publication.

William DiPuccio

Abbreviations

HF   Nevin, John W. "Human Freedom." In *Human Freedom and A Plea for Philosophy: Two Essays*. Mercersburg PA: P. A. Rice, 1850. Originally published in *The American Review: a Whig journal devoted to politics and literature* 7 (April 1848): 406-18.

IP   Gerhart, Emanuel V. *An Introduction to the Study of Philosophy with an Outline Treatise on Logic*. Philadelphia: Reformed Church Publishing Board, 1857.

LW   Appel, Theodore. *The Life and Work of John Williamson Nevin*. Philadelphia: The Reformed Church Publishing House, 1889.

MP   Nevin, John W. *The Mystical Presence. A Vindication of the Reformed or Calvinistic Doctrine of the Holy Eucharist*. Philadelphia: J. B. Lippincott & Co., 1846.

MR   *The Mercersburg Review* (1849–1878) and *The Reformed Quarterly Review* (1879–1896).

NT   Erb, William H., ed. *Dr. Nevin's Theology, Based on Manuscript Class Room Lectures*. Reading PA: I. M. Beaver, 1913.

PFP   Nevin, John W. "A Plea for Philosophy." In *Human Freedom and A Plea for Philosophy: Two Essays*. Mercersburg PA: P. A. Rice, 1850. Originally published in *The American Review: a Whig journal devoted to politics and literature* 7 (Feb 1848): 143-55.

PR   *The Biblical Repertory and Princeton Review*

Psy   Rauch, F. A. *Psychology; or, a View of the Human Soul*. Fourth edition with a notice by John W. Nevin. New York: M. W. Dodd, 1846.

ST   Hodge, Charles. *Systematic Theology*. Three volumes. New York: Scribner, 1872–1873; repr.: Grand Rapids MI: Wm. B. Eerdmans Publishing Co., 1981.

WM   *Weekly Messenger of the German Reformed Church* (1840–1848), *German Reformed Messenger* (1848–1867), and *Reformed Church Messenger* (1867–1875).

Introduction

A Crisis in Hermeneutics

Many people have difficulty conceiving how a bishop who has repudiated nearly every line of the Nicene Creed could recite that same creed in good faith every Sunday; or, how a priest or minister who has vowed to teach and uphold the apostolic faith could approve of homosexual behavior; or, how an evangelical who holds strenuously to the letter of Scripture could become an advocate of women's ordination. A sea change has swept over much of the church in the last forty years. But, like the theological liberalism of the early twentieth century, this move toward secularization and cultural accommodation was not an attempt to jettison Scripture and tradition, but to *reinterpret* it.

As a result, there is a hermeneutical crisis in the church and the academy. Pluralism and individualism, the golden calf of Western society, have become an idol in the temple. Interpretations and methodologies are multiplying *ad infinitum* (some would say *ad nauseam!*).[1] There is no longer a normative context, method, or authority for understanding Scripture and tradition. Contradictions and incongruities abound. At times it would appear we are on the brink of religious solipsism.

Those who celebrate this ambiguity, diversity, and inclusiveness forget that even their most cherished beliefs are now on the chopping block. For example, in my own church (Episcopal) a large number of clergy, ethicists, and theologians have attempted to vindicate homosexual behavior and premarital sex by appealing to such virtues as love, toleration, and social justice. Our interpre-

---

[1] For a survey of modern hermeneutical systems, see Anthony Thiselton, *New Horizons in Hermeneutics* (Grand Rapids MI: Zondervan, 1992).

tation of revelation, they remind us, is necessarily ambiguous and provisional because the Bible does not disclose God's mind and will to us; rather, it is the record of human response to God's revelation. Like those ancient communities who first received the word of God, our response is contextually limited by the changing social, historical, and cultural conditions of our time. Our experience is theologically and hermeneutically normative. Consequently, traditional standards of sexuality must give way to new standards which reflect the realities of our particular situation.

Given these constraints, however, is it still possible to unambiguously maintain that God is a God of love, toleration, and social justice? When we consider the boundless, senseless misery of our world, the Holocaust, and the daily starvation and abuse of innocent children, is it not reasonable to conclude from our *experience* that if there is a God, then He is not at all like the God of love, toleration, and social justice to whom contemporary thought often appeals? If the church has so completely misunderstood the nature of human sexuality which is merely finite, then perhaps it has also failed to discern the true character of God who is both mysterious and infinite. Moreover, why should love, toleration, and social justice be elevated to the exclusion or neglect of other characteristics (such as holiness, chastity, etc.) except to serve some political agenda (a hermeneutics of suspicion) or reduce Christianity to a form of natural law? In the end, the hermeneutics which seems to make greater love, toleration, and inclusiveness possible is forced to deconstruct the very foundation on which it stands.

A *transcendental* hermeneutic is needed if we are to avoid the incongruities and nihilism inherent in a system founded on the vicissitudes of human experience. It is with this in mind that we enter into the thought of John W. Nevin, the architect of what has come to be known as the "Mercersburg Theology" (see below). In Nevin's view, Christianity is not a "long search" for meaningful existence, but a true *incarnation* of the divine in human life, thought, and language. Revelation, therefore, is not buried or obscured by the fog of human experience. Instead, it illuminates our experience and renders it transparent. As Nevin pointed out, Jesus claimed to be "the light of the world." His uncreated radiance is the source of all truth. "He who follows me, shall not walk in darkness, but shall have the light of life" (John 8:12). The dim and lurid light of sinful humanity can never be the first light of faith, knowledge, or theological reflection. How, after all, as Nevin once asked, can Jesus be the Light of the World if we must look *first* to the light of our own experience in order to find Him?

Nevin's transcendental and even mystical hermeneutics is presented here to the church and the academy as a postcritical but orthodox alternative to modern and postmodern systems. His philosophical, historical, and theological depth will appeal to a wide range of contemporary thinkers who are engaged in hermeneutical reflection. His critique of American culture and religion will interest social historians, philosophers, and theologians. Catholic and Orthodox readers will appreciate Nevin's paradigmatic use of the Incarnation along with his eucharistic and liturgical emphasis. Protestant's will value his stress on the centrality of the word. Pentecostal and charismatic theologians will appreciate his sophisticated supernaturalism. Finally, evangelicals will find in Nevin's hermeneutics a welcome alternative to the hermeneutics of Common Sense Realism.

This work, which is based on my doctoral dissertation,[2] is part of a renaissance in Mercersburg studies. The formation of the Mercersburg Society (1983) and the publication of the *New Mercersburg Review* marked the beginning of this era. Since then, four major works on Nevin's early colleague, Philip Schaff, have been published.[3] An important collection of essays on Nevin's thought and a social theology of Nevin have recently appeared.[4] Other pub-

---

[2]See William DiPuccio, "The Dynamic Realism of Mercersburg Theology: The Romantic Pursuit of the Ideal in the Actual" (Ph.D. diss., Marquette University, 1994).

[3]George H. Schriver, *Philip Schaff: Christian Scholar and Ecumenical Prophet* (Macon GA: Mercer University Press, 1987); Henry W. Bowden, ed., *A Century of Church History: The Legacy of Philip Schaff* (Carbondale: Southern Illinois Universtiy Press, 1988); Klaus Penzel, ed., *Philip Schaff: Historian and Ambassador of the Universal Church. Selected Writings* (Macon GA: Mercer University Press, 1991); Stephen R. Graham, *Cosmos in the Chaos: Philip Schaff's Interpretation of Nineteenth-Century American Religion* (Grand Rapids MI: Eerdmans, 1995).

[4]Sam Hamstra, Jr. and Arie J. Griffioen, eds., *Reformed Confessionalism in Nineteenth Century America: Essays on the Thought of John Williamson Nevin,*

lications are also in preparation, including a monograph on his pastoral theology and a collection of general essays on Mercersburg theology.[5] A critical edition of Nevin's collected works is currently under consideration.

Historical Background[6]

The America of 1850 was a frontier by today's standards. Comprised of only 30 states, there still remained vast tracts of largely unexplored territory, unconnected by highway or rail. Americans were, for the most part, very parochial in their view of the world. Infected by the individualism of Jacksonian democracy, bounded and isolated by two major oceans, and preoccupied with the building of a continent, they were generally oblivious and even hostile to the new philosophies which had taken hold in Europe a generation before. Many thinkers were still in the grip of the Enlightenment, though the next twenty to thirty years would bring about profound changes.

The Mercersburg Theology was a German Reformed system of thought which flourished in the 1840s and 1850s in south-central Pennsylvania. (Mercersburg was the location of the seminary where Nevin taught.) With links to both German and English thought, Mercersburg was characterized by its high-church, incarnational, historical, and philosophical approach to theology. Dominant characters included philosophical theologian John Williamson Nevin (1803–1886), church historian Philip Schaff (1819–1893), philosopher Frederick A. Rauch (1806–1841), and philosophical theologian Emanuel V. Gerhart (1817–1904).

One of the lasting contributions of the Mercersburg theology was its attempt to mediate between different currents in nine-

---

American Theological Library Association Monograph Series (Lanham MD: Scarecrow Press, 1995); Richard E. Wentz, *John Williamson Nevin: American Theologian* (Oxford University Press, 1997).

[5]Theodore Trost, ed., *Tradition and Trajectory: The Mercersburg Movement in the 21st Century* (forthcoming).

[6]For a general history of Mercersburg theology, see James H. Nichols, *Romanticism in American Theology: Nevin and Schaff at Mercersburg* (Chicago: University of Chicago Press, 1961).

teenth-century theology. The Romantic theology of Schleiermacher and Augustus Neander, the so-called mediating theologies of Karl Ullmann, Isaac Dorner, Karl Liebner, and Richard Rothe, and the idealism of Schelling, Hegel, and even Samuel Taylor Coleridge were used in the service of a Reformed theology which, in its own right, attempted to fuse Protestantism with ancient Catholicism.

John Williamson Nevin[7] was, undoubtedly, the theological genius behind Mercersburg theology. The oldest of nine children, he was born in Pennsylvania of Scotch-Irish stock. At the age of fourteen he entered Union College. Due to a recurring illness, which plagued him for more than half of his life, he was forced to spend two years on the home farm following graduation. In 1823 he began a three-year course at Princeton where he mastered Hebrew, though with great reluctance. Between 1826 and 1828, he served as professor of Hebrew Language and Literature while his own professor, Charles Hodge, studied in Europe. After his ordination in the Presbyterian church, Nevin supplied the pulpit at Newville, Pennsylvania for almost two years. In 1830, he was called to the chair of Hebrew and Biblical Literature at the newly formed Western Seminary in Allegheny. He continued there until 1840, during which time he supplied nearby congregations, edited a weekly literary journal called *The Friend*, received his doctor of divinity from Jefferson College, and began his study of German theology.

In 1840 Nevin accepted a call from the German Reformed church to succeed Professor Lewis Mayer at the Mercersburg Theological Seminary. He enjoyed a brief, but significant, friendship with Frederick Augustus Rauch (1806–1841) whose German idealism would exercise a considerable influence on Nevin's theology. In addition to his own obligations, Nevin took on Rauch's duties as president of Marshall College. The school was continually in need of financial support and Nevin labored for years, with less

---

[7]For biographical information, see Theodore Appel, *The Life and Work of John Williamson Nevin* (Philadelphia: Reformed Church Publishing House, 1889), hereafter *LW*; John W. Nevin, *My Own Life: The Early Years*, (1870; repr.: Lancaster PA: Historical Society of the Reformed Church, 1964); William M. Reily, "John Williamson Nevin, D.D., LL.D," *Magazine of Christian Literature* 2 (September 1890): 324-27.

than adequate compensation, in an attempt to stabilize the failing institution. The arrival of Philip Schaff from Germany in 1844 provided some relief.

Nevin entered on a number of controversies during this decade which made him unpopular in some quarters. He registered his opposition to "New Measures" revivalism in *The Anxious Bench* (1843),[8] calling for a return to the Reformed system of catechism. He defended Schaff's controversial inaugural address and wrote a lengthy introduction to Schaff's now-famous work, *The Principle of Protestantism* (1845). In 1846 he published one of his most controversial books: *The Mystical Presence: A Vindication of the Reformed or Calvinistic Doctrine of the Holy Eucharist.* This brought him into direct conflict with his old mentor, Charles Hodge. The dispute generated hundreds of pages of journal articles and drove a permanent wedge between Mercersburg and Princeton.[9]

In his *History and Genius of the Heidelberg Catechism* (1847),[10] Nevin again expressed his high regard for Reformed confessionalism and challenged the church to uphold it. Perhaps the most stinging polemic was contained in *Antichrist, or the Spirit of Sect and Schism* (1848).[11] Here Nevin argued for a unified, catholic church. Schism is rooted in a heretical disregard for the Incarnation. Discontinuity in the church is no more than practical gnosticism.

Nevin's high-church tendencies continued to burgeon into the early 1850s. They came to full expression in his journal articles, especially those published in the *Mercersburg Review* in 1851 and 1852. There can be little doubt that Nevin came close to capitulating to Catholicism. This accounts, in part, for his resignation from the seminary in 1851. The Protestants of his day were vehement in their criticism of the Roman church. To Nevin, who

---

[8]See John W. Nevin, *The Anxious Bench*, 2nd ed. (Chambersburg PA: M. Kieffer & Co., 1846).
[9]See John W. Nevin, *The Mystical Presence. A Vindication of the Reformed or Calvinistic Doctrine of the Holy Eucharist* (Philadelphia: J. B. Lippincott & Co., 1846); hereafter *MP*.
[10]See John W. Nevin, *History and Genius of the Heidelberg Catechism* (Chambersburg PA: Publication Office of the German Reformed Church, 1847).
[11]See John W. Nevin, *Antichrist, Or the Spirit of Sect and Schism* (New York: John S. Taylor, 1848).

found strains of true piety even in medieval Catholicism, this was evidence of a nearly total defection from the ancient life of the church. If the Reformation stood in continuity with the medieval church as it claimed, then we should expect to find at least some sympathy with Catholicism and the sacramental church life. But the total absence of such sympathy, indeed the violent repudiation of these very elements, caused Nevin to wonder about the legitimacy of Protestantism.

Despite his "Romanizing" tendencies, the Synod in Lancaster overwhelmingly gave Nevin a vote of confidence upon his withdrawal from the seminary. He continued to serve as president of Marshall College until it was moved to Lancaster in 1853. In 1855 Nevin himself moved to Lancaster and later (during the Civil War) joined the faculty of Franklin and Marshall College as professor of Philosophy, History, and Aesthetics. In 1866 he was elected president and continued in that position for ten years. During that time he was involved in a major dispute over the use of liturgy in the German Reformed church.

In his remaining years (1870–1886), Nevin's attention turned mainly toward the inspiration and interpretation of the Scriptures. As a Presbyterian, he wrote a number of lengthy articles on the Bible and its interpretation before coming to Mercersburg in 1840. His later interest in hermeneutics is, in one sense, a return to this earlier emphasis on the word while teaching at Western Theological Seminary.

Nevin engaged in a lifelong polemic against American religion and culture. The majority of his writings, especially during the Mercersburg period (1840–1853) were directed against what he believed were systemic errors in theology and philosophy. Specifically, his target was the Enlightenment *Weltanschauung* fostered by Scottish Common Sense Realism. This was the philosophical and theological tradition in which he was trained at Princeton and it represented a well-defined consensus in early nineteenth-century American philosophy and theology.

It was not the pietism of Princeton or its Presbyterian confessionalism which Nevin objected to (though he considered these to be tainted by subjectivism and rationalism), but the nominalistic bias (see below) of the Princeton theology embodied preeminently in his former mentor, Charles Hodge. By contrast Nevin rarely attacked Transcendentalism or Roman Catholicism. In many ways, his mysticism, idealism, and high church theology were much closer in spirit to the beliefs of these institutions than to Princeton.

Nevin believed that the Common Sense worldview was tied inexorably to the American ethos. With its bold and sharply defined view of reality, its confidence in the senses, and its emphasis on utility and practicality, the Common Sense tradition was eminently qualified as the representative philosophy of the young republic. Nevin's polemic against Princeton and Scottish Realism was as much a commentary on American culture, thought, and education as it was a critique of Princeton's theology. In a way, the Common Sense tradition represented everything that was wrong with American theology and culture. As Nevin saw it, Common Sense contained the seeds of materialism, religious skepticism, and individualism, which in the end could only serve to destroy church and society.[12]

The Philosophical and Hermeneutical Issues

In order to grasp the significance of Nevin's incarnational theology for language, hermeneutics, and American culture, we must briefly consider the historical and philosophical context of his ideas.[13] Though more than a century has elapsed since Nevin's time, we are still facing many of the same philosophical and hermeneutical questions that Nevin grappled with in the nineteenth century. Moreover, the seemingly obtuse philosophical issues which Nevin addressed have profound and sometimes unexpected consequences for hermeneutics and American culture. Materialism, skepticism, and individualism—issues that are still

---

[12]Nevin's argument stands in full contrast to Mark Ellingsen's recent claim that Common Sense was and still is an eminently suitable philosophical vehicle for conveying the Christian faith in America. See Mark Ellingsen, *A Common Sense Theology: The Bible, Faith, and American Society* (Macon GA: Mercer University Press, 1995).

[13]For a more thorough and nuanced exploration of Nevin's philosophy, theology, and intellectual background, I would refer the reader to my dissertation (n. 2, above).

alive and well in Western society—are, at least in part, the product of cultural presuppositions rooted in the Enlightenment.

Following Kant, one of the burning questions posed by nineteenth-century philosophy was the relation of the mind to reality: Can we know things as they really are? To what degree is our knowledge determined or conditioned by our experience or the structures of our own minds? These epistemological considerations played an active role in shaping Mercersburg theology. Insofar as this was true, Nevin and his colleagues identified with the modern philosophical tradition.

The problematic relationship between reality and mind also reveals another dimension of the challenge Nevin faced: the radical dualism between mind and matter, God and world, inherited from the philosophy of René Descartes (1596–1650). Modified forms of Cartesian dualism had been virtually assumed by Locke and Kant. Owing in part to the pervasive influence of Scottish Common Sense Realism (a form of empiricism) on American culture, dualism became a defining characteristic of American theology and philosophy, as well as popular revivalism and spirituality. Nevin's goal, however, was to bring this dualism to an end by demonstrating the organic unity (but not identity) of mind and matter, God and creation.

This synthesis was accomplished, in part, by adapting Kant's philosophy. Unlike their evangelical Reformed opponents at Princeton who, for the most part, attempted to circumvent Kant by clinging to eighteenth-century Scottish Realism, Mercersburg went right through Kant. By critically adapting the idealism of Hegel and Schelling, Nevin and his colleagues emerged on the other side of the Kantian philosophy with new metaphysical optimism. Thus the solution to the problem of mind and reality as we have it in the Mercersburg theology was shaped largely by post-Kantian idealism.

Standing behind this, however, was a deeply spiritual form of Christian Platonism. Nevin found Plato conducive to the mystical inclinations which grew out of his Puritanical religion. He struggled with the subjective rationalism that evolved from eighteenth-century pietism. While he was sympathetic to pietism, he rejected its one-sided subjectivity. However, in English divines like the Platonist John Howe (1630–1705) and Archbishop Robert Leighton (1611–1684) he found a corresponding objectivity which brought to life the reality of the spiritual realm. As Nevin explains it, "It had to do with *ideas* at least, which were held to be of objective force, and not merely subjective notions and fancies."[14]

So, for Nevin this epistemological problem turned primarily upon the ontological reality of *universal ideas* and their relationship to the world of space and time. Without general concepts like "humanity," "tree," "beauty," and "justice," human knowledge could not exist. These are the categories which enable us to unite the manifold fragments of our experience into intelligible wholes.

But, are these universal ideas *objective* and independent of individual minds, or simply the *subjective* products of human thought? Are they merely generalized descriptions of things, built up and collated from observations of actual phenomena, or the source and cause of all such phenomena, actual and potential? And, what is the relationship between the ideal (which is universal) and the actual (which is finite)? These became the defining philosophical questions for Nevin and Mercersburg theology.

By framing the epistemological question in this way, the Mercersburg theologians drew their philosophical line between *realism* and *nominalism*.[15] After all, the distinction between these two philosophies turns upon the reality and nature of universal ideas. For the most part, Nevin aligned himself on the side of realism which maintains that (1) universal ideas are objective and ontological realities rather than creatures of the mind. (2) These ideas constitute the essence or nature of individuals and natural laws. (3) Universal ideas, therefore, are the foundation of all knowledge.[16]

---

[14]Nevin, *My Own Life*, 122, 12. On Nevin's synthesis of empiricism and post-Kantian Platonism, see DiPuccio, "Dynamic Realism," 62-124. On the early development of Nevin's piety and philosophy, see the series of articles in *The New Mercersburg Review* 17 (Spring 1995).

[15]Historians have ignored the formative role realism and nominalism played in nineteenth-century American religion. However, as this work demonstrates, and as the primary literature of this era clearly shows, the realist/nominalist paradigm poses a viable set of historical, philosophical, and theological categories for analyzing certain intellectual movements in nineteenth-century American theology.

[16]A distinction should be made between ontological and epistemological

In opposition to this, nominalism, which was closely aligned to the empirical tradition and Common Sense philosophy, is predicated on the assumption that (1) only individual things are real. (2) Since every individual is unique, there can be no common nature or essence among them. Nominalism concludes, therefore, that (3) the common names used to designate groups of individuals according to similar attributes are merely subjective abstractions.

These principles are derived from commonsense experience: we move in a world of individually existing things, not in a world of universals, according to nominalists. Consequently, as William J. Courtenay observes concerning William of Ockham, the father of modern nominalism, "it is similarity and universality that need to be explained, not individuation."[17] Indeed, the cornerstone of Ockham's philosophy is that our primary cognition is of individual things rather than universality.[18]

These categories would determine the historical shape of Nevin's theology and his unrelenting critique of American culture and religion. On the one side stood the medieval realism of the Platonic-Aristotelian tradition which was assumed by German idealism; on the other side was the nominalism of the Ockhamist tradition which included the empiricism of Locke, Hume, and Scottish Common Sense.[19] Standing in the middle was Descartes' dualistic philosophy, which while affirming the reality of universals was unable to reconcile the ideal with the world of sense and time.

---

realism. The former is a realism of *natures* in which objects in time and space are said to have an ideal essence. This is the position taken by medieval realism and Mercersburg. The latter is a realism of *things* which asserts that the only objects of experience are concrete and individual. This is the position taken by Common Sense Realism and representative realism (Locke). See Joseph Owens and Lawrence H. Starkey, "Realism," in *The New Encyclopedia Britannica* (Chicago: Encyclopedia Britannica, Inc., 1980) 15:540.

[17]William J. Courtenay, "Ockham, William of" in *Dictionary of the Middle Ages* (New York: Charles Scribner's Sons, 1987) 210.

[18]Meyrick H. Carre, *Realists and Nominalists* (London: Oxford University Press, 1946) 118-19.

[19]On the historical and philosophical connection between Ockham, Locke, and Common Sense Realism, see DiPuccio, "Dynamic Realism," 11-45. Locke's nominalism will be considered in chap. 2.

Like the moderate realists of the Middle Ages, then, Nevin affirmed both the objective reality of the ideal and its organic union with actual existence.[20] Empiricism, on the other hand, generally denied the objective reality of universal ideas. Nevertheless, where a connection with Christianity was maintained (e.g., Locke, Common Sense) it continued to affirm the reality of the supernatural and divine. From Mercersburg's perspective, though, this affirmation was a shallow one. Owing to its Cartesian assumptions, the empirical tradition could never maintain a real interaction—that is, an inward or historical union—between God and the world.

Implications

Nevin recognized the far-reaching implications of nominalism and realism for hermeneutics, philosophy, religion, and culture. Accordingly, part I of our study will focus upon the linguistic and semiotic ramifications of these paradigms in the context of the Incarnation, the sacraments, and the interpretation of Scripture. Of first importance, from Nevin's standpoint, is the nature of language and divine revelation. This issue was grasped by Ockham himself, who, like Locke, concluded that *our knowledge* of God is strictly a mental construction. As Copleston describes it, "We do not attain a reality (*quid rei*), but a nominal representation (*quid nominis*)."[21] It is not as though these representations are meaningless; rather, they are void of any intuitive knowledge of the divine *reality*.

Even before Ockham, Thomas Aquinas clearly discerned this characteristic. Contrary to nominalism, Aquinas insisted that "the act of the believer does not terminate in a proposition but in a thing. For as a science we do not form propositions, except in order to have knowledge about things through their means, so is

---

[20]Respecting the identity and scope of universals, however, Nevin did not characterize every individual as the instantiation of a universal idea. On his critical synthesis of realism and nominalism see DiPuccio, "Dynamic Realism," 154–69.

[21]Frederick Copleston, *A History of Philosophy*, 9 vols. (New York: Image Press, 1946–1974) 3:89.

it in faith."[22] Consequently, Aquinas (as well as Duns Scotus) maintained that our theological distinctions correspond (at least analogically or formally) to the divine attributes.

But, Ockham and Locke believed that God Himself is not the object of our theological inquiry. The object of our analyses is our *concept* of God. The unbeliever can theologize just as well as the believer. The difference, however, is that the believer knows the propositions are true (that is, they correspond to reality) because he or she accepts them on *authority* by faith as God's revelation.

American advocates of Scottish Common Sense were, for the most part, no better. Nineteenth-century Presbyterian theologians often identified the object of faith with the *propositions* of Scripture rather than with Christ Himself. Charles Hodge and others equated the objective side of Christianity with biblical propositions.[23] Like Locke, Common Sense theology viewed revelation as essentially cognitive. Faith consists in believing *that* something is true, rather than being the *means* by which we participate in the realities to which such doctrines point.[24] Such biblical rationalism reasons from abstractions to reality rather than from reality to ideas. Thus a doctrine is said to be true because the Bible teaches it, rather than saying that the Bible teaches it because it is true.

This is not to say, of course, that either Locke or Princeton regarded the words of Scripture as empty abstractions or creatures of the mind. They represented an objective reality, be it historical or spiritual. By virtue of divine authority, the propositions of Scripture were viewed as constitutive knowledge, not simply as heuristic devices. Nevertheless, by shifting the object of faith and the foundation of theology from the historical and spiritual

---

[22]Thomas Aquinas, *Summa Theologica* (New York: Benziger Brothers, 1948; repr.: Westminster MD: Christian Classics, 1981) II-II, 1, 2, ad.2.

[23]Hodge, "What Is Christianity?" *PR* 32 (1860): 119.

[24]Charles Hodge, *Systematic Theology* (New York: Scribner, 1872–1873; repr.: Grand Rapids MI: Eerdmans, 1981) 3:84-85, 44, hereafter *ST*. Says Hodge, Faith is "an affirmation of the mind that a thing is true or trustworthy, but the mind can affirm nothing of that which it knows nothing." At the same time, though, he inconsistently maintained that a person's belief in Christ is based "on the highest possible evidence; the testimony of God himself with and by the truth to his own heart; making him see and feel that it is the truth." Hodge, "Thornwell on the Apocrypha," *PR* 17 (1845): 274.

realities of Christianity to the Scriptures (that is, the *noumenon* to the *nomen*), they unwittingly lapsed into a form of nominalism which, if not actual, was at least *functional* in its effects. For them, as for Ockham and Locke, language became an end in itself instead of a bridge to the spiritual world.

Common Sense was not the only problem to be reckoned with. Kant also stood ensconced in the nominalist tradition of Ockham, Locke, and Hume. Though he had successfully assailed the citadel of empiricism by demonstrating the inability of reason to move from finite knowledge to a knowledge of the transcendent, he also destroyed the metaphysical bridge between phenomenal and noumenal reality leaving nothing but uncertainty in its place. Speculative knowledge of the supersensible, he maintained, can never be constitutive (that is, real). Universals are only regulative constructs since universality cannot be derived from finite experience. God's existence is "merely a *problematical* assumption (hypothesis) regarding the highest cause of things." Though it is possible to have an "assertorial" knowledge of our moral duty (moral imperative), this leads only to faith in "the idea of God" as the "*minimum* of knowledge" necessary to evoke a sense of moral duty. Such faith cannot "certify the objective reality of this idea through theoretical apprehension."[25]

Kant's philosophy had serious implications for Christian *revelation*. As Gerhart pointed out, Kant had reduced all constitutive knowledge to finite categories. Consequently, everything that lies beyond this sphere—the Absolute and Infinite—can "have no objective significance." The bottom line is that both dogmatic and speculative theology are banished from the "catalogue of the sciences" and "the possibility of a supernatural revelation in the Person of Christ is denied."[26] By means of Christ, however, the infinite is revealed *in* the finite. In Nevin's words, "Through the Son there is a real knowing of the Father, and so of the whole

---

[25]Immanuel Kant, *Religion Within the Limits of Reason Alone*, trans. with introduction and notes by Theodore M. Greene and Hoyt H. Hudson, and an essay by John R. Silber (New York: Harper & Row, 1960) 142n.; see also 65n., 48, 179.
[26]Emanuel V. Gerhart, "Mansel's Limits of Religious Thought" *MR* 12 (1860): 295.

trinity; not indeed the infinite knowing which belongs to the Son; but still in its finite degree of one nature with that."[27]

Though Nevin's argument was primarily with the type of nominalism found in Common Sense, his general critique of nominalism was also a repudiation of Kantian religion. Kant's epistemological limitations continue to play a formative role in contemporary theology. Indeed, any system of thought which maintains that God is wholly other, that He is in every respect beyond human thought and language, and that the character, will, and intent of God (that is, all things necessary to salvation) have not been unambiguously revealed, is Kantian in spirit insofar as it perpetuates Kant's dichotomy. That is to say, God, the *ding an sich*, transcends the categories of human thought; consequently our understanding of Him can only be regulative (that is, phenomenal, subjective, experiential) rather than constitutive (that is, noumenal, objective, real).[28] Existentialism, postmodernism, some forms of feminist and liberation theology, and a countless multitude of unnamed "systems," belong to this genre.

In part II, we will consider the religious and cultural impact of realism and nominalism by examining Nevin's unrelenting critique of American society and spirituality. The Marxist philosopher Friedrich Engels (1820–1895) once referred to medieval nominalism as the first form of materialism.[29] Since universal ideas are merely creatures of the mind, our knowledge of reality depends ultimately on sense data. The first function of reason, then, is to operate upon the material world, for it is the senses rather than the mind that

---

[27]Nevin, "Christ the Inspiration of His Own Word," *MR* 29 (1882): 21. See also Gerhart, "Mansel's Limits," 315.

[28]For a critical evaluation of this religious epistemology see Gerhart, "Mansel's Limits," 294-315. Gerhart demonstrates that if the infinite is indeed beyond human conception, then it is impossible to define God negatively as being independent of all relations. For, attributes, states, or relations cannot be denied to what the mind has no conception of. Moreover, if all the attributes, states and relations of an object are not known, then it is logically impossible to deny any.

[29]Friedrich Engels, *Ludwig Feuerbach and the Outcome of Classical German Philosophy*, Marxist Library, 15 (New York: International Publishers, 1935) 84; cited in Etienne Gilson, *The Unity of Philosophical Experience* (New York: Charles Scribner's Sons, 1950) 285. As Gilson points out, Engels mistook Duns Scotus for Ockham in this citation. The relationship between nominalism and materialism will be examined in chap. 4.

establish the vital connection with the world. It is precisely this preoccupation with the material world, and the corresponding belief that only individual (that is, sensible) things are real, that leads to materialism. Consequently, the empirical tradition, which became part and parcel of the American Enlightenment, was naturally predisposed toward incipient materialism. Nevin believed that when Common Sense is carried to its *logical* completion, it must deny the reality of the supernatural, resolving it into the life of nature.

By defining universals as mental constructs used to classify things with similar characteristics, nominalism also paved the way for epistemological skepticism. Since universal ideas are no longer external objects of cognition, they are not capable of public verification. Therefore, they are nothing more than subjective concepts or social conventions at best. But the mind needs these concepts to unite the fragmentary perceptions of reality into an intelligible whole; in other words, without general ideas thought is impossible. Therefore, to question the objectivity of these ideas throws doubt on the objectivity of all our knowledge. The intelligibility of reality becomes problematic. As Locke's philosophy showed, once ideas are regarded as the mediate *products* of our own minds instead of the objective *forms* of reality itself, our own concepts—rather than the real world—become the objects of our perception.[30]

In short, if our knowledge depends primarily on the way *we* classify and name things, then *we* shape reality more than reality shapes us. The question is no longer: What is this? Rather: What is my perception of it? Thus, some philosophers could hold that we do not, in fact, know individual objects and ideas, but only *our ideas about them*. We cannot know reality as it is *in and of itself*.

Finally, since nominalism begins by assuming that only individual things are real, it is no surprise that nineteenth-century "Baconian" theology, which clung firmly to the Common Sense

---

[30]In other words, ideas are *that which* we apprehend when we are conscious of reality, instead of *that by which* we apprehend things. In the first instance, ideas function as instrumental signs (*medium quod*), in the second, as formal signs (*medium quo*). Thus the idea we have of an object is nothing less than the noetic *form* of the object itself. We do not see the idea, but the object through the idea.

tradition, regarded humanity, society, and the church as a collection of individuals instead of an organic whole.[31] Mercersburg regarded this error as the root of radical individualism and sectarianism which would destroy the unity of both the church and American society. Humanity, as Nevin said, is not "a huge living sand-heap," but "the power of a single life."[32]

These, then, are the criticisms Nevin levied against the proponents of Common Sense religion. As an antagonist of nineteenth-century revivalism he is often viewed, even by modern historians, as a dissenter, thanks in part to his famous and oft-quoted work, *The Anxious Bench*. But the story does not end here. Nevin's dissatisfaction with American culture and religion were only preparatory to his own positive theology which was rooted in the Incarnation. So, after brushing away the charred remains of Common Sense theology, he was ready to construct a new edifice. To view his "system" as anything less than positive and vibrant would be a historical oversight.

A Transcendental Hermeneutic

With these concepts in mind it would be easy to conclude that Nevin's hermeneutics is rooted in the "traditional" dichotomy between theory and practice, rather than the more existential approach used by contemporary systems like Liberation theology. As one introductory text characterizes it, in traditional theology, "One first determines what the Christian tradition means and what it has to say in this particular situation, then one applies that insight to the situation. Liberation theology, by contrast, holds that pertinent and fruitful theological reflection cannot happen unless one is already involved in liberating action on behalf of the oppressed."[33] In the words of Jose Miguez Bonino, "there is no

---

[31]Baconians prided themselves on following Francis Bacon's (1561–1626) inductive method of scientific investigation. Baconianism was popular among Common Sense Realists and Presbyterian theologians.

[32]Nevin, *MP*, 164.

[33]Brennan R. Hill, Paul Knitter, and William Madges, *Faith, Religion, and Theology: A Contemporary Introduction* (Mystic CT: Twenty-Third Publications, 1990) 349.

truth outside or beyond the concrete historical events in which men are involved as agents. There is, therefore no knowledge except in action itself, in the process of transforming the world through participation in history."[34]

The dichotomy between theory and practice is precisely what Nevin opposed. His hermeneutic was, from first to last, existential, historical, and experiential. With Liberation theology, he regarded the community, rather than the individual, as the locus of Christ's saving power. Indeed, his understanding of the church as an embodiment or incarnation of Christ's life is, in some ways, analogous to the recognition of God's special presence among the poor and oppressed in Liberation, Feminist, and Black theology.

But, there are important differences as well. Nevin's theology and hermeneutics begin with the concrete reality of the new creation revealed in Christ's incarnation. This reality was so vivid, so overwhelming, and so tangible to Nevin, that it could not but be existential. The life of Christ is thus repeated in the life of each believer through the mystical union. In baptism we are buried with Him and rise with Him. Our sufferings are the sufferings of Christ. According to Nevin, the salvation of believers is "carried forward by a mystical reproduction in them of the grand facts of his history; he is born in them, suffers in them, dies in them, rises in them from the dead, and ascends in them to the right hand of God in heaven."[35]

Like Barth, Nevin maintained that there is no dimension of the Christian faith—Trinity, heaven, angels, final judgement, etc.—that we have not tasted in Christ. These are not abstractions or theories for the mind alone, but the realities in which we live, move, and have our very being. The Scriptures, Nevin said, are not a system of abstractions for the understanding, but a self-evidencing "system of [supernatural] realities, which as the order of nature are

---

[34]*Doing Theology in a Revolutionary Situation* (Philadelphia: Fortress, 1975) 88; quoted in Samuel Escobar, "Liberation Theology," in Alister E. McGrath, ed., *The Blackwell Encyclopedia of Modern Christian Thought* (Cambridge: Basil Blackwell, 1993) 331.

[35]Nevin, "The New Creation," *MR* 2 (1850): 5; see Schaff, *What Is Church History? A Vindication of the Idea of Historical Development* (Philadelphia: J. B. Lippincott and Co., 1846) 36-37.

to be first apprehended experimentally in the interior life of the soul, and *afterwards* drawn forth and defined to the eye of the understanding."[36] The Bible is a "transcript" of the "truths of religion . . . an actual impression taken from the things themselves just as they are."[37]

Consequently, in order to understand the Scriptures, the exegete must stand in veritable union with Christ. Like Peter, he or she must own Him as the Son of God from the inner depths of the soul. "The divine truth," says Nevin, "(joined always to the divine love) is made through faith to be actually in the soul as a part of its own existence, like light in the eye."[38] Truth holds "in the participation of His being, as this issues forth from Him in the way of living speech."[39]

By contrast, contemporary forms of Liberation theology equate "existential" and "concrete" with "social, economic, cultural, and political." This *sitz im Leben* then becomes the controlling and limiting context of our theology and hermeneutics. So, for example, classic Liberation theology logically begins with a social and economic analysis of the third world guided by Marxism or the social sciences. Christian feminism, like secular or mainstream feminism, often commences with the shared experience of male domination and oppression. This, then, becomes the hermeneutical *context* by which the "text" of the Christian tradition and the Scriptures are read and interpreted.

In these examples, the "existential situation" is defined by a bottom-up view of reality in which the kingdom of God is understood primarily as the redemption of social, political, and economic

---

[36]Nevin, "Is the Bible of God?" *The Friend*, 30 Jan. 1834; brackets mine.

[37]Nevin, "Religion a Life," *The Friend*, 15 Jan. 1835. On the existential dimension of Nevin's theology, see David Layman, "Revelation in the Praxis of the Liturgical Community: A Jewish-Christian Dialogue, with Special Reference to the Work of John Williamson Nevin and Franz Rosenzweig" (Ph.D. diss., Temple University, 1994) chap. 5.

[38]Nevin, "Christianity and Humanity," *MR* 20 (1873): 480. Conversely, those who will not receive the doctrines of the Bible "show themselves destitute of its life, its power, though they hold fast strenuously to the letter"; William H. Erb, ed. *Dr. Nevin's Theology, Based on Manuscript Class Room Lectures* (Reading PA: I. M. Beaver, 1913) 116, 106, hereafter *NT*.

[39]Nevin, "The Testimony of Jesus," *MR* 24 (1877): 8.

structures, and liberation from injustice and oppression. It is no surprise then, that these "secular theologies" often have more in common with so-called "liberal politics" than with traditional Christianity. In the name of Social Justice they offer a form of social salvation that could very well be provided with or without Christ. As historian Elizabeth Fox-Genovese indicated in her critique of Christian feminist scholarship, it uncritically appropriates a historical narrative which has been shaped by the concerns of *secular* feminist thought. "To be blunt," she says, "they seem to be 'adding' religion to an almost finished picture rather than exploring the ways in which religion might refine and even radically revise the picture."[40]

Nevin, on the other hand, commences with a top-down view of reality. The kingdom of God is the descent of the heavenly sphere into the earthly life of humanity and nature; it is a new creation, a supernatural world of powers revealed from above. The "central meaning of the gospel," says Nevin, is "the disclosure of a new world of powers in the living Christ, transcending supernaturally the universal constitution of nature, and carrying in itself both the promise and possibility of victory for our fallen humanity over all the evils under which it is found groaning so hopelessly through the ages, in every other view."[41] This new creation, according to Nevin, must "take up into itself the entire compass and power of the old creation; not destroying its constituent elements and laws, but fulfilling their inmost sense rather and raising them to their highest power."[42]

Have we become so absorbed (or obsessed) with our own experience that we are no longer able to imagine, to use Nevin's words, "forms of truth and modes of being, of an immeasurably

---

[40]Elizabeth Fox-Genovese, "Two Steps Forward, One Step Back: New Questions and Old Models in the Religious History of American Women," *Journal of the American Academy of Religion* 53 (1985): 465-71; quoted in Margaret Lamberts Bendroth, "Women in Twentieth-Century Evangelicalism," *Evangelical Studies Bulletin* 13 (Spring 1996): 4.

[41]Nevin, "The Inspiration of the Bible: The Internal Sense of Holy Scripture," *MR* 30 (1883): 10.

[42]Nevin, "Noel on Baptism," *MR* 2 (1850): 250; see idem, "The Apostle's Creed," *MR* 1 (1849): 323; idem, "Man's True Destiny," *MR* 5 (1853): 494-99; idem, "Trench's Lectures," *MR* 2 (1850): 608-11; idem, "Catholicism," *MR* 3 (1851): 11-15.

higher order than any with which we become acquainted through the medium of sense."?[43] As Nevin so eloquently declared, "the world of life exhibited in the Bible, stretching as it does through endless duration, and breaking forth immeasurably on every side, beyond the utmost boundaries of the material and sensible creation, is such as must be allowed, *if any better than an airy figment*, to throw a complete shade over all the objects and pursuits of time. It is nothing, or it is *everything*. Grant it to be real, and at once the entire aspect of life . . . changes."[44] If this is the case, then cultural, social, and economic factors can never rule or finally determine our views and actions, though from an incarnational standpoint, they can surely inform and condition them.

The transforming, invasive, and overwhelming reality of the new creation in Christ is, in Nevin's view, the existential meta-context for all theological reflection. This primal reality is concretely manifested in the church through word and sacrament. Once its presence is felt, declares Nevin, it becomes "impossible to resist the feeling, that the 'powers of the world to come' are actually at hand in its functions and services" just as the powers of nature are truly present in their own order.[45]

---

[43]Nevin, "Essay on the Interpretation of the Bible," *The Friend*, 11 July 1833.
[44]Nevin, "Is the Bible of God?" *The Friend*, 23 January 1834.
[45]Nevin, "Wilberforce on the Incarnation," *MR* 2 (1850): 187.

Part I
Transcendental Hermeneutics

Chapter 1
The Hermeneutics
of the New Creation

All hermeneutical systems originate in some philosophical (if not metaphysical) view of reality. Whether explicit or implicit, one's view of reality will impact the outcome of his or her hermeneutics. For example, assumptions about the indeterminate, plastic nature of truth and reality lie behind many postmodern systems of hermeneutics. These reader-response methods build upon the creative process of perception and cognition. Since reality and textuality are, in a sense, a construct of mind, since all understanding is interpretation, and since all facts are theory-laden, "meaning" is open-ended, fluid, and subjective.[1]

The metaphysical foundation of Nevin's hermeneutics (as well as the "Mercersburg Theology") is the incarnation of Christ. The Incarnation is the defining moment of world history. It is the archetype of the cosmos as well as the foundation of a new hermeneutic. Out of it emerges the controlling law or principle of reality itself. According to this principle, which we will call the *law of embodiment* or *reification*, the ideal and spiritual are said to be externalized in time and space (that is, the actual). "To be *real*," says Nevin, "the human as such, and of course the divine also in human form, must ever externalize its inward life." The more spiritual a state is, the more it is moved by an inward necessity to actualize itself in this way.[2] Without the Incarnation, "God can be

---

[1]For a general characterization of postmodernism, see Richard Tarnas, *The Passion of the Western Mind* (New York: Ballantine, 1993) 395-410. For a concise summary of contemporary theological ideas, see, Alister E. McGrath, ed., *The Blackwell Encyclopedia of Modern Christian Thought* (Cambridge: Basil Blackwell, 1993).

[2]Nevin, *MP*, 3-4. This concept is discussed more fully in his work on "Human

for men only an abstraction, an unreality, a mental figment, and so of course an idolatry." Christ, in Nevin's estimate, is a "living transcript and mirror of the Divine."[3]

So, whereas nominalism begins by denying the metaphysical reality and power of universal ideas, Nevin believes that the ideal constitutes the dynamic cause and essence of reality. Whereas Cartesianism rents the ideal and the actual asunder, Nevin maintains that they are organically and concretely united. Like Schleiermacher and his friend Friedrich Lücke (d. 1855), Nevin regarded Christ as the *Urbild*—the ideal or archetypal man. Through the Incarnation the ideal and the spiritual (which culminates, so to speak, in the divine life) are historically embodied or reified.

Consequently, Mercersburg theology views nature, humanity, the church, the sacraments, and even the Scriptures as nothing less than the historical concretion of the spiritual world. Moreover, it is from this law of reification that Nevin draws his hermeneutical conclusions regarding the nature of language, the function of sacraments and symbols, and the inspiration and interpretation of Scripture.

The Incarnational Paradigm

In keeping with his incarnate view of reality, Nevin regards the natural world as the efflorescence of the spiritual and supernatural orders of existence which lie behind it. This idealist notion has profound implications for Mercersburg's theology of the new creation. The created order is not a closed system but finds its first and final cause only in communion with God. The whole idea of redemption, therefore, is to raise the fallen creation into just such a sacramental communion with the powers of heaven.

But such a conjunction between God and creation can never be more than outward and mechanical unless it also joins with human will and intelligence. Humanity is the microcosm of nature. So, the redemption of humanity involves the redemption of the created

---

Freedom," in *Human Freedom and A Plea for Philosophy: Two Essays* (Mercersburg PA: P. A. Rice, 1850) 3; hereafter cited as HF.

[3]Nevin, "The Bread of Life: A Communion Sermon," *MR* 26 (1879): 21.

order as well.[4] For nature, this communion between the infinite and the finite is, so to speak, mechanically or instintively appropriated. But, for humanity the life of God must be *in* the human soul by *free* appropriation. And, this must be accompanied by the recognition that this divine life is not, in fact, its own.[5] Existentially, then, the life of the Logos, in order to be truth *for us*, must enter into the stream of history and take hold of humanity's life in its totality. As a new informing power in the world, it must translate those fallen structures into a higher form without violating the integrity of the created order or the free will of humanity.[6]

The springboard for this view of the Incarnation is the formula of Chalcedon (ca. 451 A.D.) which was held in high regard by the Reformed church. Though rarely mentioned, Chalcedon is in every respect normative for Mercersburg's Christology. Its traditional authority is assumed by Nevin and his associates. According to this ancient conciliar definition, the relationship between Christ's human and divine nature is *a*symmetrical. In other words, the center of hegemony lies on the divine rather than the human side enabling the Logos to assume human nature while maintaining his ascendancy throughout the theanthropic union.

This asymmetry demonstrates that humanity is not autonomous apart from God. Human nature requires communion with the divine nature in order to be complete. Far from forming a rupture with the created order, then, supernatural revelation is *necessary* in order for humanity to be fully human.[7] To this end, Christianity actually perfects history. It is not an addendum, but the deepest sense of the world's life—the inner core of humanity itself. It is not merely law or doctrine, according to Nevin, but a living, organic constitution. It comprises the first idea of the world

---

[4]See Gerhart, "Religion and Christianity," *MR* 11 (1859): 488-89, and *MR* 12 (1860): 258-60; Nevin, "The Testimony of Jesus," 14.

[5]Nevin, "Worldly Mindedness," *Weekly Messenger of the German Reformed Church*, 15 July 1840 (hereafter *WM*); idem, "Brownson's Quarterly Review," *MR* 2 (1850): 56-57; idem, "The Spiritual World," *MR* 23 (1876): 523.

[6]Nevin, *HF*, 30-39; Nevin, "Catholicism," 6-11; Gerhart, "Religion and Christianity," 257-260; Nevin, *Antichrist*, 21-23.

[7]See Nevin, *MP*, 202-209. The supernatural is not simply a break in the chain of cause and effect. That would make free will supernatural; see Nevin, "Natural and Supernatural," *MR* 11 (1850): 196.

and forms the ground of all other spheres of human life. More importantly, however, the Incarnation is the only power which, by taking up the onward progress of human life, can bring it finally to unity and perfection in God. The cure for sin must run at least as deep as the curse.[8]

The supernatural, then, transforms the natural; it does not destroy it. In Christ, the organic union which connects these spheres together constitutes, in the language of Chalcedon, one *life* without, at the same time, dissolving the distinction of *natures*. The Incarnation, by virtue of raising the earthly into union with the heavenly "has become the ordained law in like form also of the new spiritual creation universally; its archetype or original pattern, and at the same time its omnipotent principle and plastic cause."[9]

Just as God, in a manner of speaking, became human in Jesus Christ, so the supernatural, by descending into the sphere of nature, takes up or sublimates the created order so as to become, in a manner of speaking, natural.[10] The idea of such an organic sublimation became the source of much misunderstanding and controversy between Nevin and his opponents. His "Alexandrian" interpretation of Chalcedon sounded too much like ancient monophysitism which maintained that Christ had only one nature rather than two (human and divine). His former instructor and colleague at Princeton, Charles Hodge, accused Nevin of Eutychianism and pantheism for failing to distinguish between the two natures of Christ. The brilliant but boisterous Roman Catholic thinker, Orestes Brownson, also accused him of pantheism for allegedly merging divinity and nature, Christ and the church (see chapter 5).

---

[8]Nevin, "Trench's Lectures," 608, 610-11; idem, "The New Creation," 11; idem, "Worldly Mindedness," 24 June 1840; idem, "Natural and Supernatural," 186-87, 191-92.

[9]Nevin, "The Testimony of Jesus," 20.

[10]Nevin, "The Apostle's Creed," 323; Erb, *NT*, 15. See Nevin, *Antichrist*, 12. Thus the necessity of an external means of grace (i.e., preaching the word and ordinances): "It is strictly in conformity with the natural law that the application of redemption is made to depend on external as well as internal media." Erb, *NT*, 282.

But these accusations were, from Nevin's standpoint, driven by a dualistic metaphysic that had come to dominate most American theology. Following Descartes, the empirical tradition was inherently predisposed to view the spiritual as something outside of the physical. Hence, body and soul, spirit and nature, humanity and divinity, could come to no actual union. Through the widespread diffusion of Scottish Common Sense Realism (a form of empiricism) in American culture, many philosophers and theologians, including Nevin's counterparts at Princeton, had become the unwitting proponents of Descartes' dualism.

Nevin equated this false system of spirituality with gnosticism. The whole economy of nature is set aside resulting in a harsh dualism. The two natures of Christ, representing the economy of grace and nature, never come to an organic union. They stand outside one another in a "Nestorian" Christology. Under this view, the sacraments and the church (which are said to embody the economy of grace) are emptied of any abiding power. The new creation is not regarded as the *telos* of the old, nor does Christianity fulfill humanity's inward sense. Instead, the supernatural is simply superadded to the economy of creation in an abrupt and violent way. It has no affinity for nature or history, but floats above them.

This, as Nevin adroitly observed, was the form of Christianity that had taken root in American religion, and especially in American *sectarianism*. Having undervalued or functionally denied the reality and significance of the Incarnation by renting Christ's two natures asunder, it was naturally disposed to dividing the body of Christ (that is, the church) as well by separating the invisible and visible church.[11]

Needless to say, sectarianism is alive and well today, especially in the United States. Fueled by individualism and dualism, religion and spirituality are regarded by many as merely a "private" affair of the heart. Conversion is strictly a personal decision between God and the individual which dismisses or mitigates the significance of any ecclesiastical context. Consequently, the actual unity

---

[11]Nevin, *Antichrist*, 59-62; see also idem, "Thoughts on the Church," *MR* 10 (1858): 418-20.

and organization of the church (regarded by many as mere human convention) bear no direct and innate connection to one's spiritual life. The spiritual and the physical stand outside of one another. We will deal at length with this problem in chapter 6.

Pantheism and Naturalism

Perhaps one of the most useful contributions Nevin has made to Christian hermeneutics and theology is his understanding of orthodoxy as a critical synthesis of monism and dualism. Whereas Nevin's incarnational theology offended some American evangelicals, his sharp distinction between nature and supernature stood opposite to the growing tide of naturalism, pantheism, Transcendentalism, mysticism, and humanism in American society.

In Nevin's view, Christianity is a supernatural revelation of divine grace and life which *originates* from beyond the sphere of nature. Though it joins itself to the life of nature and ennobles the natural order, it is not a product of nature. Historically, this theology was shaped by a struggle with empiricism and incipient materialism, both of which were pervasive in American culture. It was a struggle Nevin engaged from his time at Western Seminary in the 1830s to the end of his life in 1886.

For pantheists the Incarnation is merely an example of a universal divine presence. However, the irreducible datum of Nevin's Christology is the classic distinction between God and creation. Christ is not the efflorescence of the world's natural life. The Incarnation represents the embodiment and entrance of an objective supernatural order into the world which was not enjoyed even by Moses and the prophets.[12] In Him was life, "in its original, fontal form." Says Nevin, he is the way, the truth, and the life, "not the index simply to these things, but the actual presence and power of the things themselves."[13]

Consequently, the presence of the new creation in the world is not only an abiding power in the bosom of nature and humanity,

---

[12]These experienced only an ephemeral and outward manifestation of the supernatural. Christianity is an eternal and intensive economy; Nevin, "Natural and Supernatural," 186. See also Gerhart, "Religion and Christianity," 257.

[13]Nevin, "Natural and Supernatural," 187, 189.

but an actual *historical* entrance of the Divine life in the world. Christian revelation is not a subjective impulse, a universal law of reason, or a form of natural theology. The Incarnation is supremely historical. Through it, the supernatural becomes natural not by putting off its own distinctive character, but "by falling into the regular process of the world's history, so as to form to the end of time indeed its true central stream." Thus the locus of Christ's redeeming life, indeed the locus of the new creation, is found only in the church. The power of Christ's redemption flows from His person outward through the organism of the church "with real immanent constancy."[14]

Once it is felt that the Incarnation is a perpetual force in the world's life which touches humanity through the church, then it becomes "impossible to resist the feeling, that the 'powers of the world to come' are actually at hand in its functions and services" just as the powers of nature are truly present in their own order.[15] The new creation in Christ, as Nevin so aptly remarked, "comprehends in itself a world of laws, actions, powers, results, etc.,—all comprehended in the mediatorial work, which flows from His person."[16]

Nevin repudiated Ralph Waldo Emerson's (1803–1882) pantheism and Horace Bushnell's (1802–1876) naturalistic Christianity. While he had little to say to Emerson, he reviewed four of Bushnell's works: *Christian Nurture* (1847), *An Argument for "Discourses on Christian Nurture"* (1847) which was later incorporated into *Views of Christian Nurture* (1848), *God in Christ* (1849), and *Nature and the Supernatural* (1858).[17] In his reviews of *Christian Nurture* and *Nature and the Supernatural*, Nevin praises Bushnell's attempt to overcome religious individualism and rationalism by restoring a form of "organic" and supernatural Christianity.

---

[14]Nevin, *MP*, 246.
[15]Nevin, "Wilberforce on the Incarnation," 187.
[16]Erb, *NT*, 244.
[17]See respectively, Nevin, "Educational Religion," *WM*, 23, 30 June; 7, 14 July 1847; idem, "Dr. Bushnell and Puritanism," *WM*, 1 Sept. 1847; idem, "Publications," *MR* 1 (1849): 309-312; idem, "Natural and Supernatural," 176-210. For a review of Nevin's controversy with Bushnell see Layman, "Revelation in the Praxis of the Liturgical Community," 313-30; Nichols, *Romanticism*, 236-58.

However, Bushnell overshot his mark by resolving the super-natural into the life of nature. "It is the old creation after all then," concludes Nevin, "which notwithstanding its corruption, is found sufficient to evolve from itself, by virtue of its own general organic constitution under the presence of the proper conditions, all that is comprehended in the idea of Christianity."[18] Bushnell erred by equating nature with physical causality, thus elevating free will and human intelligence into the sphere of supernature. The net effect, of course, is to reduce the supernatural to the level of our natural life. When all is said and done, Bushnell's system virtually destroys the possibility of a transcendent revelation. In short, it is rationalism.[19]

Nevin's conflict with naturalism became even more pronounced in his later writings, reflecting the burgeoning cultural trend toward materialism and humanism in the "Gilded Age." The industrial boom after the Civil War and the growing hostility between science and religion all pointed toward a dark, apocalyptic end. It was not as if he objected to science and technology in their own right. His protest was against the usurpation of Christian philosophy and theology by naturalistic presuppositions. For him the only true order of being and knowledge, "is in reality not from below upward, but from above downwards—not a scaling of the heavens by the powers of the earth, but a flowing down upon the earth of the powers of heaven."[20]

To this end, Nevin characterizes the battle between materialism and Christianity as a struggle between two fundamental *Weltan-schauungen*: Humanitarianism, on the one hand, makes spirit the outbirth of nature, "the celestial, the sublimation simply of the terrestrial." (Today this philosophy finds its counterpart in what is popularly termed "Secular Humanism.") The faith of the Apostle's Creed, on the other hand, resolves "the highest life of the world into the down-flowing life of heaven."[21] In the "humanitarian" view, the moral and physical completion of the world is found

---

[18]Nevin, "Educational Religion," *WM*, 7 July 1847.
[19]Nevin, "Natural and Supernatural," 196-97, 202-204.
[20]Nevin, "Nature and Grace," *MR* 19 (1872): 505.
[21]Ibid., 509.

in humanity and is carried forward without the "necessary complement of a higher spiritual life descending into him from the Lord."[22] In the Christological view, the perfection of the world is consummated in the Incarnation where fallen humanity is taken up and transformed by Divine life and power.

"Humanitarianism" fails to grasp the reality and significance of the spiritual world. Without faith, it has no power to apprehend the spiritual in its immediacy. The only self-evidencing reality is the world of space and time. The spiritual becomes an abstraction, a shadow of nature, "matter attenuated into sheer nihility."[23]

For Nevin, however, the spiritual world is more boundless than nature. We look through the mundane to the unseen and eternal.[24] "The things which are seen, on the earthly side," says Nevin, "are temporal, shadowy, evanescent; while the things which are unseen, on the spiritual side, are full of boundless positive reality and life that shall have no end."[25]

This infinite life is the origin of the natural world. The relation between the two realms is like that of soul and body. As Nevin describes it, the spiritual is "first, inmost, primordially substantial and real; the natural secondary, outmost, phenomenally transient, and universally dependent on the spiritual every moment for any shadow of existence it may seem to have in its own right."[26] The spiritual world, therefore, is the "region of ends and causes from which continually go forth as effects all things belonging to the world of nature."[27] Hence, the powers of the kingdom of heaven are altogether "cosmogonic, world-historical, and world-teleologic. . . ."[28]

In this connection, Nevin pursues a Logos theology which gives full credence to divine immanence. The Logos is said to be

---

[22]Nevin, "Christianity and Humanity," 484; Nevin, "Jesus and the Resurrection," *MR* 13 (1861): 183; idem, "Once for All," *MR* 17 (1870): 124.

[23]See Nevin, "Christianity and Humanity," 473-74; idem, "The Spiritual World," 515; idem, Nevin, "Bible Anthropology," *MR* 24 (1877): 227.

[24]Nevin, "The Spiritual World," 503.

[25]Nevin, "The Testimony of Jesus," 7. Nevin's Christian Platonism is evident here.

[26]Nevin, "The Bread of Life: A Communion Sermon," 19.

[27]Nevin, "The Spiritual World," 514.

[28]Nevin, "Nature and Grace," 500.

the alpha and omega of the cosmos, embracing both nature and supernature, the spiritual and the sensible.[29] Indeed, the entire creation of God, "is one thought, in the power of which all things are held together as a single system. . . . "[30] Nature, then, is a divine *word* which shows forth the supernatural.[31] But this "law of original existence" for the cosmos is "the law also of its continued subsistence." The Divine Word is not simply an "almighty *fiat*" whose efficacy is outward and mechanical—an ephemeral manifestation of divine power. Rather, it is an eternal Word.[32] "All natural things in this way, mineral, vegetable, and animal," according to Nevin, "are what they are only in virtue of the energy of his being, pouring itself into them continually, in the form and measure of their created receptivity for such heavenly influx."[33]

But how, or in what sense, is this Word of God said to be present *in* creation? Nevin, as we have seen, rejects pantheism. He also rejects the notion, popular in some forms of Absolute Idealism, process thought, feminist theology, and ecotheology, that God is hypostatically united to all creatures in the same way that the Logos is said to be united to Jesus. Here, creation is regarded as God's body or offspring. The divine essence is directly conjoined or merged with nature. Such pan*en*theism would destroy the unique, historical character of the Incarnation. Rather than being the singular center and font of the new creation, Jesus would be reduced to an example.[34]

So, while Mercersburg's powerful emphasis on divine immanence is firmly rooted in the Incarnation, the *distinction* of natures in the hypostatic union (that is, the divine and human) necessitates a like distinction between God and creation. For this reason, Nevin

---

[29]Nevin, "Christianity and Humanity," 474-75.
[30]Nevin, "The Spiritual World," 505-506.
[31]Nevin, "Brownson's Review," 68.
[32]Nevin, "Christianity and Humanity," 475.
[33]Nevin, "Bible Anthropology," 347. "Angels and men have no power to live, except by real participation in the one absolute life which is thus comprehended for their use first of all in him who is the fullness of the Godhead bodily" (ibid., 349).
[34]See Nevin, *MP*, 169, 196; idem, "Wilberforce on the Incarnation," 182-83; idem, "Brownson's Review Again," *MR* 2 (1850): 310; idem, "The Spiritual World," 524.

could not and would not blur the line between theism and monism. Consequenlty, the Incarnation is not repeated in the life of every believer (another form of pantheism) because Christ's divine life is *mediated* to us through His glorified human life. Christ's humanity, says Nevin, is "the door through which our humanity passes into union with His divinity."[35]

In the end it was the archetypal character of the Incarnation which determined the limits of philosophical speculation for Mercersburg. Clearly, Mercersburg theology was a confessional theology ruled by the spirit of the Heidelberg Catechism and the Apostles' Creed. Hence, the traditional Christology of Chalcedon prevailed. The philosophy of the German Reformed church, as Nevin's friend and colleague Emanuel Gerhart once pointed out, regards metaphysical reflection as "subservient and favorable to orthodox scientific theology and true practical religion."[36]

The Order of Being

Having rejected pantheism, panentheism, and dualism, Nevin appropriates an ancient medieval concept (adapted from Neoplatonism) which had all but disappeared from Protestant theology: The analogy of being.[37] Since God is the creator and sustainer of all things, creation is said to bear His likeness or living imprint. God is thus present in creation, according to Nevin, analogically. This is not merely a metaphorical, figurative, or conceptual relationship, but an ontological one. Consequently, the character and attributes of God are actually made known through the created order. This, as we will see, has important hermeneutical and linguistic implications.

The analogy of being is inseparably linked to an order or hierarchy of being which points to Christ as the *first and final cause* of

---

[35]Erb, *NT*, 292. On the relationship between Mercersburg and Absolute Idealism, see DiPuccio, "Dynamic Realism," 169-86.

[36]Gerhart, "The German Reformed Church," *Bibliotheca Sacra* 20 (1863): 30.

[37]According to Richard A. Muller, this concept (usually associated with Thomism) fell out of favor with Scotists and nominalists. It played only a minor role among the Protestant scholastics to whom Hodge is largely indebted. See Richard A. Muller, *Dictionary of Latin and Greek Theological Terms* (Grand Rapids: Baker, 1985) 32-33.

all things. In this hierarchy, there is an innate attraction between lower and higher orders of existence. The lower orders adumbrate and anticipate the higher, while at the same time the higher orders take up and assimilate the lower just as an organism incorporates material from its environment. We see this process at work in the assumption of basic elements by chemical and electrical processes, in the absorption of minerals by vegetable organisms, in the digestion of vegetation by animals and humans, and finally, in the transformation of nature to the sphere of mind and will in humanity. The lower order is thus made to transcend itself through the action of a higher power, thus fulfilling the created purpose or design of each class.[38]

This is not a form of Darwinian evolution. Phylogenetic evolution (that is, development across species), though gaining currency by the mid-nineteenth century, was rejected by Nevin because it supposed that the lower orders of existence have within themselves the potential to evolve to a higher sphere. Nevin maintained, however, that all things come from God and are drawn to God. The hierarchy of being is ordered from the top down, not from the bottom up. Each level is made to transcend its own order by a power which descends into it from above rather than from below.[39]

---

[38]Nevin, "Philosophy of History. I. The General Idea of History," *College Days*, Jan. 1873: "Life here is in this way a scale of degrees, a succession of ascending planes, each of which prefigures and prepares the way for that by which it is followed." This, as Lovejoy has pointed out, involved a "temporalizing" of the chain of being in which the ideal (namely, the divine exemplars) comes to realization through a historical process. Prior to the eighteenth century the order of being was considered to be perfect and thus static. See Arthur O. Lovejoy, *The Great Chain of Being: A Study of the History of an Idea* (Cambridge MA: Harvard University Press, 1936) 244ff.; Lia Formigari, "Chain of Being," and C. A. Patrides, "Hierarchy and Order," in *Dictionary of the History of Ideas* ed. Philip Wiener (New York: Charles Scribner's Sons, 1973).

[39]See Nevin, *MP*, 200n. In his lectures on "Aesthetics" (1870–1871), he maintained that humanity is not the product of lower spheres. Rather, these are suspended from him. "This is the true argument against the Darwinian theory." Nevin, "Lectures on Aesthetics," transcribed by George D. Gurley, 1870–1871, AMsS, p. 287, Archives of Franklin and Marshall College, uncataloged. Whether Nevin's repudiation of Darwinism entails a total rejection of evolution or just its naturalistic/materialistic form is uncertain. In his later writings, Nevin's early colleague Philip Schaff was not opposed to theistic evolution.

The *analogia entis* also includes another idea which is essential to the concept of organic unity, namely, the priority of the general over the particular, or the whole over the parts. Reality does not *ascend* from formless existence to rationality, or from plurality to unity; rather it is genetically *derived* from one cosmic idea which unfolds through kingdoms, orders, classes, genus, species, and individual existence. Hence, it is the idea of the general which denominates and defines the particular in all orders of existence. God created "types" from which He brought forth the whole range of individual members. As Nevin and his colleagues concluded, this deductive order defines the nature of humanity, the church, and society.

The derivation of organic unity from the ideal represents a radical departure from both nominalism (which assumes the priority of the individual) and Cartesian dualism. It is a return to the traditional metaphysics of universal being. "The *generality* of being," says Gerhart, "is that which underlies and identifies all particular entities and phenomena in every objective sphere." This is not monism though. The analogy of being, which serves as the foundation for the generality of being, entails a fundamental *distinction* between creation and God.[40] So, on the one hand, the concept of analogy enables us to view the cosmos as a universal whole grounded upon God's absolute being. On the other hand, it is a safeguard against pantheism and monism.

Though the scale of being provides a metaphysical basis for explaining the origin and intelligibility of reality, its focus for Nevin lies primarily on the emergence of life. But, its ultimate goal is to define *humanity's place in the cosmos and, more especially, in God's redemptive program.* Here, nature comprises one magnificent parable of the spiritual world. Each sphere passes into the next (e.g., plant to animal to human) only as it is caught up and assimilated by a force *descending* into it from a superior sphere. This ascent is grounded in the idea of final causality and is part of

---

[40]Or, as Gerhart says, between derived being (which has only relative necessity) and underived being (which has absolute necessity); Gerhart, *An Introduction to the Study of Philosophy with an Outline Treatise on Logic* (Philadelphia: Reformed Church Publishing Board, 1857) 76, 75; hereafter *IP*.

a universal architecture. It is a transformation from above which, according to Nevin, adumbrates the salvation and perfection of humanity in God.[41]

Despite Nevin's appropriation of classic metaphysics, he rejected the mechanical and dualistic view of creation associated with Newtonian physics and Common Sense Realism. For Mercersburg the essential stuff of reality is neither passive matter, inert substances, nor static ideas (Aristotle and Plato), but dynamic "laws." In Nevin's hands, the analogy of being is not a static idea but a dynamic one in which the forces which uphold the cosmos spring fresh every moment from the will of God. Following German idealism, we might almost say that *being* now yields to *becoming.* Speaking of creation, Nevin concludes, "Be its essence what it may, can it be in this respect any thing more than a perpetual *Werden* [becoming], in which existence, at the same moment, *is* and *is not* at every point of its progress? We may say, then, with the fullest reason, that the different orders of existence have their ground ultimately and essentially in *ideas*, or thoughts and volitions of God."[42]

As John Polkinghorne has said in regard to modern chaos theory, the mechanistic or Newtonian view of the world is dead. "The future is not a mere rearrangement of the past; instead we live in a world of true becoming." The world is thus open to the possibility of "information input" through divine causality as well as human intentionality. In other words, with the demise of the mechanical scheme and its corresponding determinism, it is again possible to conceive of a top-down universe in which God is active and immanent throughout by way of "downward causality."[43]

---

[41]Nevin, "Nature and Grace," 490-91.
[42]Nevin, "Philosophy of Dr. Rauch," *The American Biblical Repository*, 2nd ser. 10 (1843): 428; brackets mine.
[43]John Polkinghorne, "Physical science and Christian thought," in *The Blackwell Encyclopedia of Modern Christian Thought*, 447.

Humanity in the Order of Being[44]

With this scheme in mind we can understand what Nevin meant when he described the world of nature as a vast pyramid which, beginning with inorganic matter, ascends through successive stages of organization finally reaching its summit in humanity. Humanity is the perfection and recapitulation of the orders of being which rise to meet him, and the first impulse of a new order descending into him from above.[45] By virtue of the body, his life is one with the life and laws of nature. He is thus the focal point and antitype of the natural order, comprehending and subsuming the animal, vegetable, and mineral kingdoms. By virtue of the mind and will, he is the connecting link between the natural and spiritual worlds.

In humanity, nature attains consciousness and freedom as it ascends into the sphere of reason and will. Mind is thus the full efflorescence and bursting forth of nature's innermost sense. The world was made for this mode of existence. As one writer expressed it, "The cosmos must *utter* itself through mind. The human order must mirror the fullness of cosmical truth; for, in such a view only is it possible for it, in any proper sense, to be regarded as the head and crown of the natural creation." The ego, thus, becomes "a living, but *intelligized cosmos*" whose mission (philosophically speaking) is to "give rational birth" to being.[46]

But humanity is more than a microcosm of nature. While his life—body and spirit—is and must always be bonded to nature, his

---

[44]This section is based primarily on the following texts and articles: Nevin, *MP*, 199-204; idem, "The New Creation," 7-8; idem, "The Moral Order of Sex," *MR* 2 (1850): 549-72; idem, "Man's True Destiny," 492-520; idem, "Natural and Supernatural," 176-210; idem, "The Wonderful Nature of Man," in Appel, *LW*, 515-28 (repr. from *MR* 11 [1859]: 317-36); idem, "Christianity and Humanity," 469-86; Gerhart, "The Fall and the Natural World," *MR* 12 (1860): 505-24; idem, "Man: His Relation to Nature and to God," *MR* 21 (1874): 624-38.

[45]On the significance of the division of the sexes, see Nevin, "The Moral Order of Sex," 556-64; and Frederick Augustus Rauch, *Psychology; or, a View of the Human Soul*, 4th ed. with a notice by John W. Nevin (New York: M. W. Dodd, 1846) 80-85; hereafter *Psy*.

[46]Hiram King, "The Mission of Philosophy," *MR* 23 (1876): 217, 226.

destiny is supernatural. The life of nature is thus only preparatory to the fulfillment of human destiny. The affinities, wants, and tendencies of our spiritual nature demand a higher object than mere nature. They are predisposed to a supernatural end that could only be satisfied through religion. But no amount of groping by fallen humanity can bring humanity into vital communion with the powers and reality of the supernatural. Natural religion has at best a dark vision of God which only points the way to an actual positive revelation by the supernatural itself. Such is Christianity.

In the design of creation, then, nature looks upward to humanity for its perfection while humanity looks heavenward to God. All rests on the teleological idea of creation, ordered and established by the divine archetype. As Gerhart observes, "man cannot be assumed into God unless the finite life of mankind, as originally constituted by the creative act, be adapted to the divine mode of existence." There is, he says, a *homoigeneity* between God and humanity.[47] It is in humanity, therefore, where the new creation—"the powers of the world to come"—intersect the powers of nature. This happens only through faith, by which the supernatural order of grace in Jesus Christ is mediated (that is, reified) by the Holy Spirit in the word and sacraments.[48]

The Hermeneutics of Nature

The nexus between the spiritual and the sensible means that nature, as we have suggested, is the externalization or embodiment of the spiritual and ideal world.[49] This theme is a fixture throughout Nevin's writings and forms the theological complement to his Platonic philosophy. For Nevin, though, the world of space and time is not simply a static reflection of the ideal as it was for Plato, but the dynamic embodiment of the ideal. This principle must be kept in mind when interpreting Nevin's "Platonic language."

Like Jonathan Edwards (1703–1758) and other Puritan Platonists, Nevin and his colleagues believed that nature, and especially

---

[47]Gerhart, "Man: His Relation to Nature and to God," 635.
[48]Nevin, "Nature and Grace," 503.
[49]See Nevin, "Natural and Supernatural," 189–90.

humanity, is a sacrament of the divine presence in creation.[50] Nevin's early colleague, F. A. Rauch, also shared in this sacramental vision of reality. As Nevin informs us, "Innumerable analogies, adumbrations, and correspondences, not obvious to commoner minds, seemed to be pressing habitually to his view, binding the universe into one sublime whole, the earth reflecting the heavens, and the waves of eternity echoing on the shores of time."[51]

In Nevin's view, God's presence in nature is ultimately an anticipation of God's revelation in Christ. "Nature passes into an allegory of religion."[52] Christianity, in this view, is "*absolute* reality and truth," while nature is "only relatively true and real." The true sense of nature is found only in humanity which in turn looks toward the Incarnation. "It is all a shadow and type of the real; but for this very reason, not the real itself."[53]

World Religions. This analogical relationship between nature and supernature meets us on a number of fronts. In the first place the religions of the world, though void of salvific power, are said to anticipate Christianity. The fullest expression of this idea was given by Nevin's former student and younger associate, Emanuel Gerhart, in his articles on "Religion and Christianity." According to Gerhart, unless revelation joins itself to the constitution of nature it will transcend the human capacity to comprehend it leaving our religious needs unfulfilled. God would remain unknown to us. However, the idea (or intuitive consciousness) of God is innate. Not in any abstract sense, of course, but by means of God's actual power and presence in the world. "That which may be known of God is manifest in them; for God hath showed

---

[50]Nevin, "Faith, Reverence and Freedom," MR 2 (1850): 104-105. See Jonathan Edwards, *Typological Writings*, ed. Wallace E. Anderson and Mason I. Lowance, Jr., with David Watters, in *The Works of Jonathan Edwards* 11 (New Haven: Yale University Press, 1993). For an earlier edition, see Jonathan Edwards, *Images and Shadows of Divine Things*, ed. Perry Miller (New Haven: Yale University Press, 1948; repr.: Westport CT: Greenwood Press, 1977).

[51]Appel, "A Sketch of Marshall College, Mercersburg, Pa. from 1836 to 1841. Under the Presidency of Dr. Rauch" MR 34 (1887): 540.

[52]Appel, *LW*, 466 (reprinted from Nevin, "The Church Year" MR 8 [1856]: 456-78).

[53]Nevin, *MP*, 207.

it unto them" (Rom. 2:19). Thus all religion, considered as a universal phenomena, is based on a form of revelation.

But, sin has scattered the once clear light of God's presence. In our native capacity, humanity can see no more than the dim aura of God's glory. Religion, in this view, becomes the spontaneous product of a particular people. Without an objective, historical revelation, these "ethnic" religions can never rise above the general mind of the people who embrace them. Such a religion "is suited to a people as a dream is to a man. . . . Each one projecting his own habit of life is confronted by the image of himself, and with this he is in direct sympathy." As a result, it can never satisfy the *objective* need of humanity.[54]

Christianity, in one sense, rests upon the same universal foundation as religion generally—humanity's latent consciousness of and longing for God. Sin has disrupted the human faculties, darkened the understanding, and made the will powerless.[55] Yet it has not destroyed the *imago dei*. Humanity still retains a latent capacity and longing for God, and this is the basis of religion. If this were not true, there could be no point of contact between Christ and the pagan. We would be beyond the reach of Christ's saving power.

Christ, however, is the consummation of natural revelation. In Him, as Gerhart tells us, the infinite became finite, the absolute became relative, the invisible became visible, and the eternal became temporal. In Christ, God approaches humanity under the categories and limitations of his sensori-rational nature. Christianity, therefore, answers all the wants of reason, intellect, morality, religion, science, and philosophy. Christ objectively satisfies humanity's longing for God and kindles our innate sense of God's presence. He is the highest object of faith in the only form accessible to human reason.[56] In Gerhart's words,

---

[54]Gerhart, "Religion and Christianity," 495, 483-500; idem, *Prolegomena to Christian Dogmatics* (Lancaster: Lecture Printing Society of the Theological Seminary of the Reformed Church, 1891) 8-34; see also Nevin, *MP*, 202-204; idem, "Trench's Lectures," 615-19; idem, "Natural and Supernatural," 191-92; idem, "Nature and Grace," 491-94.

[55]Erb, *NT*, 210.

[56]Gerhart, "Religion and Christianity," 483-93; idem, "The Fall and the Natural

Christianity as divine and supernatural is an absolute and infinite order of being. It is and presents to the eye of faith, as a concrete reality, the object of thought which the philosophy of all ages has in vain struggled to apprehend. What the first intuition of the reason postulates; what the laws of thinking and the processes of reason assume and begin with; what all the tendencies of man's intellectual and moral being presuppose; what the profoundest speculations of Jewish, Pagan, and Christian philosophy have sought to determine;—that the objective order of Christianity is in concrete form; and, when recognized and received, must satisfy the conditions of every scientific and philosophical problem—must answer every real question which the human reason can put concerning the Absolute and Infinite.[57]

The Church Year. Another significant analogy between nature and supernature can be seen in Christian worship, especially the church year. The idea of the ecclesiastical year, Nevin observes, rises spontaneously from the human constitution. In humanity two orders of existence flow together. While the human spirit stands above nature, the human body is the perfect outbirth of the life of nature, "the full efflorescence of its inmost life" organically united in our person. So, our mental and spiritual dispositions, though not ruled by nature, are still modified by nature. "Skies, mountains, seas, plains, forests, rivers, enter into us, and become part of our spiritual being," as do the cycles of nature through which the world passes. This is true of days and months, and especially of years. Owing to its seasons, the year is the most profound cycle in humanity's life, mirroring our several ages from birth to death. In this respect, it is the vehicle of our deepest spiritual experience.[58]

In the liturgical year, then, Nevin believes that the higher sphere links itself with the lower sphere. The natural has an affinity for the spiritual and "forms everywhere an adumbration of its invisible presence and power." (Consider, for example, the correspondence between mind and matter, and the spiritual

World," 262-67.

[57]Gerhart, "Religion and Christianity," 265; see also Erb, *NT*, 38, 40, etc.

[58]Appel, *LW*, 462-65 (repr. from Nevin, "The Church Year"); Rauch, *Psy*, 55-66, 103-105.

lessons Christ frequently drew from nature in the parables.) More importantly, though, the sacred year arises spontaneously from the human *disposition* itself and prevails among all people throughout history. Though often corrupted by false notions of religion, there is still a sense in which the annual cycles of nature foreshadow the higher destiny of humanity in another world. "Time is made to be the mirror thus of eternity."[59]

But if the revelation of Christ *surpasses* nature, as Nevin believes, in what sense is it congruous to the idea of an ecclesiastical year which is apparently rooted in nature? Here again, Nevin appeals to the order of being: Nature was made to receive just such an efflux of divine power. So, even as a supernatural revelation the Incarnation roots itself in history. By being taken up into the sphere of grace, the constitution of nature is glorified and sublimated to a higher end. The pagan religious year falls short of this by confusing nature with the divine powers nature represents. Without an objective revelation, paganism proves to be "an abortive nisus" in the right direction. It falls back into the natural realm instead of surmounting it. Nevertheless, Nevin maintains that pagan and Roman religion symbolized the idea of redemption as a struggle between the powers of darkness and evil in the winter months, giving way to the victory of light and goodness in the spring and summer.[60]

The Jewish year, on the other hand, was established by divine revelation. As a result, it was of a much higher order than the pagan. Its weekly Sabbath cycle broke the force of the physical year which ruled paganism. Yet there were unmistakable correspondences. The Passover celebrated the redemption of Israel at the same time that the pagan world celebrated the renewal of nature at the spring equinox. But unlike the pagan year which commenced in the fall or winter, the Jewish religious year passed over these seasons in silence symbolizing the mystery of redemption which, like the powers of nature, lie hidden during the winter.[61]

---

[59] Appel, *LW*, 466-68.
[60] Ibid., 468-75.
[61] Ibid., 475-76.

It is only in the Christian year, insists Nevin, that nature is finally and fully taken up into the order of grace. The death and resurrection of Christ at the time of the vernal equinox fills up the sense of the pagan and Jewish religious years. The ascension and Pentecost mark the upward progress of the sun toward its summer solstice.

The church year, therefore, is not simply an arbitrary arrangement. For Nevin, it is rooted in a natural impulse which presupposes an affinity between nature and grace. Its historical development was not primarily the product of art or reflection, but the spontaneous response of the Christian consciousness. Its true sense and power can never be measured by any logical standard alone. "It speaks, not just to the understanding of man, but far more to his feeling and heart. Its voice is for the deep places of the soul, where life reigns as a full power back of all partial forms of expression."[62]

The Nature of Language and the Interpretation of Scripture. While a fuller treatment of linguistics and exegesis is reserved for chapters 2 and 3, it is important to point out the inner correspondence between nature and the spiritual world as seen in the character of language and the interpretation of Scripture. Nevin came to believe that the common or popular conception of figurative language (that is, metaphors and tropes) "always inverts the true order of the natural and the spiritual, by making the natural to be first and the spiritual second." It amounts to nothing more than a comparison of nature with nature. The actual relation between the natural and the spiritual is, as we have already seen, just the reverse. The spiritual is first, inmost, foundational, and substantial; the natural is secondary, outmost, contingent, and phenomenal.[63]

Because there is a "true interior communication" between the natural and the spiritual, as Nevin insists, the "force of all true comparison and figure of speech" reveals this "under-sense of the world's life." It is the only "sufficient key" for unlocking the interior spiritual sense of mundane reality. Every "genuine com-

---

[62]Ibid., 478-79.
[63]Nevin, "The Bread of Life," 19.

parison," then, is a parable of the spiritual. This is eminently true
of the figurative language of Scripture since the mind of God,
which comprehends truth in its universality, is the inspiration of
Scripture.[64]

As corollary to these ideas, Nevin regards the inspiration of
Scripture as an analogue to the sustaining power of God in creation. The heavens and the earth were not created and then left to
exist on their own. "The word is still in them at every point as
their living soul; so that all visible and material things are not only
outward signs and tokens of things invisible and eternal, but the
actual expression of such things, just as a man's bodily face is the
express image of his soul." Nature is the "living, speaking mirror,"
of its inward spiritual life. If this is true of nature, how much more
is it true of the Scriptures which are divinely inspired! Consequently, hermeneutics must begin from the "inward living spirit" rather
than the "outward natural letter."[65]

As we have already pointed out, the use of language to present
supernatural truth under the form of a human or natural transaction implies a capacity for the lower order to be the medium of the
higher order. Gerhart called this fitness "resemblance" in order to
distinguish it from identity. The two spheres are "generically and
infinitely" different yet "analogous." The parable occupies a
unique place in this scheme, forming a union between these disparate orders. In the natural we have the form of the parable. In
the spiritual we have its substance.[66] As Nevin later said, "The
significance of all parables rests in a real, and not simply imagi-
nary or notional correspondence between the natural and the
spiritual, as they are made to come together always in their
constitution."[67]

The Organic and Human Analogy. Finally, the nexus between the
natural and the spiritual provides the foundation for a whole range
of analogies between organic and spiritual life—all of which
presage the new creation in some way. In this we not only see the

---

[64]Ibid., 17-18n.
[65]Ibid., 19-20n.
[66]See Gerhart, "The Interpretation of the Parable," *MR* 10 (1858): 578-99.
[67]Nevin, "The Bread of Life," 25.

contrast between the mechanical and the organic, which is commonly associated with Romanticism, but also a metaphilosophy of organism in which the entire cosmos, as we have already remarked, is regarded as an organic system.

So, in the lower organic sphere, the process of digestion and assimilation, by which a higher organism incorporates a lower order of existence, reflects the assumption of nature by the supernatural. The vital unity between the vine and its branches is an image (*Abbild*) of the heavenly which finds its true archetype (*Urbild*) in the relationship between Christ and the church.[68] The idea of corporeal and intellectual food derives its energy and force from the potency which belongs to food in the highest spiritual sense, namely, the Lord himself. The divine Logos, the Word, is thus the actuating life of all our nourishment. His blessing rests upon it in an inward and living way so that even natural bread is sacramental—the sensible likeness of the eucharistic food.[69]

Humanity stands above every other analogy in nature. Mind is not just the completion of nature, but "a new order of existence." In humanity, "the world process, the divine idea which underlies creation, puts on a new form." This is not pantheism, says Nevin, but "Pan-Anthropism." Humanity is a "microcosm" of the world.[70] More importantly, though, the human mind (consisting of reason and will) is the most perfect mirror of the Universal Mind of God.[71]

In view of this fact, a number of important analogies follow. For example, the union between head and body is said to reflect

---

[68]Nature is not just a figure, but "the very reflex of this mystery itself." Nevin, *MP*, 229-30.

[69]Nevin, "The Bread of Life," 16-17.

[70]Nevin, "Philosophy of History. I. The General Idea of History," *College Days*, Jan. 1873; idem, "Lectures on Aesthetics," 8, 282. Though the tendency in past years has moved away from anthropocentrism toward biocentrism, a number of physicists and astronomers now believe that human intelligence may indeed occupy a unique and preeminent place in the cosmos (the "anthropic principle"). See, John D. Barrow and Frank J. Tipler, *The Anthropic Cosmological Principle* (New York: Oxford University Press, 1986); M. A. Corey, *God and the New Cosmology: The Anthropic Design Argument* (Lanham MD: Rowman & Littlefield, 1993); and Robert Naeye, "OK, Where are They?" *Astronomy* (July, 1996): 36-43.

[71]Nevin, "Faith, Reverence and Freedom," 104-106. Cf. Augustine, *De Trinitate*, 14.

the relation between Christ and the church. The mystery of the nuptial bond is a sacramental symbol of the heavenly marriage of Christ and the church. Natural vision is analogous to faith. And the reciprocal union of heart and lungs is an analogy of the will and understanding.[72]

Hermeneutical Implications

The Incarnation, according to Nevin, was not simply a transient supernatural appearance. It involved a true organic entrance into the life of the world. "The object of the Incarnation was to couple the human nature in real union with the Logos, as a permanent source of life." It is the aboriginal miracle of Christianity by which all other miracles in this supernatural economy are made possible.[73] So too, it is the paradigm or archetype of both metaphysics and hermeneutics.

The genius and power of Nevin's system rests in the fact that the spiritual world is foundational to all else. As Paul once said, "the things which are seen are temporary, but the things which are unseen are eternal" (2 Cor. 4:18). Behind our mundane world is an immense and unfathomable "spiritual" cosmos which is, in a manner of speaking, more real and more concrete, than the world of sense. The heavenly is not a metaphor of the earthly; on the contrary, the earthly is a metaphor of things invisible and eternal. In other words, it is *we* who are the "metaphor," God is the "reality."

Many ancient interpreters, as Nevin once observed, knew this and viewed nature and history as embodying the power of this higher world. The hermeneutical consequences of this worldview are profound. The *Song of Solomon*, for example, was usually regarded not only as a love song, but also as an allegory of Christ and the Church—none other than "the house of God" and "the gate of heaven" as Matthew Henry once called it. Until the nineteenth century, this spiritual interpretation of the *Song* prevailed almost universally throughout the church. Why? Because the union

---

[72]Nevin, *MP*, 230-333; idem, "Bible Anthropology," 344. This last analogy was derived from Emanuel Swedenborg whose influence we will consider in chap. 3.

[73]Nevin, *MP*, 165, 206; Erb, *NT*, 28, 42.

of Christ and the church is not merely a reflection or figure of the nuptial union; rather, the nuptial union is the image of this higher spiritual union (see Eph. 5:31-32). The former derives its true sense from the latter, just as the earthly tabernacle derived its full meaning only from the heavenly tabernacle (see Mat. 23:9; Eph. 3:14-15, 4:6; Heb. 8–9). After all, humanity was created in the image of God, not God in the image of humanity.

Like the bright cloud which encompassed Christ in the transfiguration, the sensible becomes the parable by which spiritual things are conveyed to the understanding. Following the pattern of the Incarnation itself, the historical sense (*inseparably* joined to this higher spiritual sense) is not diminished or set aside; rather, it is sanctified and ennobled.

Mercersburg's sacramental understanding of language bears directly on the recent controversies in the church concerning the meaning and nature of "religious language," especially as it relates to the use of "gender-inclusive language." God, it is said, is beyond human understanding and description so that all language about God is "figurative" or "metaphorical." Names such as "Father" do not literally describe the character of God. Instead they reflect the religious experience of a male-dominated culture which identifies the God of the Bible with male authority. In short, the use of "Father" projects *our* familial experience (which is patriarchal) onto God.

Nevin's sacramental and analogical understanding of language stands in stark contrast to this bottom-up theory. His view suggests that our understanding of familial relations is rooted in God Himself who is the *archetypal* "Father." Consequently, divine Fatherhood is not simply a projection of *our* familial experience. Rather, God embodies the very concept of Fatherhood. By comparison, our familial experience is only an imperfect approximation of this. Consequently, "Father" reveals the *identity, inner life, and personality* of God in a way that other titles cannot.

From a feminist perspective, however, God as "Father" only serves to perpetuate an unjust system of male domination. Yet, for Paul, the male-female "hierarchy" (again employing a top-down paradigm) is patterned after the Trinitarian relationship (1 Cor. 11:3) and the relation between Christ and the Church (Eph. 5:23-

25). This is a "hierarchy" rooted in unity, self-sacrifice, and mutual love, not power or inferiority. It entails an equality of essences, but a distinction of roles and responsibilities. (This mutuality is acknowledged by Paul in 1 Cor. 11:11-12 and Eph. 5:21.) To characterize it as a power relationship does an injustice to its true character. Christ does not oppress the Church or treat her like a servant; nor does the Father oppress the Son or treat Him like a slave. By analogy, the same must apply to male-female relationships. Both Jesus and Paul made it clear by teaching and example that he who leads must do so by serving and sacrificing himself for others. Any appeal, past or present, to the Trinitarian hierarchy as a rationale or even vindication for oppression is a distortion of Paul's teaching.

Finally, out of Mercersburg's sacramental and organic view of creation comes the possibility of an environmental theology. The realization that the physical world reflects God's character, glory, and goodness, provides the basis for an ecotheology that respects and recognizes the intrinsic dignity of creation as a work of God. At the same time, the order or hierarchy of being (something generally eschewed by most contemporary thinkers) establishes a framework for ordering the use of natural resources in two ways. First, because human beings occupy a unique position in the created order, they are morally responsible for the supervision, cultivation, and maintenance of nature. Second, since the survival and happiness of human beings is dependent upon the survival and contentment of lower orders of existence the two interests must be carefully weighed and balanced when they conflict.

In applying Nevin's principles to these contemporary issues, we have, needless to say, pressed beyond the primary literature and even Nevin himself. For, example Nevin made it clear that he had little sympathy with women's rights.[74] Like Augustine, he held that man represents the universal side of human nature while woman represents the individual side. Thus the image of God centers more in man, *separately* considered, than in woman. Man's

---

[74]See "The Moral Order of Sex"; and "Woman's Rights," *American Review* 2 (October 1848): 367-81.

mind tends toward thought and reason, while woman's tends towards feeling and temporal affairs.[75]

Nevin's view originates, at least in part, from Rauch's Hegelian observations on the differences between the sexes. These differences are considered a modification of mind owing to the permanent influence of nature.[76] Rauch's descriptions are thus made the basis for moral prescriptions. However, a comparison of the two authors shows that Nevin is more severe in limiting the role of women to wife and mother. While Rauch affirms that the highest happiness of woman is motherhood, he also recognizes that many women have excelled in learning and especially in law (mathematics, astronomy, metaphysics, history, and medicine, however, are generally not agreeable to the feminine genius). Nevin fails to mention these exceptions and seems unwilling to grant any.

Even within Mercersburg theology, then, we find slightly diverging interpretations of the order of being and its practical significance. These differences may have been as much a product of personality (Nevin was very austere) as they were of critical reflection. Though Nevin's view of women and their roles was certainly typical of his day, one cannot help but wonder how his perspective on this issue (along with his understanding of the order of being), might have been modified by giving fuller consideration to the Trinity and the relationship between Christ and the church.

---

[75]Nevin makes no explicit reference to Augustine. See Augustine, *De Trinitate* 12.3.3 and 12.7.10-12.

[76]See *Psy*, 80-85.

Chapter 2
Sacramental Hermeneutics

Because Christianity is essentially incarnate, it must externalize itself in the world historically. In creation, there can be no reality without such an inward-outward union. "To be *real*," as Nevin says, "the human as such, and of course the divine also in human form, must ever externalize its inward life." The more spiritual a state is, the more it is moved by an inward necessity to actualize itself in this way.[1] In Christianity, this actualization takes place through the church which is the embodiment of Christ's ideal life in the history of the world. It is only *through* the church, the Body of Christ, that the powers of the world to come are mediated to the individual. The means of grace—the word and sacraments—are the reification of this supernatural economy. The ideal becomes actual in space and time—a veritable incarnation of Christ's divine-human life.

The Incarnation serves as the archetype of the sacraments and the word by uniting distinct things (that is, the created and divine, unlike in their natures) into an indivisible, organic whole without transmutation or separation. It denominates the relation between the sacramental sign and the grace which it signifies, as well as the relation between the words of Scripture and the divine life they embody (chapter 3).

Nevin spent a great deal of time and energy defending this incarnational view of the sacraments against the prevailing American tendency toward subjectivity and rationalism. Whereas the symbolic memorial view denied any real presence of Christ in the Lord's Supper, Nevin believed that when the Eucharist is transacted, we become partakers of His body and blood. Christ, in

---

[1]Nevin, *MP*, 3-4.

other words, is truly present in the transaction of the Lord's Supper.

This disagreement was not merely theological. It was, as we shall see, hermeneutical, linguistical, and metaphysical. Nevin regarded symbolic memorialism as a form of nominalism which repudiates the objective nature of the ideal and its organic union with actual existence. Specifically, sacramental nominalism denies that the reality which is signified by the elements is truly conveyed to the recipient. The signs point only to the *subjective* memory of Christ's atoning work rather than to the actual power and presence of His person and life which passes over to the participant by faith. In short, the idea of the sacrament as a real spiritual transaction in time and space becomes a nominal abstraction. Once the *"being* of the sacraments" is given up, says Nevin, "all turns on the *name* merely; the thing itself, the true and proper reality, resolves itself into a mere outward commandment at best, an empty shell or letter, and nothing more."[2]

In this chapter we examine Nevin's controversy with sacramental nominalism and its hermeneutical implications. These implications involve an incarnational understanding of language, on Nevin's side, which sets the stage for his sacramental view of Scripture in the next chapter. Consequently, his view of Scripture, indeed, his view of reality, cannot be understood apart from his sacramental theology.

The Sacraments and the Mystical Presence

The sacraments exemplify the law of reification by which the ideal presses with an inner necessity to become embodied in time and space. For Nevin a sacrament is a visible sign of an invisible grace. But this definition only begins to explain his theology. In its ecclesiastical usage, *sacramentum* belongs to the Greek idea of *mysterion*—that is, something that is hidden.[3] The sacraments, therefore, are the medium by which the hidden powers of the

---

[2]Nevin, "Doctrine of the Reformed Church on the Lord's Supper," *MR* 2 (1850): 546; see also 542.

[3]Erb, *NT*, 359-60.

spiritual world are revealed. They are not empty or abstract signs, but "set us in communion with the positive actualities of that world" of grace.[4] What Nevin says about baptism is true of the sacraments generally, namely, "there is a real rending of the heavens—the canopy that separates the world of nature from the world of grace."[5]

Not all religious symbols are sacraments. Sacraments are by nature divine institutions. Their power comes from God and their efficacy depends on the Holy Spirit. They are seals or pledges of God's promised blessing intended for use only by those who are members of the covenant.[6] They are inseparably connected with the idea that the whole life of the Christian, from birth to death, "is to be embraced in the power of the church."[7] Yet, the distinction between the sacraments proper and other religious rites or expressions of religious life "is not so great that there may not be an approach of the latter to the former."[8]

Indeed, Nevin believes that the "sacramental idea" is broader than the two sacraments of the church (that is, baptism and the Lord's Supper). The sacraments do not exhaust the entire presence of the supernatural in the world. "The whole constitution of the world is sacramental, as being not simply the sign of, but the actual form and presence of invisible things." It is for this reason that the church has not made a clear distinction between "the two regular sacraments" (baptism and the Lord's Supper) and the secondary sacraments (marriage, ordination, etc.) which the church itself has designated. Though they may not be sacraments in the proper sense of the word, they are still entitled to respect as being in some sense sacramental.[9]

---

[4]Nevin, "Dorner's History of Protestant Theology," *MR* 15 (1868): 597. Even in the political world, emblems (flags, bonds, etc.) "mean nothing and are worth nothing, without the actual political resources which exist altogether independently of them in real historical form."

[5]Nevin, "The Old Doctrine of Christian Baptism," *MR* 12 (1860): 200.

[6]Erb, *NT*, 362-63. The efficacy and objectivity of a sacrament does not depend on the disposition or intention of the administrator but on the general intention of the church.

[7]Ibid., 370.

[8]Ibid., 365.

[9]Erb, *NT*, 372-73.

Citing the Oxford Tractarian and hymn writer John Keble (1792–1866), Nevin points out that the Fathers were deeply imbued with this sacramental sense. They brought Plato's philosophy to realization, though in a vastly higher sense than its original form. Everything for them existed in two worlds, namely, the external world of sense, and the spiritual world of mind. Creation was not only a figure, emblem, or symbol; rather, God is truly in it. The whole world is full of sacraments.[10]

This sacramental view of reality is also the basis of the liturgy. Like the sacraments, the liturgy is an externalization of the divine economy which grows out of the general life of the church.[11] As Nevin's early colleague, F. A. Rauch, once indicated, it should not be a mechanical creation, but like a work of art should be ruled by one central idea.[12]

Nevin regarded the Eucharist as a divine mystery and inveighed against American Protestantism for its rationalistic and subjective view of the Holy Supper. In his view, the nature of the Incarnation and the church stands or falls with our view of the sacrament of the Lord's Supper. Since the Eucharist "forms the very heart of the whole Christian worship," our understanding of it will ultimately condition and rule our view of the church and the Incarnation. Indeed, our entire idea of theology and ecclesiastical history is influenced by the "sacramental question."

If the sacrament is regarded as subjective only, if the powers of the world to come are not made present in time and space, then according to Nevin, the Incarnation and the church are only abstractions or, at best, devices contrived to bring about a higher end. The church can never be more than a human society in this

---

[10]Nevin, "Dorner's History of Protestant Theology," 625-26. Nevin does not reference his citation of Keble. On the sacramental view of reality in antiquity, see Armand A. Maurer, "Analogy in Patristic and Medieval Thought," in *Dictionary of the History of Ideas.*

[11]Nevin, *MP*, 5; Erb, *NT*, 415, 418-19. The Old Testament cultus exemplifies this principle. The tabernacle and the entire sacrificial system with its equipment and liturgy was a dim but real historical embodiment of the heavenly order (see Heb. 8–9).

[12]Nevin, *Vindication of the Revised Liturgy, Historical and Theological* (Philadelphia: Jas. B. Rodgers, 1867) 8-9; Appel, *Recollections of College Life at Marshall College* (Reading PA: Daniel Miller, 1886) 249; cf. Erb, *NT*, 415.

view. However, if the Eucharist is seen as a mystery by which the grace of God is actually made present, then the Incarnation and the church must also be regarded as divine, historical constitutions.[13]

For Nevin, the doctrine of the real presence in the sacrament rests squarely upon the idea of the *unio mystica*. "Christianity," he tells us in the first chapter of *The Mystical Presence*, "is grounded firmly in the living union of the believer with the person of Christ; and this great fact is emphatically concentrated in the mystery of the Lord's Supper."[14] Hence the sacramental doctrine of the Reformed church is inseparably connected with this idea of "an inward living union between believers and Christ in virtue of which they are incorporated into his very nature, and made to subsist with him by the power of a common life."[15]

Nevin marshaled an impressive battery of historical evidence to vindicate the Reformed theology of a real presence over and against the symbolic memorialism of nineteenth-century American religion.[16] His historiography took him beyond the sixteenth century. His intent was to demonstrate that the doctrine of the real presence, though appearing in different historical forms, was an integral part of the church's life and practice from the beginning. The Reformed doctrine of the Eucharist is as full and deep as the church itself.[17]

Finally, Nevin maintains that the virtue of the sacrament is appropriated only by an active faith. The sacrament is a medium of communication with Christ only for believers. Faith, therefore, is necessary to receive its efficacy. Those who come to the table

---

[13]Nevin, *MP*, 3-4; Erb, *NT*, 397, 403-404. Nevin's argument here reflects his existential philosophy: When all is said and done, our view and praxis of the sacrament says more about our view of the Incarnation and the church than any abstract theological doctrine. Nevin intended to demonstrate that even though evangelical Christianity claimed to defend the orthodox or Reformed view of the church and the Incarnation, their sacramental theology contradicted this.

[14]Nevin, *MP*, 51.

[15]Nevin, *MP*, 54; see also ibid., 122-24.

[16]Ibid., 63-64.

[17]Nevin, *MP*, 127-38; idem, "Doctrine of the Reformed Church on the Lord's Supper," 545-46; see also idem, "Wilberforce on the Eucharist," *MR* 6 (1853): 161-87.

unworthily (whether they are regenerated or not) receive only the sensible signs of the Eucharist which they eat and drink to their own condemnation. But, faith does not clothe the sacrament with its power. "The force of the sacrament is in the sacrament itself." Faith is only the *condition* or *instrument* by which we appropriate its effects, not the *principle* of its objective force. Just as the healing virtue of Christ was available only to those who exercised faith, so faith is the necessary condition for receiving the sacrament.[18]

The Conflict with Sacramental Nominalism

Nevin's sacramental writings represented one side of a major controversy with Princeton over the nature of the Lord's Supper. His reformulation of the Reformed doctrine of the Lord's Supper, was not an attempt to alter the Reformed tradition. Rather, as the subtitle to *The Mystical Presence* says, it was, "A Vindication of the Reformed or Calvinistic Doctrine of the Holy Eucharist." Once "vindicated," though, Nevin proceeded to recontextualize the historic Reformed position within a framework of Romantic idealism. (In doing so, he was applying his own principles of historical development in which the essential life-form of a system is conserved throughout its changing historical forms.)

The historical dimensions of this debate are beyond the scope of our present investigation. What concerns us, from a hermeneutical standpoint, is the sometimes subtle but unmistakable controversy over semiotics. Beneath the theological issues is a battle over the nature of language and symbol as they are defined by realism and nominalism.

The eucharistic controversy between Nevin and Hodge, then, represents another chapter in the struggle between Mercersburg and nominalism. Nevin's biographer characterized the controversy as a conflict between an "extreme nominalist" in the Lockean tradition and a "moderate realist" in the Platonic tradition.[19] Theologically, the dialogue turned on two major points: (1) the nature

---

[18]Nevin, *MP*, 183, 61, 120n.
[19]Appel, *LW*, 294. Hodge, however, was not an extreme nominalist. Nevertheless, Appel discerned the shape of this debate with uncanny insight.

of human personality; and (2) the relationship between divine grace and sacramental signs.

Both of these issues—anthropological and sacramental—relate directly to the question of language and hermeneutics. In the first chapter we unfolded the linguistic and hermeneutical implications embedded in Nevin's cosmology. So too there are linguistic and hermeneutical implications embedded in Nevin's sacramental theology. Nevin's work suggests that the eucharistic liturgy of the Catholic church is rife with such implications. There is a basic Christian metaphysic which emerges out of the fabric of the church's historic worship. Apart from this, the sacramentalism of the church would be rendered powerless and even meaningless. Consequently, for the Christian, philosophy is not simply an instrument or heuristic device (contra postmodernism) which could adopt any world-hypothesis as a supreme fiction.

(1) Anthropological Realism

Briefly stated, the underlying matter is whether the ideas of "person" and "life," especially as they relate to Christ, are to be regarded as simply an aggregate of individual qualities (nominalism) or a hypostatic reality (realism). If the former, then these ideas are essentially abstractions—conventional terms used to classify a family of like properties. If the latter, then "person" and "life" are the ontological realities out of which these individual properties and attributes flow.

Nominalism. As a self-avowed adherent of "moderate" or "realistic dualism,"[20] Hodge, like Nevin, believed in the reality of natural laws. In his view they are more than creatures of the mind, linguistic conventions, or probabilities. They are objective forces and powers. He rejected, therefore, the Common Sense view of his colleagues who maintained that such "laws" are not the efficient cause of phenomena, but merely a rule or pattern by which an unknown cause operates. A "law," according to Baconian philosophy, is a generalized *description* derived from observed, actual phenomena rather than the source of all phenomena, actual and potential. Thus, universals have no ontological reality. They are

---

[20]See Hodge, "Nature of Man," *PR* 37 (1865): 115.

merely generalizations built up and collated from inductive observations of sensible facts. The efficient causes of nature remain hidden in the infinite multiplicity of natural phenomena.[21]

But Hodge often fails to carry his philosophical presuppositions into his theology. On the one hand, he subscribes to the Reformed doctrine of the Trinity and the Incarnation, both of which regarded the idea of "person" as an individual hypostasis. On the other hand, however, he proceeds as if Christ's person and life were only a collection of separate attributes rather than an indivisible whole. Christ thus became a person in name only. So, regardless of his belief in the reality of universal laws and the unity of Christ's person, Hodge's eucharistic theology is decidedly nominalistic and dualistic.

Hodge's theological and historical position clearly demonstrate that whatever concrete unity he may ascribe to Christ's person, evaporates into a nominalistic abstraction. First, he draws a sharp distinction between Christ crucified and Christ glorified; that is, between the sacrificial *atoning* efficacy of Christ, and the *vivifying* efficacy of his person as taught by John Calvin. In the Lord's Supper, believers are said to participate in the former, but not in the latter.[22] Furthermore, he makes it clear that we have no communion with Christ's humanity, but only with his divine nature.[23]

Hodge's error lies in his reduction of Christ's person to a collection of attributes or qualities that can be separated and rearranged at will. How can we fail to be united with Christ's

---

[21]See Theodore Dwight Bozeman, *Protestants in an Age of Science: The Baconian Ideal and Antebellum American Religious Thought* (Chapel Hill: University of North Carolina Press, 1977) 62-70. As Reid indicated, "All the distinct knowledge we have or can attain of any individual is the knowledge of its attributes; for we know not the essence of any individual. This seems to be beyond the reach of the human faculties." Thomas Reid, *Essays on the Intellectual Powers*, essay 5 ("Of Abstraction"), §2 ("Of General Conceptions") in *Reid's Inquiry and Essays*, ed. Ronald E. Beanblossom and Keith Lehrer (Indianapolis: Hackett, 1983). In the same volume, see Reid, *Essays on the Active Powers*, essay 1 ("Of active Powers in General") §6 ("Of the Efficient Causes of the Phaenomena of Nature").

[22]Hodge, "Doctrine of the Reformed Church on the Lord's Supper," *PR* 20 (1848): 249, 251.

[23]Ibid., 255-56, 258.

humanity if we are truly united to His person which includes both His humanity and divinity (without confusion or division)? In Nevin's words, "What is personality if it be capable of this broad dualism?"[24] Though Hodge insists that Christ's benefits cannot be severed from His person,[25] he is nevertheless willing to sunder His two natures as well as His crucified and glorified person.

A second indicator of Hodge's nominalism is his concept of "life." Unlike Nevin, he does not consider "life" to be a real genus. For him it is not a substance or an essence, but a predicate or quality. This move enables Hodge to sharply distinguish Christ's human and divine life. So, rather than seeing two natures organically united in one theanthropic life, he could emphatically deny that the Reformed church held, in any sense, "that our union with Christ involves a participation with his human body, nature, or life."[26] Having said this, however, he is left with the difficulty of explaining how we could be partakers of Christ's flesh (which for Hodge was simply its atoning efficacy) apart from his humanity. As Nevin observes, Hodge reduces communion with Christ's body and blood to a "bold metaphor."[27]

In his review of *The Mystical Presence*, Hodge effectively resolves the idea of life into an extrinsic property. He seems to imply that we partake not of Christ's real flesh and blood, but only of its *influence*. As the years passed, he continued to refine this position in a consistently nominalistic direction. (During this time we also find a growing awareness in his writings that his disagreement with Nevin grew largely out of their divergent views of realism.) In 1865, writing on the "Nature of Man," he took his stand against the realistic position, arguing that "Life is a predicable, not an essence. It supposes a subject of which it is predicable."[28] Several years later, in his *Systematic Theology*, he cites the English botanist and natural historian H. Alleyne Nicholson

---

[24]Nevin, *Antichrist*, 13; see idem, "Doctrine of the Reformed Church on the Lord's Supper," 446, 450-51.

[25]Hodge, "Doctrine of the Reformed Church on the Lord's Supper," 249, 254-55.

[26]Ibid., 255.

[27]Nevin, "Doctrine of the Reformed Church on the Lord's Supper," 451.

[28]Hodge, "Nature of Man," 125.

(1844–1899), who maintained that vitality is "something super-added and foreign" to matter. Like electricity it requires a conductor as the condition of its manifestation. It is not, therefore, an intrinsic property of the material substance to which it adheres.[29] These refinements only served to vindicate Nevin's charge that, contrary to the Reformed position, Hodge had reduced the idea of Christ's life (at least with regard to His human nature) to a simple influence on the believer.

Nevin's Realism. Hodge, as we would suspect, viewed Nevin's Christological realism with utter suspicion. He accused the Mercersburg doctor of adopting Friedrich Schleiermacher's pantheistic theology in which divine life and human life are but two modes of the same principle.[30] Nevin objected. His use of Schleiermacher (as well as Hegel, Schelling, and Coleridge) was guided by a critical and historical orthodoxy.[31] These protests notwithstanding, Hodge held firm to his accusations and later lumped Nevin together with both Hegel and Schleiermacher concluding, "Theologians of this class deny that God and man are essentially different."[32]

It is plain that Hodge did not understand Nevin's realism or the law of reification. The genius of this philosophy is not to reduce all distinctions to a monad as Hodge supposed, but to hold distinct entities in organic union while maintaining their differences. It stands midway between dualism and pantheism, being a synthesis of these opposing systems. Hodge, however, stood firmly on the side of Cartesian dualism. He consistently emphasized the

---

[29]Hodge, *ST*, 3: 731. This should not be interpreted to mean that Hodge regarded life merely as a physical force. This he specifically denied. In his lengthy discussion on materialism (Hodge, *ST*, 1:246-99), he sides frequently with those who believe that life is the result of an immaterial, vital principle (see esp. 285-99).

[30]Hodge, "Doctrine of the Reformed Church on the Lord's Supper," 259, 264-67, 278.

[31]Nevin, *Antichrist*, 3-12. As Nevin points out, his normative principle was not the *identification* of God and humanity, but their *organic union* in the Incarnation and the real historical entrance of the Divine life in history.

[32]Hodge, *ST*, 2:429; but cf. his apologetic tone in a lengthy footnote to Nevin, ibid., 3:655n. See also Hodge, "Nature of Man," 128. For Hodge the use of Schleiermacher and German theology was in itself enough to convict Nevin. Hodge's aversion to German thinking was downright visceral.

separation, rather than the unity, of metaphysical natures as well as the separation of distinct substances. He was unable to unite humanity and divinity, body and soul, matter and life, form and substance.[33] Consequently, his notion of Christ's person was nothing more than the sum of individual attributes. As Nevin retorted, if he was guilty of Eutychianism (confusing Christ's two natures) as Hodge had charged, then Hodge was no less guilty of Nestorianism (severing Christ's two natures).

For Nevin, personality clearly involves the notion of an ideal hypostasis, that is, a metaphysical foundation from which individual qualities arise. However, the unity of Christ's person does not thereby entail a confusion of his *natures*. Here is where Hodge's accusations prove to be wide of the mark. Though all personalities involve will, intelligence, and self-consciousness, they are distinguished by their separate natures—human, divine, angelic.[34] In other words, the distinguishing nature of a being constitutes a deeper ground than personality.[35] The two natures of Christ, which subsist without confusion or separation, are mediated to us through a single, unified personality or life. Consequently, the object of our communion is neither the divine nature of Christ nor his humanity separately taken; it is the theanthropic person of Christ.[36]

Hodge was not theologically opposed to the unity of Christ's person. It was, after all, an article of orthodoxy.[37] However,

---

[33]As Holifield points out, Hodge's theology of discontinuity was also rooted in the tendencies of the Reformed tradition which emphasized the contrast between creation and redemption, God and humanity, the visible and invisible church; E. Brooks Holifield, "Mercersburg, Princeton, and the South: The Sacramental Controversy in the Nineteenth Century," *Journal of Presbyterian History* 54 (Summer 1976): 239-40.

[34]For Nevin's treatment of angels and demons see Erb, *NT*, 168-76.

[35]See John Calvin, *Institutes of the Christian Religion*, ed. John T. McNeill, trans. Ford Lewis Battles, Library of Christian Classics 20 (Philadelphia: Westminster, 1960) I.xiii.2,6. Calvin carefully distinguished person (which he called a hypostasis or subsistence) from essence. Without this division the persons of the Trinity would be reduced to modes or attributes.

[36]Nevin, *Antichrist*, 12; see Erb, *NT*, 291. Nevin made it clear that for him, "life" is not the same as "nature" with regards to the "hypostatical mystery." Rather, it is commensurate with the idea of "personality."

[37]According to the Westminster Confession (VIII.ii), the "two whole, perfect,

Nevin's clarifications were of no avail. Even after twenty-five years, Hodge's opposition continued unabated.[38] At the same time, though, he insisted on the unity of Christ's person in terms that would have pleased even Nevin.[39] Nevertheless, the Princeton professor's view of the Eucharist, as Nevin saw it, belied his Christology.

Conclusion. Hodge never moved from his original position on the Eucharist either historically or theologically. For him, the locus of Christ's personality continued to rest exclusively in the Logos even after the Incarnation. This dualism continues to flourish in many forms of contemporary evangelical theology, especially where the symbolic memorial view prevails. Communion with Christ's person entails no participation in His proper humanity. With Hodge, the most they could say is that "a divine person with human affections and sympathies is near us and within us."[40]

Though Hodge considered himself to be a defender of the Reformed tradition, his historical and theological method betrayed a propensity for creative innovation and contextualization. Having imbibed the nominalism of enlightenment empiricism (along with its Cartesian dualism), he then proceeded to restate the Reformed doctrine of the Eucharist in much the same way that Nevin attempted to correct Calvin's deficiencies by using the principles of his own realism.

Hodge's historical method, however, was attended by a certain danger: for the most part Nevin was aware of his differences with the Reformed tradition; Hodge was not. Indeed, Hodge refused to

---

and distinct natures, the Godhead and the manhood, were inseparably joined together in one person, without conversion, composition, or confusion. Which person is very God and very man, yet one Christ, the only mediator between God and man."

[38]See Hodge, *ST*, 3:650-61.

[39]Ibid., 2:390-92; see also 2:382-83. Like Nevin, Hodge even identified personality with self-consciousness (ibid., 1:391, 444).

[40]Ibid., 3:638, see his treatment on the Eucharist generally (611-50), and his rebuttal of Nevin's view (650-61). Hodge's view agreed with a class of Reformed interpreters who, as J. H. August Ebrard said, "teaches the communication of both the natures of Christ in the supper, but only *as regards his theandric spirit, not as regards his theandric body*"; see Nevin, "Doctrine of the Reformed Church on the Lord's Supper," 501.

admit them even after they were fully exposed. Commenting on Hodge's review of *The Mystical Presence*, Nevin correctly observed, it "urges terms and propositions which are in truth of common acknowledgement, quietly filling them always with its own sense, as though they could admit no other. . . . "[41]

(2) The Conflict over Realistic Semiotics

Nevin's conflict with sacramental nominalism, as I pointed out in the beginning of this section, turned on two major points: anthropology and semiotics. Needless to say, the two issues cannot be entirely separated. Our concept of "humanity" and "person" are conditioned by the way we use and understand language. By distinguishing between anthropology and semiotics, however, I intend to address the specific *relation between the sacramental sign and the thing it signifies*. So, having considered the anthropological dimension of the sacramental controversy we now turn to the question of semiotics.

The relation between signs/symbols and the reality they signify is fundamental to the definition of a sacrament. This relationship is governed by the connection between the ideal (in this case the spiritual reality) and the actual (namely, the finite sign or symbol), which brings us back around to the issue of realism and nominalism. For, when the objective reality of universal ideas is denied, general terms (e.g., tree, humanity, etc.) come to stand only for mental abstractions which may not correspond to a reality outside the individual. In other words, nominalism affirms only the reality of individual things (this tree, that human). Universal ideas have no ontological reality, they are merely names we use to designate individual things with *similar* characteristics. Realism, on the other hand, affirms the objective reality of the ideal. General terms, therefore, refer not simply to individuals with similar attributes, but to their ontological essence (hence individuals are said to be human because they embody the universal idea of humanity).

When these concepts are applied to the question of sacraments, two corresponding theologies emerge. In the first instance the sacramental symbol points only to a mental abstraction (nominal-

---

[41]Nevin, "Doctrine of the Reformed Church on the Lord's Supper," 447.

ism); in the second instance it is united to an objective spiritual reality (realism). These views represent the symbolic memorial doctrine of "Puritan" theology (as Nevin called it), and the Reformed concept of the real presence which Nevin maintained.

By severing the ideal (objective grace) from the actual (sacramental signs), American theology had, for the most part, reduced the sacrament to a memorial supper which turned upon the individual experience of the participant. Whereas the Reformed view maintained that the grace of God (that is, the ideal) is made present objectively through the signs of the sacrament (that is, the actual), the symbolic memorial view insisted that these signs point only to the subjective experience of the worshipper.

Because the sacramental question involves the relationship between a sign and its referent, it has implications for the broader philosophy of semiotics.[42] John Locke (1632–1704), who laid the foundation for nominalistic philosophy in America, drew a telling distinction between what he called "real" and "nominal essences."[43] A nominal essence is the idea by which *we* define the necessary qualities of a thing so that without these qualities it would be, by definition, something else. A real essence, on the other hand, is "that constitution of the parts of matter, on which these qualities and their union depend." Locke maintained that the real essence, like substance, cannot be known. Consequently, it is the nominal essence—our idea of the thing—which proscribes the bounds of the species. The result is that general terms (that is, universals) are merely names. They have no extramental reality.[44]

---

[42]We cannot enter into the various distinctions between symbols, emblems, signs and signals made by Rauch (*Psy*, 248-52). Suffice to say that sacramental signs are regarded as symbolic because the sign and the thing signified are *homogeneous*, e.g., as when a light is used to represent life. Linguistic signs are *semiotic*, because there is no resemblance between the form (i.e., the signs) and the contents they represent. According to Nevin, "Signs are wholly external, while the relation of a symbol to the thing signified is more or less internal." Erb, *NT*, 213.

[43]See W. Von Leyden, "What is a nominal essence the essence of?" in *John Locke: Problems and Perspectives*, ed. John W. Yolton (Cambridge: Cambridge University Press, 1969) 225-33.

[44]John Locke, *An Essay Concerning Human Understanding* ed. with an introduction by Peter H. Nidditch (Oxford: Clarendon Press, 1975) 3.6.6, 2-3, 8-9, 20, 27, 36; 4.7.9. "[G]eneral and universal belong not to the real existence of things, but are the inventions and creatures of the understanding, made by it for

There is a direct and striking correspondence between linguistic nominalism and sacramental nominalism, and between linguistic realism and sacramental realism. In the case of Locke's representational realism, the primary referent of language is the individual's idea of a thing (its nominal essence) rather than the thing itself. Hence, general terms refer only to my perception of reality which, we would hope, bears some connection to the noumenon. Similarly, in sacramental nominalism the sign refers to my subjective experience of grace (nominal essence) which is in some way connected to the objective reality of grace revealed historically in Jesus Christ (real essence).

According to the symbolic memorial view, the sacramental signs point to the *objective*, historical work of Christ (that is, the real essence) which is subsequently wrought in the soul of the believer through grace. Nevertheless the sacrament itself has no objective efficacy. It involves no real offer of grace made *present* in and through the transaction. Indeed, whatever benefit may accrue from participating in it is wholly dependent on the worshipper's state of mind. Hence, the signs do not actually convey what they represent. Instead, their primary function is to evoke a deeper devotion and affection towards Christ on the part of the communicant (that is, the nominal essence). Memorialism, which begins as an objective form of rationalism, degenerates into subjectivity.

Even granting the modifications made by the Common Sense school (e.g., Thomas Reid and Samuel Tyler) to Locke's empiricism, we have not moved substantially closer to Nevin's realistic position. For though, according to them, we come to perceive the reality of a sensible object by an original and natural judgement, we do not thereby comprehend it in its *ideal* ground. That is to say, we do indeed know this or that human as a real sensible object with intellect and personality, but we do not know the ideal essence of this person (that is, universal humanity) by which he or she comes to exist. For the most part, general terms refer only to

---

its own use, and concern only signs, whether words or ideas" (3.3.11). Cf. his overall definition of language: "*Words in their primary or immediate Signification, stand for nothing, but the* Ideas *in the Mind of him who uses them* . . . " (3.2.2). See also 2.11.9; 3.3.6, 12.

generalizations built inductively from individual instances. They point to descriptions (patterns) of actual phenomena, rather than the ideal ground or law which comprehends all potential as well as all actual phenomena.

Furthermore, since a universal term refers only to actual phenomena, its definition is dependent on the experience of the individual or community. Without a single, objective, underlying reality, its meaning may differ according to individual perception or social convention. The meaning of language is derived primarily from its usage.[45] Linguistic and sacramental signs, therefore, refer to the subjective experience of the individual or, at best, the community.

In contrast to this, a realistic system of semiotics regards signs as the means by which we apprehend a given universal. Ideas are the transparent medium (*formal* sign) through which we perceive things (including other ideas) and come subsequently to attach signs or symbols (*instrumental* signs). The sign and its corresponding reality are thus inwardly coupled. The meaning of language is derived primarily (though not exclusively) from its referents in reality. As a result, there is a direct correspondence between things that are real (e.g., objects, ideas, God) and the words we use to signify them.[46] Human language, Rauch tells us, "expresses the true Being of all that exists." Each genus can have only one corresponding conception, but many names. These names

---

[45]This, despite inductive attempts to ground such definitions in actual attributes. A striking example of this is seen in historical attempts to redefine humanity in order to justify slavery, genocide, and abortion. Reid, in a foreboding passage, contemplates the difficulty of defining *humanity* in connection with legal questions that may arise regarding "monstrous" births: "Although this be, in reality, a question about the meaning of a word, it may be of importance, on the account of the privileges which laws have annexed to the human character. . . . It is, indeed, very difficult to fix a definition of so common a word; and the cases wherein it would be of any use so rarely occur, that perhaps it may be better, when they do occur, to leave them to the determination of a judge or of a jury, than to give a definition, which might be attended with unforeseen consequences"; Reid, *Essays on the Intellectual Powers*, essay 5, §2, in *Reid's Inquiry and Essays*.

[46]For a nontechnical but insightful treatment of the relationship between words and meanings from a realistic perspective, see Mortimer J. Adler, *Ten Philosophical Mistakes* (New York: Macmillan, 1985) 54-82.

are objectively and inseparably linked to their corresponding conceptions by the power of memory.[47]

In this respect, Nevin's theory of semiotics is the polar opposite of the nominalistic theory which tends to sever language from reality. His understanding of language exemplifies the law of reification by which the spiritual or ideal is externalized in time and space. Though words are not ideas and ideas are not words, Nevin believes that the two are inseparable. Language, he said in 1842, "is a constituent part of the life of the soul itself." Like a germ "the rational nature of man expands itself from the beginning in the form of thought and speech." Therefore, "To think, is to speak."[48]

Nevin's concept of ideas is, of course, rooted in his Christian Platonism. He regards thought as universal and objective. The connection between these ideas and the words used to represent them is more than accidental, it constitutes a *bond of being*. "Language," he tells us, "is thought itself corporealized and made external, and it must be penetrated of course with the same organic life in all its parts." It is the nisus of the soul developed and modified through the particular environment in which it lives. Hence, "no language can be regarded as a full, perfectly symmetrical, and absolutely transparent, corporification of the true inward life of thought."[49] "A perfect language would be like a garment of light, unfolding with clear transparency the life it was formed to invest and represent."[50]

---

[47]Rauch, *Psy*, 262, 267. According to Rauch, memory resolves the conflict between realism and nominalism by virtue of its ability to unite many names to one objective concept. Nevin's linguistic theory was based on Rauch's philosophy and was developed shortly after Nevin published the second edition of Rauch's *Psychology* in 1841.

[48]Nevin, *The German Language. An Address Delivered before the Goethean Literary Society of Marshall College, at Its Anniversary, August 29, 1842* (Chambersburg PA: Publication Office of the German Reformed Church, 1842) 4; see also Erb, *NT*, 178. Cf. Rauch, *Psy*, 256: "As reason produces our conceptions, so it produces inseparably with them also their corresponding words."

[49]Nevin, *The German Language*, 5. See also Rauch, *Psy*, 251-52, 256-57.

[50]Nevin, *The German Language*, 8. Coleridge had a similar view of language. See Samuel Taylor Coleridge, *Aids to Reflection*, in *The Complete Works of Samuel Taylor Coleridge*, ed. W. G. T Shedd (New York: Harper & Brothers, 1858) 1:248-51; and his essay in the same volume, "Hints towards the formation of a more Comprehensive Theory of Life," 377; idem, *The Friend*, in *The Collected Works of Samuel*

What are the sacramental implications of these ideas? In the sacraments, says Nevin, the bond between the sign and the grace it signifies "is more interior than that between a common sign and that which it represents."[51] The issue before us is, first, whether the sacramental signs evoke an objective reality, and, second, in what sense this sign is conjoined to its corresponding reality. Sacramental nominalism does not disavow the reality of Christ's person and life. It does, however, deny that what the signs represent is actually conveyed *in* the sacramental transaction. The signs point only to the *subjective* memory of Christ's atoning work rather than to the actual power and presence of His person and life which passes over to the participant by faith. The idea of the sacrament as a transaction in which the powers of the heavenly world are actually manifested in time and space is rendered utterly abstract.

In Nevin's theology, the Incarnation functions as the archetype for the sacraments insofar as it denominates the union of God and creation. Just as the Logos assumed common humanity and ennobled it while yet preserving the integrity of the created order, so the grace of God assumes the common elements of the sacraments and sanctifies them without destroying their integrity. The sacramental union between the elements and the divine grace is not, of course, on the same order as the hypostatic union between Christ's natures. Rather, the relationship is analogous. Nevertheless, a confusion of these natures would destroy the integrity of creation. So too, a complete separation would destroy the potential unity of creation because the perfection of creation is predicated on communion with God.[52]

Herein lies the error of transubstantiation and symbolic memorialism, according to Nevin. The latter destroys the unity and purpose of creation by severing the sacramental elements from divine grace in a dualistic fashion. The former, as Nevin sees it,

---

Taylor Coleridge, ed. Barbara E. Rooke (Princeton: Routledge & Kegan Paul, 1969) 1:458-59.

[51]Erb, *NT*, 360.

[52]The natural cannot fulfill its own ends except as it is conjoined with the spiritual. To sanctify something, says Nevin, is to raise it "from mere nature to the region of the spirit, by the word of God and prayer"; Nevin, "The Bread of Life," 18.

amounts to a miraculous deification of creation.[53] "The spiritual can never be imprisoned, or *banned*, in the bosom of the mere natural." Hence the water of baptism can never be the "principle or efficient" cause of regeneration just as the bread and wine could never themselves be the glorified life of the Lord.[54]

The Sacraments and Occasionalism. So, on the one side, the Roman and Lutheran views err by identifying "Christ's presence in the Eucharist with the elements" themselves. On the other side, the "Puritan" theory falls over into an outright dualism. Modern rationalism and sectarianism, observes Nevin, "so sunders form and substance in the life of the church as to make the first a mere outward accident to the second, if not an actual incumbrance."[55]

Between these two extremes there was the theory of sacramental *occasionalism* which was embraced by Hodge, but repudiated by Nevin. Hodge never claimed to be an occasionalist, nor is there any historical evidence to suggest that he followed either Arnold Geulincx (1624–1669) or Nicolas Malebranche (1638–1715). In fact, he specifically rejected the theory of occasional causes because it overturns the efficiency of secondary causes by referring all activity to God alone.[56] However, as I have indicated before, Hodge stood firmly in the tradition of Cartesian dualism. Consequently, he inherited the same question as Descartes' successors: What is the connection between God and creation and how do they interact?

This question had a direct bearing on Hodge's sacramental theology and the problem of semiotics. Indeed, the whole concept of historical mediation, Incarnation, and instrumentality—so essential to Nevin's sacramental theology—was at stake. Unlike the Calvinistic view of the sacraments, occasionalism denies that there is a sacramental and objective *bond* between the sign and the grace

---

[53]See Nevin, *MP*, 184-85. As he says elsewhere, "There is a palpable contradiction in making Christ identical with matter or symbol. This is heathenism." Erb, *NT*, 394, 392. Some question remains as to how well Nevin understood transubstantiation. This is difficult to ascertain owing to the brevity of his remarks.

[54]Nevin, "The Bread of Life," 32.

[55]Nevin, *MP*, 184; idem, "Doctrine of the Reformed Church on the Lord's Supper," 546; see also ibid., 542; idem, "Noel on Baptism," 239.

[56]Hodge, *ST*, 2:281-82.

it signifies. However, the theory does not thereby resolve the sacramental transaction into a subjective memory. Rather, the use of the sign is said to be synchronized with the immediate and objective bestowal of grace by a divine intervention. Sacramental occasionalism is essentially dualistic for it maintains that the two realities involved (in this case the elements and the divine grace) are so fundamentally "different in kind that they cannot causally interact."[57]

Hodge did not question the objectivity of the sacrament. But he did believe that the sign and its attending grace are essentially unconnected. There is no sense in which the elements themselves become the mediate agent of Christ's grace either locally or dynamically through the sacramental transaction. As he explains it, unlike the Lutherans who believe that the "power of the word, is inseparably joined with the signs," or the Romanists who say that the sacraments themselves contain the grace they convey, the Reformed teach that the "attending power of the Spirit" can be separated from the signs.[58]

As Brian Gerrish has pointed out, Nevin specifically repudiated sacramental occasionalism.[59] The relationship between the terrestrial sign and the celestial grace is not merely external. They are "not simply joined together in time, as the sound of a bell, or a show of a light, may give warning of something with which it stands in no further connection." The outward elements and the grace that is inwardly received are not made present to the soul as two entirely separate realities; rather the "inward and outward, by the energy of the Spirit, are made to flow together in the way of a common life."[60]

Hodge, on the other hand, was an exponent of what could only be described as *intermittent* occasionalism.[61] This was his undoing.

---

[57]Peter Angeles, *Dictionary of Philosophy* (New York: Barnes and Noble Books, 1981) s.v. "Occasionalism (mind/body theory)."

[58]Hodge, "Doctrine of the Reformed Church on the Lord's Supper," 274.

[59]Gerrish, *Tradition and the Modern World: Reformed Theology in the Nineteenth Century* (Chicago: University of Chicago Press, 1978) 200n.31.

[60]Nevin, "Doctrine of the Reformed Church on the Lord's Supper," 449-50; idem, *MP*, 182, 118; see also idem, "Doctrine of the Reformed Church on the Lord's Supper," 437.

[61]Gerrish calls it "radical occasionalism"; Gerrish, *Tradition and the Modern*

Not only did he separate the sacramental sign from its attending grace, but he maintained that since the efficacy of the sacrament is dependent upon the cooperation of the Holy Spirit, "the power is in no way tied to the sacraments. It may be exerted without them. It does not always attend them, nor is it confined to the time, place, or service."[62]

According to Hodge, then, the sacraments are not *always* objective. They may be administered apart from the operation of the Holy Spirit at times, in which case they are only subjective memories. The signs are thus reduced to nominalistic abstractions. (Hodge, of course, did not see it that way.) The power is not "in the transaction" but "beyond it altogether," as Nevin says. In the end it degenerates into a mental abstraction which turns on the mind of the worshipper. Princeton, he charged, strips the sacraments of "efficacious virtue." The relation between the sign and the grace they represent is "altogether outward and loose; they point to it only like dead fingerboards, or as signs in algebra, giving notice of truth which is not in themselves, and can have no presence save by the mind and will of those who are led to think of it in this way."[63]

In itself, occasionalism does not reduce the efficacy of the sacrament to a subjective mental state. However, by refusing to acknowledge an antecedent *guarantee* or divine *pledge* of grace, Hodge's view may well have been closer to the symbolic memorial view than to Calvin's doctrine of the real presence. Catching the scent of subjectivity, Nevin charged Hodge with reducing the sacrament to a mental construct by offering a noetic presence as the only alternative to Christ's local presence. The result was a doctrine of the "real absence" instead of the "real presence" of Christ![64]

As it stands, Hodge's theology of the Lord's Supper was not out-and-out memorialism. Despite all appearances, Hodge was not about to reduce faith to rationalism. In his view, faith includes

---

World, 62.
[62]Hodge, "Doctrine of the Reformed Church on the Lord's Supper," 257.
[63]Nevin, "Doctrine of the Reformed Church on the Lord's Supper," 452.
[64]Ibid., 436-37, 444, 448-51, 485, 502.

both knowledge and assent as well as a "real appropriation of Christ."[65] Nevin may have exaggerated the degree of Hodge's subjectivity. But, taken together with his other nominalistic tendencies, the Mercersburg doctor was more than justified in questioning the direction of his theology.

Conclusion. On the Efficacy of the Sacraments

Nevin's struggle to articulate a Reformed doctrine of the Eucharist was for him the unfolding of a supernatural reality revealed for faith. Through the sacraments, the theanthropic life of Christ is actually made present in time and space. Nevin's theology is the existential reality of the new creation coming to expression in thought and language. As he later said, "The apprehension of faith is not from knowledge, but in order to knowledge."[66] This, after all, is the nature of theology as Nevin saw it. In other words, the object of theology is neither speculation nor abstraction, but the realities themselves—that is, the ontic and the holy.[67]

Nevertheless, Nevin was not about to dispose of creeds or theological definitions in favor of experience and theological relativism. This would contradict the very basis of his system which assumes that reality is intrinsically intelligible. But, Nevin recognized the fundamental *priority* of being over knowing: It is "not what we may know, but what we habitually feel. . . . It is not enough," he continues, "to hold a correct creed; not enough, to have a scientific insight into the nature and grounds of the Christian system; the thing needed is a direct contact on the part of the spirit with the realities themselves with which religion is concerned."[68]

By locating the center of theology on the objective realities of the Christian faith rather than their subjective apprehension,

---

[65]Hodge, "Doctrine of the Reformed Church on the Lord's Supper," 436-37, 247.

[66]Nevin, "Nature and Grace," 502. The fact of the Trinity, says Nevin, was *manifested* through the Son before it was comprehended dogmatically.

[67]See Nevin, "Is the Bible of God?" *The Friend*, 23 Jan. 1834; 13 Mar. 1834; idem, "Religion a Life," *The Friend*, 25 Dec. 1834, 15, 22, 29 Jan. 1835.

[68]Nevin, "Worldly Mindedness," *WM*, 1 July 1840.

Mercersburg theology distanced itself from the nominalism that had come to characterize American theology. In a profound article on the relationship between Christianity and consciousness, Nevin's colleague and former student, Thomas G. Apple (president of Franklin and Marshall College, 1878–1888), traced the difference between the two systems to the influence of empiricism.

Contemporary American pietism (that is, revivalism), according to Apple, shifts the ground of certainty from the idea of objective faith as held by the Reformers (that is, connecting the testimony of the Spirit to the word and sacrament), to feeling and subjective experience. Much of this problem stems from Locke's philosophy which holds that all knowledge comes only by experience. It denies the distinction between essential nature or life on the one hand, and experience on the other. By teaching that the soul is a *tabula rasa*, Locke set aside the idea of an objective human nature which lies at the foundation of personal life. Hence, the only reality is individual experience.

If this is true, then we must ultimately reject the organic unity of the race as well as the Christian belief that a nature deeper than the individual is fallen. Having done this, we are also forced to repudiate the objective constitution of Christianity itself along with the objective side of the Christian life (that is, the redemption of human nature rather than merely the individual). Such subjectivism, as Apple rightly concludes, undermines both the sacraments and catechetical religion.[69]

In contrast to this, he proposes an intuitive psychology which elevates being above human intelligence and experience. The subconscious life is considered the significant, maybe even predominant, portion of our overall life. Since God-consciousness is an intuition of the real presence of the infinite in the human soul (an idea derived from Schleiermacher), the mystery of the new birth penetrates deeper than conscious experience. In this respect it is analogous to natural birth. "Nature is deeper than knowledge.

---

[69]Thomas G. Apple, "Christian Life Deeper than Conscious Experience," *MR* 30 (1883): 59-62. This philosophy, observes Apple, was joined to rationalistic Deism and destroyed faith in the supernatural. He credits Schleiermacher with eliminating these errors by restoring the essential nature of Christianity as life.

From nature proceeds conscious knowledge and conscious acts." The fall corrupted the whole of human nature out of which comes evil thoughts and deeds. Hence regeneration, if it is to be redemptive, must be as deep as the effect of the fall.[70]

So, our relationship to the spiritual world holds, for the most part, in the subconscious or unconscious sphere of our life. As Apple tells us, "there are springs of life that are nourished down in the inner depths of the spirit, of which we have no conscious knowledge except in the effect or results in experience." When we feed upon the body and blood of Christ in the sacrament, the grace conferred is not necessarily connected with a sensation or feeling. One should not mistake spiritual nourishment for religious excitement. The same may be said of infant baptism and the Incarnation. In both cases, God is at work in the secret depths of the human soul before the child attains consciousness. Again, the analogy to nature is relevant. Before the child comes to know "the name or meaning of parent," Apple tells us, "the loving beams of a mother's eyes, the sunshine of her countenance, the tender tones of her voice, have power to evoke a life of love." Can it be, he asks, any less with our Heavenly Father?[71]

Apple concludes by suggesting that the "certitude of the believer" according to Reformed theology, "is not exactly a certitude of knowledge, but of faith." As with justification by faith, the "matter of certitude" is not the subjective state of the believer, but the "objective fact" of his or her salvation wrought by Jesus Christ. The Christian life, therefore, is not dependent on our conscious experience.[72]

Apple's and Nevin's distinction between the objective reality of faith and its subjective appropriation is intended as a safeguard against experiential forms of faith and theological rationalism. At the same time, however, both believed that the reality of the Christian faith emerges ineluctably into human language. Indeed, those who will not receive the doctrines of the Bible, says Nevin, "show themselves destitute of its life, its power, though they hold

---

[70]Ibid., 42-47.
[71]Ibid., 47-51.
[72]Ibid., 54-55.

fast strenuously to the letter."[73] The point of Nevin's sacramental hermeneutics it that the spiritual and the ideal must clothe itself, must embody itself, in the medium of human expression. Consequently, language is neither an end in itself (analytical philosophy; literary hermeneutics), nor a circular system of signs and symbols with no entrance or no exit (deconstructionism), but a *bridge to reality* and a gateway to being. To say anything less would reduce the Incarnation and the sacraments to nominal abstractions or magical singularities at best.

---

[73]Erb, *NT*, 116,106.

Chapter 3
The Interior Sense of Scripture

It would not be too much to say that contemporary hermeneutics is, for the most part, dominated by some form of Cartesian and Kantian presuppositions. From Descartes comes the insistence that all knowledge begins with the subject. From Kant comes the belief that all knowledge is perspectival. As a result any reading of the text may be validated since it is no longer possible to adjudicate between interpretations.

Interpreters are thus caught in an endless loop as they attempt to analyze the *process* by which texts are understood rather than the texts themselves. As Mark Ellingsen has noted, "On such grounds the interpreter has no immediate access to texts (to the *Ding an Sich*), and so can never hope to identify the meaning of a text. For, given Kantian presuppositions, interpreters must necessarily provide their own constructive contribution to the interpretive result."[1]

For Nevin, on the other hand, the Scriptures are the incarnation of the Divine life in human language. They are "the very embodiment in natural form of a supernatural spiritual power and glory surpassing immeasurably the reach of all merely natural intelligence or thought."[2] Here, as throughout Nevin's hermeneutics, the Incarnation serves as the fundamental paradigm. Like the two natures of Christ, the words of the text are organically joined to the supernatural life they embody. All this presupposes, of course,

---

[1]Ellingsen, *A Common Sense Theology*, 31.

[2]Nevin, "Christianity and Humanity," 476; see idem, "The Pope's Encyclical," *MR* 27 (1880): 39: The Bible "can be nothing less than the divine itself ensouled in human speech, as really as the words of Christ were that, when he stood among men on earth, and spake as never man spake."

that the ultimate nature of truth as it is found in the Bible is not simply abstract or notional, but a real incarnation, namely, Christ Himself.

On the other hand, when truth is reduced to information or doctrinal abstractions, faith becomes a mere belief *that* something is, rather than a participation in the reality itself. The spiritual presence which penetrates the language of the text with its own life is attenuated into subjectivity. Instead of being the historical medium of the *viva vox Dei*—the life and power of God revealed for all time—the Bible becomes a codex of facts. This, in short, was the rationalistic hermeneutic against which Nevin so vehemently protested.

Like Schleiermacher and other romantic exegetes, Nevin believed that the presuppositions which guide the biblical interpreter must emerge out of the essential character of Christianity itself. The meaning of Scripture can only be grasped when we hear it speak from its own element which is the life and power of Christ. The proper context of Scripture, therefore, is none other than the new creation in Jesus Christ considered in its universal scope. This is the presupposition of all sound interpretation.

Even more fundamental than an understanding of the Bible's grammar and history (though these are necessary) is a true faith which holds directly to Christ in and through the apostolic life and teachings of the church. Those who disregard or minimize the necessity of this first principle, or who adopt a worldview based upon other foundational principles (e.g., rationalism, humanism, historicism), can never grasp the true life and meaning of the Scriptures.

Though the cultural and philosophical context of these hermeneutical issues changed from the time when Nevin taught at Western Theological Seminary in the 1830s, to the time of his "hermeneutical essays" four decades afterwards, his fundamental principle remained essentially the same: the realization or incarnation of the spiritual and the ideal in actual existence. So far as he was concerned, there was little difference between the rationalistic methods of interpretation espoused by Common Sense theology, and the hermeneutics later espoused by historicism, humanism, and Darwinism. The former—which was shaped in part by the influence of eighteenth-century German historical criticism—was only a nascent form of the latter. As we will see, both were rooted in naturalistic presuppositions which are inimical to the idea of Christianity. Nevin saw the line of development here just as clearly as he saw cultural materialism and religious skepticism growing out of the incipient materialism of Common Sense philosophy (see part II).

Nevin's biblical hermeneutics is quite unlike anything found in contemporary theory. Reality, as we saw in the first chapter, is a top-down affair in which there is an actual correspondence between heavenly things and earthly things, between the spiritual and the physical. The Scriptures, therefore, are not simply the product of social and cultural forces, they are not merely a reflection of the mind of the early church; nor can they be said to represent a human search for truth or the cumulative experience of religious communities. Instead the Bible is a system of realities. The authors of Scripture "contemplated divine truth through the medium of divine affections, and the objects of faith stood forth upon the vision of their souls, in all the reality that belongs to objects of sense."[3] The hermeneutical implications of this principle form the subject of our present inquiry.

The Development of Nevin's Sacred Hermeneutics: The Word as Sacrament

The continuity between the incarnate Word (Christ) and the word written was the basis of Nevin's sacramental view of the Scriptures. During his debate with Charles Hodge over the nature of the Lord's Supper in the late 1840s, the Princeton professor accused Nevin of departing from the Reformed tradition because he had insisted that the grace received through the Eucharist is in some sense unique.[4]

---

[3]Nevin, *The Claims of the Bible Urged Upon the Attention of Students of Theology. A Lecture, Delivered November 8, 1831, at the Opening of the Winter Session of the Western Theological Seminary of the Presbyterian Church* (Pittsburgh: D. & M. Maclean, 1831) 23.

[4]Hodge, "Doctrine of the Reformed Church on the Lord's Supper," 275. Brian Gerrish has shown that Hodge was on solid ground here for Calvin had forcefully

But for Nevin the Eucharist stood in direct continuity with the *unio mystica* (that is, the mystical union between Christ and believers). He readily admitted, therefore, that in the Reformed tradition "the grace represented in the sacraments is described as being of the same general nature with what has place in the life of believers at other times." This assumption, however, is no bar against the idea that the sacrament has a "*special* significance and power" and carries in it a "special exhibition of grace" for the support and repair of our communion with Christ.[5]

These facts notwithstanding, there is more than a kernel of truth to the charge that in his early attempts to articulate the meaning of the Lord's Supper, Nevin neglected to consider the sacramental power of the word in Reformed theology. While this may have been a mere oversight (polemics is always a one-sided affair), Nevin himself later (1879) acknowledged the fact in what could only be described as a striking admission.[6] As if to regain the ground he had lost, his later theology (beginning around 1870) was devoted almost entirely to expounding the sacramental presence of Christ in His word. The *unio mystica* formed the link between sacrament and word: the *life* of Christ which is present in every believer, is also present in both the word and sacrament as their actuating spirit.

The meaning of the Eucharist, as Nevin later defined it, is to "actualize, or make real" the idea of spiritual nourishment or food,

---

expressed the same idea in several of his writings. See Gerrish, *Tradition and the Modern World*, 62-63.

[5]Nevin, "Doctrine of the Reformed Church on the Lord's Supper," 498. J. H. A. Ebrard pointed out that Nevin's eucharistic doctrine differed from the Lutheran view in that the Holy Supper is an act by which the life-union with Christ is renewed, rather than being a new kind of corporeal union in addition to the *unio mystica*. See the translation of his review in Appel, *LW*, 271; see also Nevin, "Doctrine of the Reformed Church on the Lord's Supper," 457n.

[6]Nevin, "The Bread of Life," 28n. The text merits reproduction in full: "In our past controversies with regard to the Lord's Supper, we may not have done justice always to what must be considered in this way the true and real pre-eminence of the Word above all sacraments. In contending for the faith delivered to the saints in regard to the sacraments, we may have failed to intone properly what the presence of the Lord in his WORD means, without which there is no room to conceive of his presence among men in any other form. Should this have been so, let us trust that it may be so no longer."

which according to Scripture is a real participation in the life of Christ. "For it is the word of God divinely joined with the elements which makes the sacrament, according to the ancient Christian fathers." In their view, the procession of the word was a "continuous going forth of life from the Lord." When it was joined to the sacraments, it became their "living soul." In this respect, Nevin considered the word to have preeminence over the sacraments.[7]

Nevin's theory of language also played a major role in his later concept of "Sacred Hermeneutics." He viewed language as the icon, the actual medium, through which we apprehend the Divine numen or life. Under the Hegelian influence of F. A. Rauch, his early colleague at Mercersburg, he formulated a definitive concept of language in 1842: "Language," he said, "is thought itself corporealized and made external, and it must be penetrated of course with the same organic life in all its parts."[8]

Nevin made it clear that he viewed both the Scriptures and the sacraments as corollary expressions of the theanthropic life of Christ. "Christ utters Himself by the grace of the Spirit through the media of the Word and sacraments." His words are spirit and life (John 6:63). Christ's life is thus the substance of the word making it difficult to distinguish between "the Word spoken and the Word incarnate." As in the sacraments, the Spirit of Christ is the "soul" and animating spirit of the "external Word." The external sign, in this case the spoken and written word, must be united to the Spirit so that the internal and external are *in* the other, not locally but mystically.[9]

But even more powerful than the word written is the word preached. It is a fuller incarnation of the life of Christ in the world. Words come from living beings and so embody the life from which

---

[7]Nevin, "The Bread of Life," 28. This view is sometimes referred to as "Dynamic Symbolism." See L. Michael White, "Real Presence," in *Encyclopedia of Early Christianity*, ed. Everett Ferguson et al. (New York/London: Garland Publishing, 1990).

[8]Nevin, *The German Language*, 5. The term "Sacred Hermeneutics" was used by Nevin himself in an article by the same name. See Nevin, "Sacred Hermeneutics," *MR* 25 (1878): 5-38.

[9]Erb, *NT*, 286-87, 314.

they emanate. Truth is thus "the externalization of thought in the form of a word." The spoken word, according to Nevin, is more efficacious than the written, because the ear is a more inward sense than the eye. Sound reveals the inner constitution of things.[10] Thus, even the written word must be pronounced in the mind.

"The preaching of the Word," in Nevin's view, "implies the actual presence of the life which it represents. . . . It embosoms the mind of the soul from which it proceeds." There is a need, then, to embody the word in living preachers in order to be effective. Christianity, after all, was first "exhibited in living men" before it was inscripturated. However, this can take place only within the context of the church which is the living organ of the word.[11]

Nevin's Mystical Tendencies

Nevin's later interest in hermeneutics and biblical interpretation was accompanied by an ever-deepening sense of the mysterious nature of Scripture. Owing to these "mystical tendencies," as his biographer tells us, he turned away from the "fleeting shadows" of this world to the sphere of the eternal and heavenly. Consequently, he became more enamored with "spiritual, mystical, and symbolic" interpretations of the Bible.[12]

These revolutions in his thinking were not new. As a Christian Platonist, Nevin always looked beyond (or rather *through*) the world of sense in order to discern the true significance of reality. For him, the meaning of the Bible was never bound simply with its grammar or history. Nevertheless, a number of events between 1861 and 1872 seemed to drive him, in ever-increasing degrees, toward a more profound and mystical consideration of the Scriptures.

---

[10]Cf. Rauch, *Psy*, 211: "While the eye opens the universe with its thousands of objects, the ear is their common echo, and communicates their internal being . . . for, whatever can emit sound, from the gushing water, and the singing bird, to man, expresses by it the degree of its vigor, the manner of its life. The ear excites, therefore, more deep sympathy than the eye."

[11]Erb, *NT*, 357-59. This disproves the general misconception that Mercersburg placed little emphasis on the pulpit owing to their elevation of the sacraments.

[12]Appel, *LW*, 740-41.

The Civil War, the death of two of his sons (Richard Cecil in 1867, John Williamson in 1872),[13] the first Vatican Council with its declaration of papal infallibility,[14] and the unrelenting liturgical controversy in his own church, appear to have diminished his overall confidence in the church's historical progress, forcing him, so to speak, to seek Christ's presence in the Scriptures here and now. The Word of God, as Nevin said in 1878, is the "only medium of direct communication with heaven."[15] Yet, with this graduated loss of historical optimism he also became more millenarian in his thinking. He placed his hopes more in the Second Coming of Christ than in the historical evolution of a Reformed Catholicism (a prospect inspired by his former colleague, Philip Schaff).[16]

In addition to these negative considerations, there was also a constructive force at work in Nevin's life at this time which helped to promote his interest in hermeneutics and Scripture. This force was none other than the "personification of mediating theology," Richard Rothe (1799–1867). Rothe had studied with Carl Daub, Hegel, and Schleiermacher. In 1863 he published his *Zur Dogmatik* which contained expanded essays on "Revelation," and "Scripture" that were originally published in *Theologische Studien and Kritiken*.[17] These essays, with orthodox modifications, formed the basic framework for Nevin's hermeneutical writings. Rothe viewed reve-

---

[13]Appel, *IW*, 740. In 1848 Nevin lost his infant son, Herbert, to the measles; ibid., 64, 762-63.

[14]See Nevin, "The Old Catholic Movement," *MR* 20 (1873): 240-94; idem, "The Pope's Encyclical," 5-50.

[15]Nevin, "The Supreme Epiphany; God's Voice Out of the Cloud" *MR* 25 (1878): 244.

[16]See Reiley, "John Williamson Nevin," 327. These later millenarian expectations coincided with a rising interest in biblical prophecy among some conservative theologians (especially dispensationalists, Calvinistic Baptists, and Presbyterians) after the Civil War. See Nevin, "The Bread of Life," 42. On the prophetic movements of the late nineteenth century, see T. P. Weber, "Bible and Prophetic Conference Movement," in *Dictionary of Christianity in America*, ed. Daniel G. Reid (Downers Grove IL: InterVarsity Press, 1990).

[17]See Richard Rothe, *Zur Dogmatik* (Gotha: F. A. Perthes, 1863). Nevin's hermeneutics also bore a close resemblance (in many places) to Schleiermacher's program. For a brief but penetrating description of Schleiermacher's hermeneutics, see Thiselton, *New Horizons in Hermeneutics*, 204-36.

lation as a personal encounter and a divine disclosure. It is an incarnational event which necessitates, in addition to an objective *manifestation*, a corresponding receptivity in individuals which he regarded as *inspiration*. Though he refused to identify the Bible with revelation and insisted that it contained many errors, he believed that as a record of revelation it provides a medium through which God can speak to the religious affections. This personal presence, however, is centered in Christ where, as Claude Welch says, "manifestation and inspiration utterly coincide."[18]

Nevin's interest in Rothe also kindled an appreciation for the Swedish mystic, Emanuel Swedenborg (1688–1772).[19] According to Appel, Nevin's attention was probably directed to the mystic in the early 1870s by Rothe's writings. Subsequently he secured a Latin edition of Swedenborg's works. He found them to be both edifying and full of original genius. In Nevin's own words (as related by Appel), Swedenborg stood in the company of Dante and Kant as "one of the greatest poets and philosophers" who ever lived, "if not the greatest." According to Appel, Nevin's last works (after his retirement in 1876) illustrated his newly found "mystical and theosophic tendencies, as well as his allegorico-mystical Exegesis." However, as Appel rightly points out, Nevin did not leave the letter of Scripture or history behind in his Christian mysticism.[20] The Apostle's Creed and the Incarnation continued to function as the central paradigm of his thought.

Nevin's interest in Swedenborg was part of a larger historical movement in nineteenth century America which Sydney Ahlstrom calls "The Swedenborgian Impulse." The seer's influence, though often unacknowledged, was widespread, ranging from Transcendentalism to medical quackery. In an era of revivalism and constant flux, Swedenborg made the universe spiritually intelligible. He was hailed as a free thinker who liberated the mind from the narrow confines of traditional dogma. At the same time, however,

---

[18]Welch, *Protestant Thought in the Nineteenth Century* (New Haven CT: Yale University Press, 1972) 1:289. Welch is quick to add, however, that Christology was not as central to Rothe's theology as it was to many of his contemporaries.

[19]See Reiley, "John Williamson Nevin," 324-27.

[20]Appel, *LW*, 740-42; see Nevin, "Reply to an Anglican Catholic," *MR* 21 (1874): 421-22.

he ignited new interest in biblical exegesis. Through Swedenborg's spiritual interpretation, Christ is said to make his Second Coming through the inspired Scriptures.[21] Like Rothe, then, Swedenborg identified revelation as a form of God's personal disclosure.

Whatever influence one may attribute to Swedenborg, it seems apparent that his writings acted more as a *catalyst* which awakened tendencies in Nevin that had been long slumbering. Nevin appropriated the ideas of Swedenborg with the same critical thoughtfulness he applied to other thinkers such as Schleiermacher and Rothe. As the evidence we have examined above clearly demonstrates, Nevin's later "mysticism" and his view of Scripture stood in direct continuity with his earlier theology.

"Allegorico-mystical Exegesis"

Nevin's adaptation of Swedenborg's hermeneutics raises important questions about the complexion of his own system and its place in the history of interpretation. Like Origen and Swedenborg, Nevin believed that the text of Scripture contains more than one level of signification. The similarity originates in a mutual sympathy for the Platonic or Neoplatonic tradition which supposes that there is an ideal or spiritual reality standing behind the world of space and time. Origen distinguished three levels of significance, corresponding to the three parts of human nature: body, psyche, and spirit.[22] Swedenborg's divisions corresponded to three distinct orders of being which are reflected in all creatures: the natural, the spiritual, and the divine or celestial.[23]

---

[21]Sydney E. Ahlstrom, *A Religious History of the American People* (New Haven CT: Yale University Press, 1972) 483-86; Emanuel Swedenborg, *Arcana Coelestia*, 4060; idem, *True Christian Religion*, 776-77, 779-80; idem *Apocalypse Explained*, 1183; idem, *Spiritual Diary*, 1647; idem, *Invitation to the New Church*, 29, 38, 44, 52. Swedenborg's works, originally written in Latin, are available in numerous editions and translations. All of them, however, employ a standard reference system divided by paragraphs rather than page. Unless otherwise noted, citations are from Emanuel Swedenborg, *A compendium of the theological writings of Emanuel Swedenborg*, ed. Samuel M. Warren (New York : Swedenborg Foundation, 1875).

[22]J. N. D. Kelly, *Early Christian Doctrines* (San Francisco: Harper & Row, 1978) 73; see Origen *De principiis*, 4.1.11; 4.2.4.

[23]Swedenborg, *Doctrine of the Sacred Scriptures*, 6, 7; idem, *True Christian Religion*, 212. See also Roberts Avens, *Blake, Swedenborg, and the Neoplatonic*

These distinctions are echoed in Nevin's interpretive method which, being patterned after the Incarnation, is typically twofold. The Scriptures, he said, possess an "inner" and "outer" sense which he frequently compared to the "natural" and "spiritual," or the "body" and "soul."[24] While his debt to Swedenborg is never openly acknowledged in these later writings, he made no secret about his sympathy for Alexandrian exegesis. Ancient exegesis, despite its apparent arbitrariness and disregard for grammar, logic, and common sense, "did full homage in its confused way to the idea of an infinite supernatural in the oracles of God. . . . " Even an Origen, says Nevin, transcends modern interpreters such as Hugo Grotius, J. A. Ernesti, and Moses Stuart. The error of modern hermeneutics in this regard is that it views words as "simply outward signs of things . . . mere *voces et praeterea nihil* . . . spectacular unrealities." Consequently, they are not amenable to any "art of interpretation."[25]

Despite Nevin's affinity for Platonic thought forms, he never fully embraced the allegorical hermeneutics of Swedenborg or the Alexandrian school. Allegorical interpretation supposes that the meaning of a text transcends the historical level. As Angus Fletcher remarks, it is "a symbolic surplus beyond the literal level." Since most allegories are "images of the cosmic order," the key to their structure usually lies in a system of ideas outside the immediate context. Thus, the older Greek term for allegory (ὑπόνοια, *hyponoia*) refers to the opaque character of language. The true meaning is veiled behind or buried beneath the literal sense. Allegory is especially amenable to Platonism and Neoplatonism: the Platonic notion of ideas and the fullness of being exhibited by the cosmic hierarchy (the so-called "principle of plenitude") provide a vast reservoir of hidden meanings for the allegorist. The sensible becomes a self effacing sign for the transcendent.[26]

Tradition (New York: Swedenborg Foundation, n.d.).

[24]Cf. Swedenborg, *True Christian Religion*, 192-94; idem, *The New Jerusalem and Its Heavenly Doctrine*, 25.

[25]Nevin, "Sacred Hermeneutics," 9n., 14, 36. Appel also compared Nevin's mystical exegesis to the Alexandrian school, see Appel, *LW*, 742.

[26]Angus Fletcher, "Allegory in Literary History," in *Dictionary of the History of Ideas*, 1:41-43.

The multiple senses which arise out of this allegorical method should not be confused with the polyvalent character of the text associated with postmodern hermeneutical theories (especially reader-response criticism). These systems assume that the text has no objective existence or meaning. Which is to say, meaning is not something that inheres *in* the text, but stands in *front* of it. It is either created by the reader as he or she engages the text; or, it is said to be an existential event which emerges from the interaction ("dialogue") between text and reader. Allegorical hermeneutics, on the other hand, makes objective truth claims about the meaning and significance of the text. Multiple senses are not the product of an existential encounter with the text, but arise out of the manifold character of the realities to which the words of Scripture refer.[27] The exegete does not open a window merely into a literary world projected by—"in front of"—the text, but into the real world of the text (historical and spiritual). As Thomas Aquinas observed:

> The author of holy scripture is God, in whose power it is to sig-nify his meaning, not by words only (as man also can do) but by things themselves. So, whereas in every other science things are signified by words, this science has the property that the things signified by the words have themselves also a signification. . . . The multiplicity of these senses does not produce equivocation or any other kind of multiplicity, seeing that these senses are not multiplied because one word signifies several things; but because the things signified by the words can themselves be types of other things.[28]

While Nevin's hermeneutical approach involves many of the elements associated with the Platonic approach discussed above, it also represents a significant departure from the allegorical method. Like the Platonic allegorists, Nevin certainly maintained that the spiritual sense is more than metaphor. It comes from an "inherent correspondence of the natural with the spiritual." Those literalists who stigmatize the inner sense or "under-sense" of

---

[27]The exception being the mystical etymologies and arithmology employed by some writers.

[28]*Summa Theologia* I.1.10; emphasis mine.

Scripture as "mystical extravagance" do not understand the spiritual order of the world generally.[29]

In keeping with his incarnational philosophy, however, Nevin rejected the metaphysical dualism which permeated Platonic philosophy. The spiritual and natural orders are not severed but organically united—the ideal is *in* the actual. Natural light, as Nevin points out, is indeed the reflection of spiritual light on a lower plane (a Platonic notion). But it is more than just the sign or emblem of this spiritual reality for men's thoughts, it is "its very effigy as we say, for their life."[30] Consequently, when Nevin adapts Origen's comparison between the Scriptures and the manifold character of human nature, he does so with the understanding that body and soul originate in a single principle of life.

This integral unity, which was an essential component of Mercersburg theology, was reflected in Nevin's hermeneutical essays. The words of Scripture are to Christ what the body is to the soul. "Each side of the relation needs the other; just as form needs essence, to be real, and essence at the same time needs form, to come into the light of actual existence. But the essential and inward, nevertheless, must everywhere rule the formal and outward as the soul rules the body."[31] The inspired word of God, said Nevin in one of his last articles, reflects the life of the seed which has two sides—the one "external, material, visible, the other inward, non-material, and wholly beyond the reach of the senses." The inward is "the entire motive-force of its germination and growth, the sole vitality of all that can ever come of it as blade, leaf, flower, or fruit."[32]

---

[29]Nevin, "The Supreme Epiphany," 236; idem, "The Bread of Life," 44-45. The doctrine of "correspondences" was one of the central principles of Swedenborg's philosophy; see his *Clavis Hieroglyphica* (written ca. 1744); *True Christian Religion*, 201-202; *Doctrine of the Sacred Scriptures*, 8. See also Inge Jonsson, "Swedenborg, Emanuel," *The Encyclopedia of Philosophy*, ed. Paul Edwards (New York: Macmillan Publishing Co. & The Free Press, 1967).

[30]Nevin, "The Supreme Epiphany," 228.

[31]Ibid., 242. This twofold division of the word was rooted, of course, in the hypostatic union. The inner illumination of the outward letter is exemplified in the glorification of Christ's humanity on the mount of transfiguration (ibid., 244).

[32]Nevin, "The Pope's Encyclical," 43. He cites the parable of the sower in which the seed is called the word of God.

Unlike the Platonic or Alexandrian notion of language in which the *spirit and life* of the text stand behind it as a mystery eclipsed and enshrouded by symbols, Nevin looked upon the language of Scripture as the formal expression, the concrete incarnation, of its inner life. The interior sense of the Bible is not behind, beyond, or even before the word, but *in* the word. Consequently, Nevin placed a greater value upon the grammatical and historical significance of the text than either Origen or Swedenborg.[33]

The practical impact of this incarnational philosophy was to push Nevin's exegesis more in the direction of typology than allegory. In allegory, the historical level of the text plays a only a minor role in interpretation. In typology, however, history is taken more seriously. It is regarded as the external medium of God's redemptive plan. The object of typology is to uncover the Christological correspondence between the two testaments in order to demonstrate the historical continuity of this plan. Typology, then, differs from allegory by accenting the historical, that is, one historical figure is regarded as the prophetic type of another.[34]

Nevin's typological approach is exhibited in his 1878 article, "The Supreme Epiphany; God's Voice Out of the Cloud." This is the most exegetical of his later essays and contains many of Swedenborg's interpretations. For the most part, he is occupied with finding the Christological and spiritual sense of historical things, events, and institutions that are *intentionally* symbolic, or

---

[33]This tendency is also reflected by the history of biblical interpretation: The ancient church came under the influence of Platonic philosophy in which, as Kenneth Hagen points out, "the particular thing (in Scripture, the letter of the text) is a mirror of reality. The reality is the fuller meaning." However, late medieval exegetes were influenced by Aristotle, who held that this reality is seen only in and through the thing itself. Thus, the letter of the text is the medium, rather than simply a mirror, of the reality to which it refers. See Kenneth Hagen, "The History of Scripture in the Church," in *The Bible in the Churches* (New York: Paulist, 1985) 5, 9.

[34]See Kelly, *Early Christian Doctrines*, 70-72. But as Fletcher has observed, the distinction is by no means unequivocal. See Fletcher, "Allegory in Literary History," 47. See also M. Simonetti, "Allegory–Typology," in *Encyclopedia of the Early Church*, ed. Angelo Di Berardino (New York: Oxford, 1992) 1:25: "any interpretation which is typological in content (in that it recognizes an OT fact as the *typos* of a NT fact) is necessarily allegorical in hermeneutical procedure (since it gives that fact a meaning other than the literal one)."

readily lend themselves to a symbolic interpretation: The transfiguration is said to be a mirror of Christ's incarnation as well as a symbol of divine revelation generally (that is, the cloud is the "natural side of the divine revelation . . . while the glory of the Lord in it is its interior spiritual side . . . "). All the details of Ezekiel's temple (Ezek. 40–48) and the Mosaic tabernacle have a spiritual significance. The holy anointing oil and incense (Exod. 30:22-38), for example, represent the glorified humanity of Christ (that is, the spices symbolize truths ordered from the outermost senses to the innermost good, while the olive oil symbolizes the divine spirit of Christ which permeates these truths with its own life). For Nevin, "The entire history of the Jewish nation, in the Bible, is said to be a hidden parable of heavenly things . . . the vehicle throughout of spiritual truths under natural cover and veil. . . ."[35]

Though Nevin's typological exegesis bordered on allegorism at times, unlike Swedenborg and other Platonic interpreters, he did not attempt to find an ocean of meaning in every word and syllable, or to dispense with the historical sense altogether in favor of some higher meaning which bears no relation to the letter of the text or its commonly received prophetic-Christological meaning.[36] On the other hand, he poured contempt upon modern methods of typological interpretation because they were rooted primarily (if not exclusively) in philological and literary presuppositions rather than an actual, internal correspondence between supernature and history. For Nevin, the letter of Scripture was not simply its philo-

---

[35]See Nevin, "The Supreme Epiphany," 222-55. The specific points of agreement with Swedenborg's philosophy and exegesis are too numerous to list here. On the transfiguration see Swedenborg, *Apocalypse Explained*, 64, 594. On the anointing oil see idem, *Arcana Coelestia*, ed., John F. Potts (New York: Swedenborg Foundation, 1915) 10250-10310.

[36]Swedenborg's massive commentary on Genesis and Exodus, *Arcana Coelestia* (filling twelve volumes in the English translation), is a good example of this form of allegorizing. Like Philo, who found Platonism in every verse of the Bible, Swedenborg found a secret spiritual significance peculiar to his own philosophy in *every* word, *every* action, "even to the smallest iota" of the text as he says; see Swedenborg, *Arcana Coelestia*, 1,2.

logical aspect, but involved all that Scripture is for natural reason including history, liturgy, and prophecy.[37]

Without discounting the influence of Swedenborg or Alexandrian Christianity upon Nevin's later hermeneutics and exegesis, his interpretation of the Bible may actually have more in common with the devotional commentaries of seventeenth and eighteenth century English and Puritan divines. After all, this was his spiritual pedigree. "He read and studied the Word of God," as his colleague Emmanuel Gerhart later said, "principally for his personal spiritual edification."[38] Nevin's resemblance to such a commentator as Matthew Henry (1662–1714) was more than formal or accidental. Though he was more Christocentric and metaphysical than the English exegete, Nevin's typological method (if not his actual interpretations) coincided with Henry's on many points. Like Nevin, Henry believed that the sensible world is a parable of heavenly things.[39]

By the late nineteenth century, however, this hermeneutical approach was rapidly falling out of favor among historical exegetes. Consequently, it was often scorned as being mysterious, allegorical, and unscientific. On the other hand, the renewed appreciation for symbol and mystery that many have experienced in our own day imparts to Nevin's hermeneutics a new sense of immediacy and relevance. Indeed, his critique of the critical method, which follows, will probably resonate with those who have sought an alternative to Enlightenment-bound hermeneutics.

The Failure of Modern Hermeneutics

Nevin's sustained polemic against grammatical-historical exegesis was preparatory to the presentation of his own method. It should be noted at the outset, however, that he had no qualms

---

[37]Nevin, "The Pope's Encyclical," 40.

[38]Gerhart, "John Williamson Nevin: His Godliness," in "A Memorial Service," *MR* 34 (1887): 18.

[39]E.g., the cloud of transfiguration, says Henry, was like a parable to the understanding of the disciples "to convey spiritual things by things sensible, as they were able to bear them"; see Matthew Henry, *Matthew Henry's Commentary on the Whole Bible* (repr.: Peabody MA: Hendrickson, 1991) 5:197 (Matt. 17:1-13).

with the use of critical exegesis, it was the reductionistic assumptions that often accompanied this method which he opposed. The cumulative impact of these assumptions, in his view, is to turn truth into a mental abstraction by severing the spiritual realities of the text from their linguistic signs. The language of the text becomes an end in itself—a mere medium of understanding—rather than the medium of Christ's true presence. When this happens, natural intelligence rather than faith becomes the only essential qualification for exegesis. But without the eye of faith the spiritual presence of Christ in His word is reduced to grammar and history. Hence the referent of the text is not Christ Himself, but an abstract representation of Him for the understanding.

By distinguishing between an outer and inner dimension of Scripture, Nevin was able to identify three corresponding methods of interpretation. The first attempts to move from the "outward natural" to the "inward spiritual." This is the central principle of the grammatical-historical system. The second attempts to modify this "bald rationalism" by coordinating these together. In the third we "throw ourselves absolutely on the inward spiritual as first in order and power." The natural man, observes Nevin, cannot receive the things of the Spirit because they are spiritually discerned (1 Cor 2:11-14).[40]

The critical theory, therefore, "is never able to come to any clear apprehension of what is meant by the spiritual-internal in the Bible, as distinguished from its natural-external." It begins, Nevin tells us, by supposing that words have two sides, formal and material, or sign and the thing signified. The formal is "outward and corporeal," the material is alleged to be "inward and spiritual." The inward side, namely, the meaning of the word, is itself divided into the literal and tropological (that is, figurative, symbolic). This distinction (also typical of today's literary interpretations), it is felt, somehow opens up a significance which is even more inward and spiritual. However, this inward side is not truly supernatural for it is accessible to the "natural man" who has

---

[40]Nevin, "Sacred Hermeneutics," 28.

no power to induct himself into the supernatural interior sense of the Scripture.

As Nevin saw it, the moral interpretation of Kant, the poetical interpretation of Robert Lowth (1711–1787) and J. G. von Herder (1744–1803), and the typological interpretations of Patrick Fairbairn (1805–1874) all fail by beginning with this fatal assumption.[41] Even today, despite a plethora of interpretive theories, one would be hard pressed to find a biblical hermeneutic which systematically incorporates the supernatural interior sense which Nevin addresses here.

Nevin's tirade against the grammatical-historical method was not, as I have already indicated, a general repudiation of scientific exegesis. He employed scientific methods in his own interpretation and held the study of language and history in the highest regard. His objection was over the inadequacy of this approach to connect the interpreter with the *spiritual realities* of Scripture. It is essentially a scheme based on naturalistic assumptions. Insofar as Christianity is human in its origin such presuppositions are sound. But they can never carry the exegete beyond the bounds of natural reason. How, asks Nevin, could Christ be the light of the world if His presence must first be demonstrated by the light of fallen, natural reason? The grammatical-historical method is really an attempt "to fill out the form of revelation, the text of the Bible, with substance or meaning drawn from the human spirit engaged with it, instead of owning and seeking in it the substance which belongs to it of right objectively from the Spirit of God."[42]

In order to be a divine revelation, says Nevin, the Scriptures must enshrine a supernatural object of faith. That object cannot be something that is added by the exegete through reason, hermeneu-

---

[41]Ibid., 34-35. Nevin had cautiously endorsed Fairbairn in an earlier article; see Nevin, "Fairbairn's Typology," *MR* 4 (1852): 76-80.

[42]Nevin, *My Own Life*, 69, 113. Thus, many of the words of Christ, according to some biblical scholars, are neither the *ipsissima verba* (actual words) nor the *ipsissima vox* (actual voice) of the historical Jesus. Rather they reflect the theology and life-situation of the ancient church. For the most part, they evolved out of the early Christian community in order to answer the existential necessities of the church and confer authority on the church's developing interpretation of Jesus. By adopting this same approach to *interpretation*, we pass over to reader-response criticism.

tics, or illumination. Faith requires a supernatural object directly implanted by the Holy Spirit and apprehended "directly in its own supernatural objectivity." Its yearning can only be satisfied by Christ Himself. Without this self-authenticating presence, the outward credibility and sense of the Bible "would be no revelation at all."[43]

So, the breakdown of the grammatical-historical method lies in its failure to unite the divine and human elements of revelation. It begins by assuming that the meaning of language is a function of its *usus loquendi* and no more. However, it is Nevin's contention that the "historical sense" of language is something more than can be quantified in grammars and lexicons. "It draws its main element always from the life and spirit which enter into the use of it in any given case." It is just here where this method fails to take into account the peculiar position of the sacred writers "as the subjects of a heavenly inspiration occupied and possessed with the full sense of supernatural and eternal things." Thus the sentiments and mind-set which belong to this divine inspiration must be considered as a *historical* factor in the task of interpretation. To ignore them would be a departure from the rules of grammatical-historical exegesis![44]

In the end, concludes Nevin, the primary fallacy of the grammatical-historical method lies in supposing that revelation is a "mere announcement of theoretical and doctrinal truth" communicated to natural intelligence in a supernatural way. Though this conclusion is no longer relevant in many quarters where we find a renewed recognition of the literary, moral and spiritual depth of Scripture, Nevin's fundamental critique of modern biblical exegesis is still sound: The "ground maxim" of this erroneous scheme, he says, is the assumption that human thought and speech are the only vehicles by which this knowledge is conveyed to our minds. Inspiration is confined to a providential leading of ordinary human thought and speech rather viewing it as "the actual descent of the Divine itself into such human thought and speech."[45] The human

---

[43]Ibid., 113-14.
[44]Ibid., 129-30.
[45]Nevin, "Christ the Inspiration of His Own Word," *MR* 29 (1882): 38-39.

element, therefore, stands entirely on the "outside" of the divine. The text of Scripture is sundered from its supernatural substance—that is, its "theopneustic sense." In the end, the supernatural is not *in the text* itself (that is, incarnated in living language) but comes after it only by way of subjective illumination.[46]

Princeton and the Evangelicals[47]

Nevin found that the "rationalistic" or "abstract" supernaturalism of late, eighteenth-century Germany fell in well with nineteenth-century American evangelicalism. Both systems tended toward subjectivity and both severed the idea of the divine from the actual life of the world. Beginning with Moses Stuart at Andover, the new hermeneutic spread quickly to Princeton and other denominational seminaries. It found a special affinity with subjective pietism (especially Methodism) where "the emotional subjectivities to the camp meeting" were easily translated "into the logical subjectivities of the divinity school."[48]

Despite the strenuous objections to Locke's representative realism (see chapter 2) made by the Common Sense school, Presbyterian Baconians unwittingly fell prey to it in their theology by equating the "facts" of Scripture with concepts (that is, doctrine) rather than realities.[49] We grant of course that these concepts were for them constitutive (that is, describing real things) rather than merely regulative (to use Kant's distinction). Nevertheless, by

---

[46]Nevin, *My Own Life*, 130-31; idem, "Sacred Hermeneutics," 9; idem, "Christ the Inspiration of His Own Word," 39.

[47]In describing Nevin's opponents (whom he referred to as "Puritans"), the term "evangelical" should be used cautiously. As Stephen Graham points out, "This definition fails both to identify the specific characteristics of what Nevin and Schaff opposed and to recognize that in many ways they considered themselves "evangelical." See Graham, *Cosmos in the Chaos*, 25n.56.

[48]Nevin, *My Own Life*, 96-100; Schaff, *The Principle of Protestantism*, ed. Bard Thompson and George H. Bricker, Lancaster Series on the Mercersburg Theology (Philadelphia: United Church Press, 1964) 186, 204. Nevin did not intend to impugn the faith of those who subscribed to this rationalistic system. But he felt that "a large amount of true faith" was "held in bondage" by it; Nevin, *My Own Life*, 118.

[49]According to representative realism, we know only our ideas of things, not the things themselves.

driving a wedge between reality and our understanding of it—that is, between the *noumenon* and the *nomen* in Scripture—they opened the door for a biblical rationalism which reasons from abstractions to reality rather than from reality to ideas. A doctrine is said to be true because the Bible teaches it, rather than saying that the Bible teaches it because it is true.

Perhaps the most telling example of this representative realism is found in Charles Hodge's theological method. Hodge identifies the truth of Christianity with the abstract concepts of Scripture rather than with the realities these concepts express. He affirms that Christianity is both "doctrine" and "life." But, by "life" Hodge does not mean the objective spiritual realities of the Christian faith. Rather, as Charles Jones points out, he means the subjectivity of religious experience. Hodge himself says that the objective side of Christianity is the divinely revealed doctrine of Scripture, while the subjective side is the life of Christ in the soul.[50] In practice, however, Hodge's theology is more spiritually objective and pietistic than his method would allow insofar as he sometimes identified the "facts" of Scripture with the realities themselves.[51] But his approach is not consistent.

Both Hodge and Nevin were fond of drawing analogies between the realms of nature and grace. Hodge models his theological method on Baconian principles by declaring induction—that is, the *a posteriori* rather than the *a priori method*—to be the only legitimate method for ascertaining facts in science as well as theology. Thus the Scriptures are to the theologian what nature is to the scientist, namely, "his storehouse of facts."[52] The task of theology, therefore, is to "collect, authenticate, arrange, and exhibit [these truths] in their internal relationship to each other."[53]

By contrast, Nevin regards the order of supernature or grace as the real, spiritual counterpart of nature. Like Hodge he affirms that the Scriptures are to the theologian what nature is to the

---

[50]See Charles A. Jones, "Charles Hodge, the Keeper of Orthodoxy: The Method, Purpose and Meaning of his Apologetic" (Ph.D. diss., Drew University, 1989) 208-209; Hodge, "What Is Christianity?" *PR* 32 (1860): 119.
[51]See Hodge, *ST*, 1:57-58.
[52]Ibid., 1:10.
[53]Ibid., 1:1; brackets mine.

scientist.[54] But this analogy carries with it a different meaning. Opposing any scheme that would render the truths of Scripture abstract, he consistently emphasizes the spiritual realities which underlie Scripture as the true object of our faith. Faith, therefore, is the organ by which we apprehend the supernatural. It is intuitive rather than simply discursive.

Hodge, for the most part, rejects this notion of faith. "Faith is limited by knowledge." "We can believe," says Hodge, "only what we know, that is, what we intelligently apprehend." Faith, therefore, "is an affirmation of the mind that a thing is true or trustworthy, but the mind can affirm nothing of that which it knows nothing."[55]

The most pointed illustration of this tendency may be found in the ardent Baconian philosopher, Samuel Tyler. Tyler proposes two sources of knowledge: experience and revelation. As aspects of Common Sense, both are believed spontaneously rather than by critical reflection. Like experience, revelation is believed "by an inward necessity independent of ratiocination." This inward necessity is derived from the illumination of the Holy Spirit and constitutes the essence of faith. But the object of faith for Tyler is not Christ Himself, but "the truth" which operates upon the mind and quickens the moral sensibilities. "True faith," according to Tyler, "is accompanied with a spiritual communion between the heart and the doctrine believed."[56] The proper method of biblical interpretation for Tyler consists in a strict adherence to grammar and logic by which the interpreter collects all the passages on a subject matter, "and from the induction of the whole" draws out the meaning of each.[57]

The legacy of this rationalist approach (though waning) is clearly discernible in some forms of twentieth-century Evangelicalism. Carl F. H. Henry, though supposedly departing from Common Sense Realism, states that the facts of Scripture are open and

---

[54]Nevin, "Essay on the Interpretation of the Bible," *The Friend*, 9 May 1833; idem, *Claims of the Bible*, 9; Erb, *NT*, 99; Hodge, *ST*, 1:1, 10-17.
[55]Hodge, *ST*, 3:84-85, 44.
[56]Samuel Tyler, "Connection between Philosophy and Revelation," *PR* 18 (1845): 407-408.
[57]Ibid., 387.

available to anyone with the mental aptitude to understand them. Although regeneration creates new attitudes toward truth and facilitates its understanding, it is not essential in this regard. In language reminiscent of Hodge he says:

> The subject matter of theology is not limited to examination only by those who are Christian believers. The truth content of theology can be investigated—as can that of astronomy and botany and geology—quite apart from the moral character of the technical scholar and his interest or disinterest in a new way of life.[58]

Spiritual-Dynamic Inspiration and Exegesis

As one fully opposed to reducing the Scriptures to mere doctrine, Nevin contends that the object that engages us is not "the notion simply of spiritual and heavenly things," but rather "those things as they are in their own actual being and objectivity." The presence of divine life and power in Scripture is "a mystical quantity inclosed in the outward letter, but forever inaccessible to the mere anatomical dissection of our schools, even though it were a thousand times more searching than at present."[59]

The *essence* of revelation, in Nevin's view, is the supernatural spirit of Christ, its *form* is the natural letter. Hence, the heavenly is seen *through* the earthly as light is refracted through clouds or precious gems. The two orders are united organically like body and soul. Thus, the distinction made by Paul between letter and spirit (2 Cor 3:6) is not simply the difference between the philologi-

---

[58]Carl F. H. Henry, *God, Revelation and Authority* (Waco: Word Books, 1976) 1:229. On the evangelical legacy of Common Sense Realism, see Ellingsen, *Common Sense Theology*; Bozeman, *Protestants*; George Marsden, "The Collapse of Evangelical Academia" in *Faith and Rationality: Reason and Belief in God*, ed. Alvin Plantinga and Nicholas Wolterstorff (Notre Dame IN: University of Notre Dame Press, 1983) 219-64; idem, "Evangelicals, History, and Modernity," in *Evangelicalism and Modern America*, ed. George Marsden (Grand Rapids MI: Eerdmans, 1984) 94-102; idem, *Fundamentalism and American Culture: The Shaping of Twentieth Century Evangelicalism 1870–1925* (New York: Oxford University Press, 1980); Mark Noll, "Common Sense Traditions and American Evangelical Thought," *American Quarterly* 37 (Summer 85): 216-38; Sydney E. Ahlstrom, "The Scottish Philosophy and American Theology," *Church History* 24 (1955): 257-72.

[59]Nevin, "The Inspiration of the Bible," 11, 28.

cal exterior of the language and the interior word or thought which produces it. Together these represent only the letter of the word. Rather, as Nevin observes, it is the distinction of higher and lower senses, natural and spiritual, "held together by a nexus . . . through vital energy descending from the higher plane to the lower."[60]

Despite this top-down perspective, Nevin's controlling belief in the Incarnation necessitates a corresponding emphasis on the historical immanence of revelation. Here, he shares some common ground with liberation theology and other praxis oriented systems. Mechanical and external concepts of revelation are, for him, inadequate. In order for revelation to be historically concrete it must unite itself with the actual life of humanity in such a way that the divine and created orders come into proper union. The human spirit must itself be a co-factor in the process so that revelation becomes "the outworking energy of the human life itself." At bottom, therefore, revelation is not the communication of information, but a divine historical event in the sphere of human life. As such, the Bible is not the substance of revelation itself, but its inspired "documentary record." In this capacity, at least, it cannot properly be the first principle of theology.[61]

Yet the nature of inspiration is significant for the task of exegesis. For Nevin, the means by which divine revelation was encoded in human language provides the key for determining the method by which such language is subsequently decoded. Minimally, inspiration involves an influence on the mind of the person which enables him to communicate facts and truths "absolutely free from error." But it is more than this. Inspiration is not simply a transient state, but a habit of life springing from the divine promise of Christ to abide with the holy writers. The human and divine are bound together like body and soul.[62]

---

[60]Ibid., 32-33.

[61]Nevin, *My Own Life*, 49-50; idem, "Brownson Again," 310-12.

[62]Erb, *NT*, 44-47. These views come out of Nevin's lectures at Mercersburg (1850-51). He later shifted his position and then retreated. There is, he concluded in 1880, a contradiction in affirming the Incarnation as a joining of the divine to the life of the world and then saying that such a revelation can authenticate itself to the world without a record which answers to its heavenly character. See Nevin,

Since language and thought are inseparably bound, inspiration must extend to thought and, through it, to language. It is not, however, necessary to suppose that it mechanically extends to every word. For Nevin, this would imply dictation. Instead, the thought freely flows from the inward life of the writer who is ultimately rooted, of course, in the divine life. Yet, because each writer embodies humanity in a particular way, revelation is modified through the historical peculiarities of each individual. When taken together, however, these writers comprise a more complete or perfect embodiment of humanity than would be otherwise possible.

This, in Nevin's view, accounts for the diversity and unity found throughout the Bible and provides a theoretical foundation for his interest in historical-critical exegesis. In keeping with the character of the Incarnation itself, though, he also believed that the mundane and historical dimensions of inspiration cannot attenuate its divine force which "looks through these always and wholly to Christ, and the spiritual world in him. . . . "[63]

Language and Interpretation

The unity of thought and language has tremendous implications for Nevin's hermeneutics. The *"in-forming* word" (thought) is the basis from which the "word processional" (language) emanates. We cannot, therefore, consider the interpretation of language apart from the "animating spirit" from which it derives its "being." Language is not merely the "algebraic sign" of this animating soul, "but the very form in which it looks out upon us with its own living presence." There is a "spiritual element," a "distinctive life," which belongs even to the outward form of language. This needs to be grasped before the language can be understood. The key to the meaning of language, then lies in the soul of words which is in them "objectively before they reach our minds."[64]

Nevin draws a graphic example of his linguistic theory from poetry. Without "poetic taste" no amount of philology or history

---

"The Pope's Encyclical," 41; Erb, *NT*, 287.
    [63]Nevin, "Christ the Inspiration of His Own Word," 41; Erb, *NT*, 44-47.
    [64]Nevin, *My Own Life*, 132-33, 110.

can reveal the sense of great poets like Homer, Horace, Shakespeare or Goethe. The language of the poet affects the minds of his readers only as they are drawn into felt sympathy with the spiritual elements of his own life. By "spiritual *infection*" they thus become poets in their own measure and so enter into the "true historical sense" of his or her language. Only the "spirit of poetry"—that is, the same mind in both the poet and the reader—can be trusted to articulate the sense of a poet's composition. All language is thus the "embodiment of spirit in word." The soul that is in literature, art, and science can only be grasped "by inward soul-intuition."[65]

If this is true of language in its capacity to convey natural truths, how much more is it true when such language is animated by the substance of supernatural truth? As in poetry the mind of God lodges itself in the Scriptures so that it cannot be understood and explained apart from this supernatural and spiritual element which is "part of its very being." The divine and the human meet together in the totality of what is spoken and so must also be apprehended "each in the other" in order to render the language intelligible.[66] Or, in the language of Ricoeurean hermeneutics, to "experience" the world of the text the reader needs to engage the text with some attitude of belief.

Nevin believed that the outward letter of Scripture can never exhaust its meaning and power because the mind of God is truly in the Bible. The situation is analogous to common human speech which involves much more than we can see or record. Our "external natural mind," as he explains it, forms only a small part of "our full inward existence." Within this, our rational mind opens "right into the spiritual world itself; and there it is, that the real complex forces, which enter as innumerable fibres into the constitution of our outward conscious thought and speech, are all the time at work for this end—though we know it not." Behind the

---

[65]Nevin, *My Own Life*, 133, 110. See idem, "Christ and His Spirit," *MR* 19 (1872): 353: "All language is intelligible only in the element of the life from which it derives its origin."

[66]Nevin, *My Own Life*, 110, 135; see idem, "The Supreme Epiphany," 248; idem, "Hodge on the Ephesians," *MR* 9 (1857): 48; see also Erb, *NT*, 106, 111; Nevin, *Vindication*, 66.

complex web of human language, therefore, "is this interior ocean of things invisible, immaterial, and eternal—the region of the universal in distinction from the single and particular, the region of ends and causes in distinction from mere effects—which is continually pressing, as it were, to come to some utterance in his outward thought and speech."[67]

The propositions of Scripture, then, are pregnant with a sense going beyond logic and grammar. Neither thought nor language alone can fully fathom them. In this way, Nevin could say that the Scriptures are mystical. Not that they are shrouded in uncertainty, rather they possess an undivided simplicity. John's gospel, for instance, has the logical sharpness of a scholastic and the depth of a mystic. He was intuitive and contemplative, seeing his object with the soul.[68]

But how is it, asks Nevin, that the divine life (which he regards as the spirit of prophecy), can "be actually resident in the words spoken, when the speech itself is at an end," much less in a printed book? In the constitution of God's word, whether spoken or written, there is "an inward nature different from all other speech or writing, nothing less in reality than a Divine life of its own, derived from the life which it is thus made to enshrine." The words of Christ are spirit and life. As such they must enclose "universally the quality of His own being." Standing in the power and glory of the heavenly and spiritual world, they are "interiorly pregnant also with the celestial fire of that life."

Obviously, existential participation in this Divine reality involves more than reading and studying the word for Nevin. It necessitates both obedience and faith. Keeping Christ's commandments is nothing less than "the simple being of the soul in the element of spirit and life thus effluent from Himself."[69] The ancients, according to Nevin, attributed wisdom to the one "who had the knowledge of the good in himself practically, as his own

---

[67]Nevin, "The Bread of Life," 45; see Swedenborg, *Arcana Coelestia*, 657, 1443, 1904, 1495, 5145, 10330; idem, *Apocalypse Revealed*, 914; *Divine Love and Wisdom*, 236-38, 261.

[68]Nevin, "The Heidelberg Catechism," *MR* 4 (1852): 167-69.

[69]Nevin, "The Spirit of Prophecy," *MR* 24 (1877): 186-87, 189, 197; see Swedenborg, *Arcana Coelestia*, 2588.

inmost being—something well understood, at the same time, to be in him only by indwelling inspiration from the Almighty."[70]

Nevin identifies this dimension of participation with faith. Like Samuel Taylor Coleridge, the quintessential Romantic, Nevin defines faith as the organ by which the supernatural element in Scripture is grasped. It is "an original capacity for perceiving the divine." There is, therefore, "an original, necessary correlation" between faith and the objective side of revelation just as there is a correlation between the eye and the light it sees. As in art and poetry, the object is not placed in the word by the interpreter nor produced by the word, rather it is already *in* the word, waiting to be grasped. The word of God possesses an *innate* potency and life by which, as 1 Peter 1:23 says, we are born again. In the words of Jesus, "He that is of God heareth God's words; ye therefore hear them not, because ye are not of God."[71]

The Hermeneutical Context

Like postliberalism, Nevin recognized that Christianity is mediated through a historical tradition and a historical community. Like postliberalism, Mercersburg rejected *in part* both the cognitive approach to religion which equates religious doctrine with propositional claims, and the experiential-expressivist approach which equates religion with a universal, unmediated encounter with the transcendent. Consequently, neither Princeton's Reformed rationalism, nor Schleiermacher's subjectivism proved wholly adequate to Nevin's theological goals.

The objective authority of faith, according to Nevin, is not the private possession of any individual. This would place the individual above the community, the part before the whole. In the order of being, however, the whole is prior to its parts. Thus the Body of Christ serves as the historical instrument and locus of divine life and faith for the world. Faith demands a historically objectified authority. Consequently, the general life of Christianity, as embodied in the church must (so to speak) stand between

---

[70]Nevin, "Bible Anthropology," 357n.
[71]Nevin, *My Own Life,* 135-37.

individual faith and the letter of Scripture. The Bible, says Nevin, "shines as a light from heaven *in the Church*, and was never intended to be a sufficient and final light for the world, as such, on the outside of the Church."[72]

To stand in continuity with the life of Christ is to stand in continuity with the church. Though the church is not infallible relative to the truth, it is, Nevin believes, indefectible. In other words, since the church is the body of Christ, the truth will always be found in her, as it is in Him, despite its mixture with error.[73] While individuals are encouraged to study the Bible, each person's understanding is meaningful only within the context of the larger community. The general is more perfect than the particular. So, as the individual cannot free himself from prejudice and sectarianism, the church can provide the proper ballast enabling him or her to maintain equilibrium against arbitrary interpretations. Yet Nevin also warned that to view the church or the creeds as an absolute power leads to "spiritual despotism." Freedom is attained when a person exercises his liberty of interpretation within the context of the church's consciousness, both present and past.[74]

The Christian exegete, then, stands in the midst of a new life greater than his or her individual existence. Consequently, he cannot understand his own position apart from the perspective of the whole. In Nevin's own words, the exegete "must be consciously within the horizon, and underneath the canopy, of the new supernatural creation he is called to contemplate. . . . " The Bible is not to be understood, by "fragments, and as seen from any and every point of view where the beholder may happen to stand." To the contrary, a true understanding "turns on the position of the

---

[72]Nevin, "Thoughts on the Church," 394; idem, "Dorner's History of Protestant Theology," 644.

[73]Nevin, "Brownson's Review," 71-73; Erb, *NT*, 37-39. This ecclesiohistorical method of interpretation does not neutralize the priority of Scripture or the objectivity of revelation. The immediate issue for Mercersburg theology was not the relative authority of the church and the Scriptures, but *how* to interpret the Bible. The church is the *operant sphere* of exegesis.

[74]Erb, *NT*, 53-54, 57-58; Nevin, "Brownson Again," 320-22; Moses Kieffer, "Dogmatic Theology. Its Conception, Sources, and Method," *MR* 12 (1860): 469-74. Nevin's statements on the relation of the Bible to the church are sometimes difficult to reconcile.

beholder himself, and his power of observing and comprehending the revelation as a whole." An interpreter "must stand in the truth, have sympathy with it, feel the authority that belongs to it in fact, in order that he may have power to do justice at all to its presence."[75]

The Apostles' Creed

By defining faith and the church as the proper context of biblical interpretation, both Nevin and his colleague, Philip Schaff, recognized that there is a prior condition for interpreting the Bible. Working, in part, off of Kant, the Mercersburg doctors were keenly aware of the fact that there is, in fact, a prior condition for all knowledge. So, just as the condition for understanding natural science lies only in the sphere of nature, the condition for understanding and interpreting the Bible lies only in the sphere of grace which is the church.[76] All written statutes, observes Nevin, are hermeneutically governed by the power of unwritten, living traditions which are applied publicly rather than by private judgement. For Nevin and Schaff, the hermeneutical lens of biblical exegesis is the apostolic tradition as it is expressed in the Rule of Faith and the Apostles' Creed.[77]

Mercersburg's interest in the Creed was rooted, to a large degree, in its German Reformed identity. The Heidelberg Catechism (Q. 22) calls the Apostles' Creed "our universally acknowledged confession of faith." Indeed the general plan of the Catechism is based on the tripartite division of the Creed (see Q. 23-24) as Nevin has pointed out.[78] In addition to this historical factor, Nevin found the hermeneutical possibilities of the Creed agreeable to his theological mind-set which was formed partially under the influence of Schleiermacher's theology. In reality, the German thinker had very little to say about the Creed. Nevertheless, by the

---

[75]Nevin, *MP*, 245.

[76]Nevin, "Cyprian," *MR* 4 (1852): 363-64; idem, "Early Christianity," *MR* 3 (1851): 551.

[77]See Nevin, "Early Christianity," 550-52; idem, "Cyprian," 434; J. H. A. Bomberger, "The Rule of Faith," *MR* 1 (1849): 44-68, 347-71.

[78]Nevin, *Heidelberg Catechism*, 149-51.

mid 1840s Nevin had come to regard it as the immediate, historical expression of the church's God-consciousness.[79]

Nevin maintains that the living tradition which underlies the Creed finds its nucleus in Peter's confession, "Thou art the Christ, the Son of the Living God." This confession, as Jesus told Peter, is the spontaneous utterance of a faith which is revealed not by flesh and blood, but supernaturally from above. The Creed, therefore, functions as the matrix of biblical interpretation because it represents the universal life of the church from the beginning. The *credo*—the "I believe,"—of the Creed is not simply the affirmation of doctrinal abstractions for the intellect, it is the substance of Christianity coming to expression in the form of faith.

In more contemporary language, we might say that the Creed is the root-narrative of the Christian faith for it unfolds the story and the inner logic of the Incarnation. It embodies the living fabric of catholic Christianity together with its *doctrine, morality, and liturgy*. Consequently, fundamental disagreements over such issues, especially as they relate to the interpretation of Scripture, must be brought before the bar of the catholic tradition (which is embodied by the Creed) in order to discern the mind of Christ in the church.

In this sense, the Creed is actually the fruit of the church's *collective* life according to Nevin—a postliberal idea to be sure. The notion of collective life, as he explains, is not peculiar to the sphere of grace, but operates throughout the natural course of human existence. It can be seen in the nature of language, social institutions, customs, and laws insofar as these are the products of a culture rather than an individual. Like the Creed, they are more than simply the arithmetic sum of their parts for they develop inwardly from a living, organic principle. They come to expression in individuals, but that expression embodies a life that is deeper and broader than any one person.[80]

Schaff expresses a similar idea when he discussed the role of different ecclesiastical traditions. The "formal" side of what he

---

[79]See Schleiermacher, *Der christliche glaube*, §135. Schleiermacher maintained that in the determination of right doctrine, the Creed "ought to be controllingly present to every mind." It contains the "authentic sense of Scripture."

[80]Nevin, "The Apostle's Creed," 215-16, 219, 315-16; idem, "Anti-Creed Heresy," *MR* 4 (1852): 606-607.

termed the "dogmatico-moral" tradition, for example, functions as the *channel* by which the contents of the Bible are conducted forward in history. This tradition is indispensable to interpretation, being the only medium through which Scripture can be understood. It embraces the "onward development" of Christian doctrine and life as comprehended in the oral traditions of the church, the ancient rule of faith, the ecumenical creeds (that is, the Nicene and Athanasian), and, above all, the Apostle's Creed. Schaff clearly grasps the hermeneutical and *a priori* nature of this tradition when he concludes, "everyone, before he wakes even to self-consciousness, is made involuntarily to feel its power. . . . [It is] *not an independent source of revelation, but the one fountain of the written word, only rolling itself forward in the stream of church consciousness.*"[81]

Nevin believes that the Reformed principle of *sola Scriptura* is correct insofar as it asserts that the "Bible is not the principle of faith, but the measure of it, and that normally rather than extreme." This means that all truths are not specifically contained in the Bible, but they are "normally contained" as the form of the oak is contained in the acorn. There is room, therefore, for the development of different traditions or denominations each of which embody the life of the church from their own particular standpoint.[82] But such advances can never transcend the original *idea* of Christianity in Christ which is expressed in the Creed. All life has a fixed form. Growth, therefore, is not the *mutation* of an organism's essential definition, but the *actualization* of its innate potential.[83]

In this respect, the Creed stands beneath Scripture and functions as the radix—the genome—of all true theology and the embryo of subsequent doctrine. It is "the fixed doctrinal matrix and mould of the Christian faith for all ages." Though there are many major doctrines which it does not contain (such as justification by faith), the measure of these doctrines is whether they flow from the living substance of Christianity which the Creed represents. This substance is the only true lens of biblical interpretation.[84]

---

[81]Schaff, *Principle of Protestantism*, 115-16; see Irenaeus, *Adversus haereses*, 3.2.4.
[82]Erb, *NT*, 55-56.
[83]Nevin, "Historical Development," *MR* 1 (1849): 514; Schaff, *Principle of Protestantism*, 98, 115-16, 201, 221-22, 225.
[84]Nevin, "Apostle's Creed," 340-42; idem, "Anti-Creed Heresy," 607-608.

For Nevin, then, the issue at stake is a hermeneutical one: With what mind will the Bible be interpreted? Will it be the mind of Christ in the church as represented by the Creed, or the mind of the individual apart from all such relations?[85] When "Puritanism" (Nevin's term for sectarian and "unchurchly" Protestantism) proudly asserts that the Bible alone is the rule of faith, what it really means, says Nevin, is that the Bible plus private judgement (that is, "common sense") is normative. For, everyone comes to the Scripture with some posture or habit conditioned by education, culture, religion, etc. (Indeed, every sect has its own interpretive tradition.) This then becomes the filter through which the voice of the Spirit is heard. "The point here, accordingly, is in truth, not the Creed against the Bible; this last we allow to be supreme; but the Creed against the inward habit and tradition of Puritanism, which, to our view, is something quite different."[86]

Contemporary Implications

Unlike many of his American contemporaries, Nevin was aware that all interpretations and interpretive methods—including those of science—are conditioned by certain assumptions (philosophical and otherwise) which cannot be critically (that is, empirically) established. It is these *a priori* principles which, in many cases, guide the definition, selection, arrangement, and interpretation of data. As a result, the philosophy and even the personal bias of the scientist or interpreter can exercise a formative influence on

---

[85]Erb, *NT*, 53; Nevin, "Anti-Creed Heresy," 608-609, 612-16; idem, *Antichrist*, 54-58; idem, "Dr. Berg's Last Words," *MR* 4 (1852): 287-88; idem, "Evangelical Radicalism," *MR* 4 (1852): 511.

[86]Nevin, "Puritanism and the Creed," *MR* 1 (1849): 598; idem, *Antichrist*, 57-58; idem, "Noel on Baptism," 242; idem, "Early Christianity," 550. Nevin also felt that any interpolation or *"subaudition"* to the Creed (e.g., denying the descent into Hades) affects "the right Christological sense of the entire symbol." It is a mockery of the Creed when sects claim allegiance to it and then proceed to fill it with their own meaning making it the mouthpiece of their own theology. The Creed must be said *"ex animo"* according to its Catholic and historical sense. See Nevin, "Reply to an Anglican Catholic," 402; idem, "Presbyterian Union Convention," *MR* 14 (1868): 105-109. Even within his own denomination, Nevin was critical of the Heidelberg Catechism's diluted interpretation of the descent into hell. See Nevin, *Heidelberg Catechism*, 151.

the conclusions of his or her research and scholarship. This is especially true when data is sparse, compelling us to creatively, and sometimes fancifully, "fill in the gaps."

Because so much of the historical evidence used in biblical scholarship and ancient history is (relatively speaking) indirect, inferential, and even tenuous, it is often sorted and adapted to support a variety of theoretical constructs. Or, to put it another way, though historical facts and grammatical constraints do indeed limit the variety and scope of our interpretations (some constructs/interpretations are impossible to sustain), they may still yield a number of competing interpretations. The ever-changing and even contradictory history of biblical criticism over the past two centuries ably bears this out.

Consequently, our exegesis, as well as our critical disposition toward the Bible, is molded, to a large degree, by our presuppositions. Conscious or unconscious, this pre-understanding shapes the criteria we use to adjudicate questions of meaning, historicity, and authorship. Every method of interpretation, therefore, is rooted in assumptions which often depend more on faith than demonstration. Nevin was on solid ground, then, in rejecting many of the presuppositions that have been surreptitiously appended to the historical-critical method in favor of the Apostles' Creed and the catholic tradition.

Conclusion. The Presence of Christ in His Word

The purpose of the New Testament, according to Nevin, is not to teach people religion, "but to set them in felt communication with the presence of Christ, that this may become for them the power of God unto everlasting life." Like Luther, Nevin believed that the Scriptures are essentially Christocentric. The kingdom of God and the historical realities revealed in the Bible are seen only through His person, just as disparate beams of light are refracted through a prism. "The revelation," says Nevin, "lay wholly in His own living person and presence, and in the self-demonstrating power which this carried with it to show that He was the Son of God."[87]

For Nevin, inspiration and illumination, as traditionally conceived, are part of one, continuous, creative act by which Christ is present in His word. The greatest question of the day, in his view, does not turn upon meaning or mode inspiration, but upon the perpetual reality of Christ's presence in the word which, when grasped by faith, becomes the fount of self-authenticating life and truth.[88] As creation is not merely a divine fiat taking effect upon the cosmos outwardly and mechanically, but a continuous stream of life filling the universe through the Word from God Himself, so the inspiration of the Bible is to be understood in the same way:

> It is the Word of God, in its ever-living supernal majesty, occupying and possessing the sacred text, not simply as the cause and origin of it at the first, but as its truly informing and actuating spirit through all time. Of the Bible it must be said always in this view, *God is there.*[89]

Jesus Himself said, his words are *spirit* and *life* (John 6:63). They are not abstractions; rather, "they stream out through all time from the fountain of life in His person." Consequently, they still sustain their original meaning and force as they hold in the mystery of His presence.[90] The Scriptures authenticate Christ because His uncreated light shines through them at every point bearing witness to their origin. The written Word is "only by light from the incarnate Word; but, then, again we learn what the light

---

[87]Nevin, "The Revelation of God in Christ," *MR* 18 (1871): 334.

[88]Nevin, "Christianity and Humanity," 482-83.

[89]Ibid., 476. Swedenborg regarded divine truth, life, love, and wisdom as a substance which flows from God, fills the universe, and descends into humanity through the will and understanding. This is part of his Neoplatonic concept of "influx" and "conjunction" which permeates all his works; see especially *Influx Between the Soul and the Body*, 7-8, 14; idem, *Arcana Coelestia*, 1904, 3484, 2888, 5150, 5846, 6472, 7270; idem, *Divine Love and Wisdom*, 340; idem, *Apocalypse Revealed*, 346; idem, *Apocalypse Explained*, 569; idem, *True Christian Religion*, 8.

[90]Nevin, "Once for All," 108; idem, "Christ and His Spirit," 354; idem, "Christ the Inspiration of His Own Word," 38; Erb, *NT*, 106.

of the incarnate Word is, only as this shines into us through the written Word."[91]

In order to understand the Scriptures, therefore, the exegete must stand in veritable union with Him. Like Peter, he or she must own Him as the Son of God from the inner depths of the soul. "The divine truth," says Nevin, "(joined always to the divine love) is made through faith to be actually in the soul as a part of its own existence, like light in the eye."[92] Truth holds "in the participation of His being, as this issues forth from Him in the way of living speech."[93]

The nature of all truth is that it is "substantial essence just as really as life, both flowing together from the Lord."[94] It is not a quality or accident, but the very *fundamentum* of things, the necessary principle of their existence, and the power by which they continue to exist. It is a "hideous satire," therefore, to speak of truth as an "outward *traditum* or *depositum*" which is handed down mechanically. Even the truth that is embodied in nature is "forever bursting the cerements which would hold it in any such inaction as this." It carries within it "an effort or nisus toward the indefinite production of ever new forms of existence."[95]

Nevin believes that this living Divine presence shining forth from the text of the Scripture, and felt by faith, is powerful enough to defy, if need be, the conclusions of biblical criticism and hermeneutics. For it is an authority holding immediately (that is, "consciously" or at the least, "*sensibly*") to the Divine power itself which is hidden in the outward text. This is not an espousal of mystical relativism by Nevin. Not only would that undermine all belief in history, but it would be a concession to subjective individualism. Rather, as we have already seen, Nevin fully appreciated the hermeneutical concept of what we now call

---

[91]Nevin, "The Spiritual World," 510.

[92]Nevin, "Christianity and Humanity," 480. Conversely, those who will not receive the doctrines of the Bible "show themselves destitute of its life, its power, though they hold fast strenuously to the letter" (Erb, *NT*, 116, 106).

[93]Nevin, "The Testimony of Jesus," 8.

[94]Nevin, "Christianity and Humanity," 480; Erb, *NT*, 98.

[95]Nevin, "The Testimony of Jesus," 8-9.

"preunderstanding." Consequently, he was critical of those who placed natural reason prior to faith in hermeneutics.

Earlier in his career this aberration was embodied by Baconianism whose theological method was rooted in English empiricism and German rationalism. After the Civil War he faced the same error in the guise of historicism, naturalism and materialism. Taken together, these philosophies were part of an ever-darkening *Weltanschauung* which he called humanitarianism: "the idea of a full completion of the world, morally and physically, in man . . . without the necessary complement of a higher spiritual life descending into him from the Lord."[96]

For Nevin the Scriptures are truly the incarnation of the Divine life in human language. His sacred hermeneutic is the instinctive culmination of what I have called "the law of reification." In his last article, "The Inspiration of the Bible: The Internal Sense of Holy Scripture," he concludes by defining the two fundamental articles of religion as set forth in Scripture: The centrality of Christ as the only medium of eternal life; and, living according to the precepts of Christ. The sayings of Christ, he concludes, are "the going forth of the divine energy resident in his person; the hearing and doing of them, the sensible conjunction with him in that vivifying medium."[97]

---

[96] Nevin, "Christianity and Humanity," 476, 483-84.
[97] Nevin, "The Inspiration of the Bible," 36-38; see also idem, "Man's True Destiny," 503-507.

Part II
The Hermeneutics of American Culture and Religion

Chapter 4
Materialism

Nevin's transcendental hermeneutics was accompanied by an on-going analysis and critique of American culture and religion. The moral and cultural decay of today's society would not have surprised him. The materialism, religious skepticism and uncertainty, and individualism of our day are the products of forces that have been at work in our nation since its inception. The philosophical origin of these maladies, in Nevin's view, lies in the widespread adoption of a nominalistic empirical philosophy. This philosophy, which exercised a formative influence in shaping American culture, has become embedded within the deep structure of our society.

In part II, then, we examine Nevin's analysis and critique of American culture and religion from the standpoint of ontology (materialism vs. idealism), epistemology (skepticism vs. realism), and relationality (individualism vs. organic holism). In each case, the diagnosis is essentially the same: Common Sense philosophy and religion magnify the actual at the expense of the ideal, the particular at the expense of the universal, and individual part at the expense of the whole. As a form of empiricism, it's ontology, epistemology, and concept of relations are, contrary to the Incarnation, rooted primarily in the senses. Nevin not only criticizes this imbalance, but addresses it by demonstrating the priority of the ideal and universal while also affirming the goodness and integrity of individual existence.

There are, then, three fundamental points of contention between Mercersburg and the nominalism of Scottish Realism which we will address consecutively, beginning with this chapter. All of them relate to the relative priority of the ideal and the actual. The first is the conflict over *ontology*: Nevin believes that the empirical tradition, with its preoccupation with the phenomenal (that is, actual), is naturally predisposed toward incipient materialism. When carried to its *logical* completion, Common Sense must deny the reality of the supernatural resolving Christianity and revelation into the life of nature. For Christianity, the only viable ontology is one that views the *fundamentum* of reality as ideal and spiritual.

The second is the conflict over *epistemology*: Nevin maintains that by denying the intelligibility and objectivity of universal ideas,[1] and equating objectivity primarily with the actual and particular, Common Sense nominalism fosters a misplaced confidence in the senses and a false notion of authority. The result is a latent but ever-increasing tendency toward subjectivity and skepticism in the realm of religion. The only antidote to this error, according to Nevin is to affirm and demonstrate the priority of the ideal over the actual. Consequently, Nevin and his colleagues advance an intuitive epistemology rooted in universal being, the immediacy of faith, and the Incarnation.

The third is the conflict over *relationality*. Nominalism begins with the assumption that only the individual is real. Accordingly, the Princeton theology regarded humanity and the church as a collection of individuals instead of an organic whole. As Nevin saw it, this is the root of radical individualism and sectarianism which would eventually destroy the unity of church and society. In opposition to this position, Nevin and his associates affirmed the organic unity of humanity, society, and the church by demonstrating the priority of the universal over the particular, the ideal over the actual.

These philosophical issues—so abstract at first appearance—in truth reach to the very core of American religion and society. This connection was discerned better by idealists like Nevin, than by nominalists. Common Sense philosophers generally scoffed at the suggestion that their system was an open door to materialism, subjectivity, and individualism. So long as they were able to maintain evangelical piety side by side with Baconian philosophy (sometimes an uncomfortable combination as we will see) the charges appeared absurd.

---

[1] On the controversy over universals and language, see the introduction, above.

While the vagaries of American materialism, skepticism, and individualism have been decried and acknowledged by many, not everyone would agree with Nevin's philosophical analysis. In *A Common Sense Theology*, Ellingsen traces what he calls the "Secular-Democratic Consciousness" to the influence of the Continental European Enlightenment rather than Common Sense Realism. In fact, Ellingsen attempts to demonstrate that the "Classical-Christian Consciousness" of American culture "reflects commitments that are at least compatible with, if not dependent upon, Common Sense Realism."[2] The genius of Nevin's approach, on the other hand, is to show that the secular consciousness is a logical concomitant of Common Sense; that the seeds of decay lie within the system itself; that once Common Sense is cut loose from its historical Presbyterian moorings it will inevitably founder on the rocks of materialism.

The Ontological Issue

Nevin's concern over the rise of materialism is rooted in a very basic philosophical question: What is the *fundamentum* of reality? For Mercersburg, the shape of this question was determined by both epistemological and theological considerations. Philosophically, Hegel and Schelling had transformed reality from real to ideal by synthesizing Kant's phenomenal/noumenal distinction into Absolute Idea. The asymmetrical character of Christ's hypostatic union (in which His divine nature was said to be foundational to His human nature) seemed to point in the same direction. In both cases the spiritual, the ideal, and the universal were regarded as going before the actual or finite in the order of being.

In nominalism, however, the fundamental reality is the actual. For Ockham, Locke and the Scottish Realists, reality begins with the individual thing. Universal ideas have no ontological status. They are creatures of the mind, dependent ultimately (more often than not) on sense data. The first function of reason is to operate upon the material world. It is the senses rather than the mind that established the vital connection with the world.[3] Given this prem-

---

[2]Ellingsen, *A Common Sense Theology*, 132.
[3]Bozeman, *Protestants*, 54.

ise, it is not unreasonable to expect a downward spiral into materialism ending, as it did in France, with infidelity. Granted, one can assert a belief in the Creator (as did Ockham, Locke, and the Scottish Realists), but the logic of the *system itself*, as Hegel adroitly pointed out, has no inherent power to sustain such a belief.[4]

With its one-sided emphasis on sensible knowledge, the incipient materialism of the Scottish philosophy prepared the way for humanism, utilitarianism and positivism. These philosophies were introduced in one form or another by the French philosopher Auguste Comte (1798–1857) and British thinkers such as Jeremy Bentham (1748–1832), J. S. Mill, (1806-73), Herbert Spencer (1820–1903), and Charles Darwin (1809-82). On the German side, there were the left-wing Hegelians such as Ludwig Feuerbach (1804-72) and Karl Marx (1818-83). However, since these systems did not begin to take root in American soil until the last quarter of the nineteenth century, we find only glimpses of them in the writings of the Mercersburg theologians.[5] Nevertheless Nevin and his colleagues believed that the empirical and utilitarian tendencies of American thought provided an open door to more radical forms of materialism.

But the immediate issue at hand was not so much the collapse of Scottish Realism into ontological materialism, but the adoption of *empirical methods* to discover spiritual truth. Such was the confidence of Baconianism. As Theodore Dwight Bozeman has shown, the same system of investigation that proved so successful in the natural sciences was employed in matters of religion and biblical studies. Through induction, collation, and comparison, Old School Presbyterian theologians attempted to scale the invisible with the ladder of empiricism.

The wholesale adoption of the empirical method in matters of religion sent a clear message to Mercersburg: The world of space and time is, in some sense, more concrete, more abiding, and more

---

[4]G. W. F. Hegel, *The Encyclopaedia Logic (with the Zusätze)*, 3rd ed. (1830), trans. with introduction and notes by T. F. Geraets, W. A. Suchting, and H. S. Harris (Indianapolis: Hackett Publishing, 1991) §60. Thus he distinguishes between this form of empiricism which he calls naive, and consistent empiricism which is materialism or naturalism.

[5]E.g., Nevin, "Nature and Grace," 505.

real than the ideal and the spiritual. How else can one account for the strident Baconian opposition to every form of idealism and Christian Platonism?[6] The answer was obvious. From the standpoint of nominalism and empiricism the ideal and spiritual seemed like chimeras when compared to what Bozeman aptly calls "the beefy firmness of *sense*."[7]

The object of the Baconian method was to first establish the veracity of revelation by appealing to miracles and prophecies. In keeping with the presuppositions of empiricism which deny the reality of universals, Baconians held that certainty begins not in the realm of the ideal or spiritual, but in the concrete world of time and space. In order to establish the veracity of faith, especially the veracity of special revelation, we must begin with the knowledge of the finite. Hence, faith and special revelation were made to rest on miraculous "evidences."

Once the integrity of Scripture was established, the data of Scripture could then be collected and arranged. Doctrinal truths were thus assembled through a process of induction and generalization. Revelation was regarded as a communication of information *about God* rather than a disclosure of God Himself. Theology, therefore, proceeds by simple induction.

Another consequence of Scottish Realism's "incipient materialism" was dualism. Under the influence of empiricism and Descartes radical separation of mind and matter, Baconians regarded miracles as supernatural interventions which punctuated an otherwise unbroken chain of causality in the material world. This view excludes any type of organic union between the ideal and actual orders of creation.[8] Consequently, the spiritual and ideal are all but eliminated from the internal nexus of history and daily life, or relegated to the sphere of private conscience as was the case in subjective pietism.[9]

---

[6]See DiPuccio, "Dynamic Realism," 30-41.

[7]Bozeman, *Protestants*, 54.

[8]This seems to be the Hodge's position who, with the Westminster Confession (V.III), speaks of miracles as being "without, above, or against" secondary causes; see Hodge, *ST*, 1:617-29.

[9]This is not to say, however, that empiricism alone is the basis of individualistic forms of religion (e.g., pietism, voluntarism). They do, though, share an affinity

Nevin critiqued Baconian religion by demonstrating that the presuppositions of Common Sense ultimately end in cultural (if not philosophical) materialism. One cannot move from the sensible to the spiritual simply by induction. The goal of Mercersburg theology, on the other hand, was not only to affirm the ideal or spiritual basis of reality, but to demonstrate its organic union with the actual world. The entire creation is the efflorescence of a vast, ideal cosmos—a sacrament of the divine. The Incarnation and Christianity thus constitute the inner life of the world. As Nevin loved to say, the "powers of the world to come" are actually present in and through the church.

The Common Sense Struggle with Incipient Materialism

Having subscribed to a form of empirical philosophy, Princeton and Old School Presbyterians placed themselves in the unenviable position of defending this system against charges of materialism. Common Sense philosophers were very sensitive to being yoked with Hobbes, Hume, Hartley, Condillac, Helvetius, D'Holbach, and "the host of infidels and atheists in France." These errors, according to the highly respected lawyer and Baconian philosopher Samuel Tyler, were the result of a one-sided application of Baconian philosophy carried to the "wildest extreme."[10]

In order to understand this acute sensitivity we must first consider the uneasy alliance which Common Sense had forged with Newtonian physics. Having adopted the "corpuscular" or atomic theory of matter, Newton conceived of natural philosophy as a description of the interaction between atoms. The resulting order was a lifeless, mathematical, and mechanical universe. Presbyterians transformed this system into what Bozeman calls a "doxological science" by "camouflaging atomism" with the spiritual canvass of "providential purpose and wise design." But with the shadow of Cartesian dualism looming in the background, Scottish Realism could mount no higher than a sort of *deus ex*

---

for subjectivism which is nominalistic. For a brief overview of American pietism see F. E. Stoeffler, "Pietism," in *Dictionary of Christianity in America*, ed. Daniel G. Reid (Downers Grove IL: Intervarsity Press, 1990).

[10]Tyler, "The Influence of the Baconian Philosophy," *PR* 15 (1843): 494.

machina. Once they accepted the Newtonian model, remarks Bozeman, "Christians found it necessary to twist and turn dexterously to avoid giving assent to its final ramifications."[11]

The greatest fear of Baconian philosophers was lapsing from this doxological view of the universe into a type of naturalism which supposed that order and mind were the result of a "fortuitous concourse of atoms." At times, advances in science seemed to do just that. New theories which reduced phenomena to material forces alone threatened to undo the belief in divine causality and destroy the sharp dichotomy between mind and matter. Matter according to the Baconians was dead, passive and lifeless. Unable to act on its own, they supposed that "all power, motion, and change," was produced by the action of mind. Natural effects, then, were the sole result of mind acting upon inert matter. However, this Cartesian dualism became increasingly difficult to maintain. In psychology for example, mounting evidence pointed to an integral connection between the power of thought and the organization of the brain. Some scientists went so far as to say that the mind was nothing more than an effect of the brain.[12]

Nevertheless, Presbyterians like Samuel Tyler sought to bring Baconianism and Christianity into harmonious union without abandoning biblical values. The Baconian emphasis on experience, he maintained, should not be construed as a regression to sensationalism. Rather, "the Baconian philosophy recognises the testimony of consciousness as fully as that of sensation. . . . Sensation informs us of the material world, consciousness, of the spiritual world. . . . " We cannot, therefore, "predicate . . . any idea derived from the material world, of the objects of the spiritual world."[13] Common Sense is not, then, constitutionally opposed to morality, revelation, or the idea of the soul which are developed from consciousness. In fact, by excluding Platonic innate ideas, according to

---

[11]Bozeman, *Protestants*, 88-89.

[12]Bozeman, *Protestants*, 89-92, 53-55. A similar controversy took place in the life sciences. The erosion of vitalism and the rise of evolution threatened to reduce life—the mysterious, seemingly irreducible principle which was added to dead matter—to a material force (ibid., 94-95).

[13]Tyler, "The Influence of the Baconian Philosophy," 504.

Tyler, Baconianism opens the door for a transcendent and external revelation as well as natural theology.

However, these assurances did little to deflect accusations of materialism by opponents. Baconian philosophers like Tyler, it is true, regarded consciousness as an intuitive source of morality, self-identity, etc.[14] This concept, which originated in Thomas Reid, successfully demonstrates that Baconian philosophers were not sensationalists since all the data of experience are not reducible to the senses. But, in the eyes of idealists like Nevin, Tyler's defense failed to address the crucial issues.

In the first place, consciousness, as Baconians defined it, failed to bridge the gap between sense and spirit. That is, it fell considerably short of uniting the believer with the spiritual realm. A heartfelt *knowledge* of the truth apart from an immediate communion with the spiritual world leaves the soul with only an abstract representation of Christ. For the most part, Presbyterian theology viewed revelation as a communication of information instead of a disclosure of the actual life and person of Christ. Tyler's claim that one must "enter into communion with divine things" meant that faith based on "spiritual discernment" perceives the truth in its own light and is accompanied by a "spiritual communion" between heart and doctrine. The object of faith is not Christ Himself, but "the truth" which operates upon the mind and quickens the moral sensibilities.[15]

In the second place, the proponents of Common Sense, insisted on applying the *methods* of empirical inquiry to the sphere of religion. Nevin, on the other hand, maintained that the distance between the sensible and the spiritual cannot be scaled by the categories of time and space. Empirical induction became the polestar which guided Presbyterians through the Scriptures. This correlation between nature and the Bible was not new. Richard Baxter (1615–1691) and a number of other Puritans believed that the Bible should be interpreted using the inductive methods of natural science. However, it was not until the nineteenth century that the

---

[14]See Nicholas J. Griffin, "Possible Theological Perspectives in Thomas Reid's Common Sense Philosophy," *Journal of Theological History* 41 (July 1990): 438–40.

[15]Tyler, "Connection between Philosophy and Revelation," 384–87, 408.

idea was fully implemented. Jacob Jones Janeway (1774–1858), at Western Theological Seminary in Pittsburgh, gave classic expression to this concept in 1828 when he compared the Bible to the facts of nature. The method of theology, therefore, is the same as the method of science: collection, arrangement, comparison, and systematization. This idea was propagated and refined by a number of prominent Presbyterians including Charles Hodge, Samuel Tyler, James W. Alexander, and James H. Thornwell.[16]

Finally, Baconian philosophers and theologians demonstrated their unwavering commitment to Newtonian science and the primacy of the senses by relying on "evidences" in order to vindicate the truth of Christianity. Evidentialism was largely a product of eighteenth century British theology designed to defend orthodoxy against the assaults of deists and pietistic enthusiasts. It was assumed that revelation, like the propositions of science, were capable of and even required empirical verification. Miracles and prophecies provided the palpable test necessary for such verification. Nineteenth-century Presbyterians continued in this tradition. While acknowledging that evidences alone are insufficient to kindle true faith, Tyler praised the work of Joseph Butler (1692–1752) and William Paley (1743–1805) as shining examples of the power of Baconian philosophy.[17] The legendary Princeton theologian Archibald Alexander (1772–1851) reflected the sentiments of Old School Presbyterianism when he said, "unless the Christian religion is attended with sufficient evidence, we cannot believe in it, even if we would."[18]

Yet, Presbyterians viewed their Baconianism not as an avenue to materialism but as a means of establishing the certainty of Christianity and restraining wayward speculation. By the 1830s, Old School theologians became aware of the threat to orthodoxy

---

[16]Bozeman, *Protestants*, 149-55; Tyler, "Connection between Philosophy and Revelation," 386-87.

[17]See Tyler, "The Influence of the Baconian Philosophy," 504-505; idem, "The Baconian Philosophy," *PR* 12 (1840): 370; see also idem, "Connection between Philosophy and Revelation," 408.

[18]Archibald Alexander, *Evidences of the Authenticity, Inspiration, and Canonical Authority of the Holy Scriptures* (Philadelphia: Presbyterian Board of Publications, 1836) 89; quoted in Bozeman, *Protestants*, 140.

posed by Unitarianism, Transcendentalism, and Romantic idealism. Thinkers such as William Ellery Channing (1780–1842), Ralph Waldo Emerson (1803–1882), J. D. Morell (1816–1891), Coleridge, Schleiermacher, Schelling, and Hegel all extolled the power of human reason and raised it to new heights. While orthodox theologians were not opposed to viewing the human intellect as a reflective image of the Divine Mind, they were wholly against any type of metaphysical and spiritual speculation that would make human reason the measure of reality. The only reliable safeguard against this form of reasoning was an appeal to the tangible "facts" of sense. Reason was shut up to the incontrovertible evidence of nature and Scripture. The inductive method, operating on the data already at hand, directed reason to firmly established conclusions. The methods of Baconian science, then, acted as a restraint against the unchecked speculations of reason.[19]

But even some of the proponents of Baconianism recognized the potential danger of adapting an empirical philosophy—a fact which could only lend credence to the charges made by Nevin and others. Charles Hodge became keenly aware of the creeping materialism in American religion and devoted over fifty pages to its general history and refutation in his *Systematic Theology* (1872–1873). Perhaps this, as well as his primary devotion to theology, explains his cautious commitment to Common Sense and his readiness to digress from it at times.

Though Locke himself was not a materialist, says Hodge, he inadvertently paved a way for its entrance into England by his theory of mind. In his attempt to refute the theory of innate ideas, Locke held that the origin of our ideas is rooted in sensation and reflection. If by reflection, says Hodge, Locke meant the cogitation of the mind upon its own ideas, then his system cannot be reduced to sensationalism. However, if reflection is simply "the process of recalling, combining, analyzing, and otherwise elaborating the impressions upon us from without," then "the two sources of ideas, or of knowledge, are reduced to one, and that one is sensation." This latter view, according to Hodge, was probably held by Locke

---

[19]Bozeman, *Protestants*, 134-38, 141-43.

and certainly by many of his followers. A less circumspect use of Locke in France ushered in an era of materialism there.[20]

But if Baconian religion proved to be a slippery slope ending in incipient materialism, the Presbyterians had installed a number of safeguards to prevent such a disaster. Though the methods of religious inquiry and the criteria of verification were governed by the principles of empirical science, advocates of Common Sense appealed to the supremacy of revelation as a counterbalance. The propositions of Scripture were considered to be the final authority in all matters. When discrepancies between science and the Bible arose, it was generally (though not always) science rather the testimony of Scriptures that stood in need of adjustment. Since both natural and special revelation came from the same God, the two must ultimately be in harmony. Consistent use of the inductive method with the proper restraints would insure such agreement.

Yet despite the supremacy of the Scriptures in Presbyterian religion, empiricism may have had the last word. Like Locke many Baconians held that the Scriptures, in order to be regarded as revelation, must first conform to the universal standards of reason set forth by the Baconian philosophy. These standards, as we have discussed, refer to the necessity of miraculous evidences and, to a lesser degree though by no means unimportant, to the internal or self-evidencing quality of the Scriptures themselves. As one writer said,

> the ultimate basis, the surest guaranty of faith in supernatural and superrational revelations, must be supernatural attestations. And we may add, that these attestations must to a large extent be so palpable and convincing, that if they are not in and of themselves *self-evidencing*, they are so [at least] in effect.[21]

The other attempt to circumnavigate the shoals of incipient materialism came about through a union of Baconian religion and pietism. Pietism was a longstanding tradition in American Presbyterianism. At Princeton it was exemplified in the life and writings

---

[20]Hodge, *ST*, 1:248-49, 253-54.
[21]Thomas M. Skinner, Jr, "The Bible Its Own Witness and Interpreter," *PR* 32 (1860): 399.

of men like Archibald Alexander and Charles Hodge.[22] Relying on the Westminster Confession, Hodge maintained that the truth of Scripture is ultimately vindicated by the work of the Holy Spirit in the heart. As a result, he bypasses or rather subordinates the appeal to evidences. "Undoubtedly the highest evidence of the truth is the truth itself." Christ's glory "reveals Him, as the Son of God, to all whose eyes the God of this world has not blinded." Miracles are designed to prove not so much the truth being taught, as "the divine mission of the teacher."[23]

But this emphasis on internal evidence was not the product of pietism alone. It was supported by the Baconian belief that "consciousness" also constitutes a form of evidence. As Mark Noll points out, Hodge's appeal to the immediate testimony of the Spirit was reinforced by Scottish philosophy's concept of "moral sense" as a type of intuition.[24] Hence, even the necessity, character, and priority of internal evidence, as Samuel Tyler once forcefully demonstrated, was derived from the principles of Baconian induction![25]

Nevin's Critique
of Cultural and Philosophical Materialism

Like Alexis de Tocqueville, Nevin saw the creeping influence of materialism on American society. The repudiation of objective ideas by Locke and the Common Sense school, the transformation of philosophy from a "science of ideas" to a science of mundane facts, the preoccupation with building the national infrastructure, and the accumulation of wealth, were all viewed as ominous portents of moral and spiritual decline. Though less radical than philosophical materialism, social or cultural materialism was no less dangerous, amounting, so to speak, to a form of practical atheism.

---

[22]See W. Andrew Hoffecker, *Piety and the Princeton Theologians: Archibald Alexander, Charles Hodge, and Benjamin Warfield* (Grand Rapids MI: Baker Book House, 1981); and Mark Noll. ed., *Charles Hodge: The Way of Life* (New York: Paulist Press, 1987).

[23]Hodge, *ST*, 1:636.

[24]Noll, ed., *Charles Hodge: The Way of Life*, 28.

[25]See Tyler, "Connection between Philosophy and Revelation," 402-408.

As a Christian Platonist and idealist, Nevin stood in the midst of a broad spiritual tradition which proved to be an inveterate critic of empiricism and the Enlightenment.[26] It was, therefore, his Christian Platonism that served as the philosophical and theological basis of his critique of materialism. Before coming to Mercersburg he made frequent contrasts between the reality of the spiritual world and the transitoriness of the sensible realm. He referred to the "slavery of matter." The inner life of the sinner, he said, "is made up entirely of thoughts and affections, that terminate on the objects of sense and the interests of the present world."[27]

As a Presbyterian, he was a strong advocate for the Christian Sabbath, the very design of which "is to break the strong and steady flow of this world's life, and to give room for 'the things which are not seen and eternal' to assert their truth." As an institution which summons the soul away from all that is "outward and passing" the Sabbath, according to Nevin, "can have little attraction for a generation that is so taken with the outward and material. . . . "[28] Nevin would probably not be surprised to see the secularization of Sunday in our own day. Leisure, sports, and recreation have replaced sacred devotion as social conventions. Commerce rages on (especially in the retail sector) without regard for the day.

Shortly after coming to Mercersburg in 1840, Nevin wrote a series of articles for the *Weekly Messenger of the German Reformed*

---

[26]See D. A. Rees, "Platonism and the Platonic Tradition" in *The Encyclopedia of Philosophy*, ed. Paul Edwards (New York: Macmillan Publishing Co. and the Free Press, 1967); and Daniel Walker Howe, "The Cambridge Platonists of Old England and the Cambridge Platonists of New England" in *American Unitarianism 1805–1865*, ed. Conrad Edick Wright (Boston: Massachusetts Historical Society and Northeastern University Press, 1989) 87-117.

[27]Nevin, *The Seal of the Spirit: A Sermon, the substance of which was preached in the Presbyterian Church at Uniontown, Pa. January 21, 1838* (Pittsburgh: William Allinder, 1838) 13. See also idem, *The Scourge of God, a Sermon preached in the First Presbyterian Church, July 6, 1832, on the Occasion of a City Fast observed in reference to the approach of the Asiatic Cholera* (Pittsburgh: Johnston & Stockton, 1832) 17. The tendency toward materialism, says Nevin, causes us to forget God.

[28]Nevin, *The Presbytery of Ohio on the Claims of the Christian Sabbath; A Report Read and Adopted April 21, 1836, at a Meeting of the Presbytery held at Raccoon Church* (Pittsburgh: William Allinder, 1836) 5.

Church on "Worldly Mindedness." The kingdom of God, he said, "is a divine life in the soul" which "rises above the sphere of sense, and finds, while it is yet in the body, a conscious citizenship in the higher, heavenly economy, which is revealed in the glorious gospel." It is not simply an aspect of our life in this world, but an order of existence in its own right. "The principles, views, sentiments and affections, by which this life works," he once observed, "are peculiar, proceeding from God and always flowing toward Him. Together they make up a complete organic existence, symmetrical, self-consistent, and altogether distinct from the experience of life under any other view."[29] By contrast the kingdom of the world is that system of life "which belongs to men naturally, as estranged from God and destitute of faith."

Many years later he continued to strike the same notes. To the contemplative spirit, the "enduring forms of creation," he says, are "felt to be apparitional only, phenomenal merely, and not substantial; signs and shadows which have their proper truth not so much in themselves as in things that lie beyond them in another order of existence altogether." This is the region of ideas which transcends the evanescent forms of sense and is rooted in the eternal Logos—the source of the power of thinking in creation.[30]

Nevin's philosophical critique of Scottish Realism began during the early days of his career at Western Theological Seminary (1830–1840) and continued to the end of his life. His attack was directed against (1) the nominalist notion that ideas are only generalizations or abstractions, (2) the empirical tendency toward sensationalism, and (3) the Cartesian dualism of mind and matter.

His growing hostility toward the Common Sense tradition is first exhibited in an article he wrote in 1843 on the "Philosophy of Dr. Rauch." Responding to accusations of pantheism lodged against his one-time friend and colleague by James Murdock (formerly of Andover Seminary), Nevin fired back with charges of materialism and dualism: "The world is so separated from God,"

---

[29]Nevin, "Worldly Mindedness," *WM*, 24 June 1840.
[30]Appel, *LW*, 610, 619 (from "Undying Life in Christ," an address delivered at the Convention of the Third Centennial of the Heidelberg Catechism, 19 January 1863, Race Street Reformed Church, Philadelphia).

in the general view," remarked Nevin, "as to be considered in fact an independent existence." So, while rejecting the theory of eternal matter on principle, Scottish empiricism embraces the error by virtue of its radical, Cartesian dualism which supposes that matter, in order to be external to God, must be passive and mechanical. Hence, it is forced to conclude that any dynamic theory which attributes innate activity and power to matter can only blur the distinction between Creator and creation.[31]

Though Nevin's Christian Platonism provided a platform for his critique of materialism, by the early to mid 1840s any shadow of dualism between the ideal and actual (such as we find in Plato) was swallowed up by his incarnational theology. For him there can be no disparity between the sensible and the spiritual. They are co-extensive. Between them there is a mutual in-being. "The whole constitution of the world," Nevin said in 1851, "is sacramental, as being not simply the sign of, but the actual form and presence of invisible things."[32] The spiritual world is the ground and pattern of the sensible world. It is a "fixed law of life, that every spiritual force which it comprehends must take some outward form, in order to become complete."[33]

With this incarnational principle well in hand, Nevin articulated his case against Common Sense empiricism in an essay entitled "A Plea for Philosophy" (1848). It was not the practical or technological benefits of the Baconian method which caught the ire of the Mercersburg professor, but its attempt to subordinate the ideal to the actual and mind to matter in every sphere of human life and thought. Baconianism begins with the erroneous assumption that philosophy is a science of empirical facts instead of a science of *transcendental* ideas. Nevin considers this a usurpation of true philosophy which he identified with the "science of the absolute" and the supremacy of "Mind" over "Matter." It is this

---

[31]Nevin, "Philosophy of Dr. Rauch," 422, 428.

[32]Erb, *NT*, 373.

[33]Nevin, *The Church: a sermon preached at the opening of the Synod of the German Reformed Church at Carlisle, October 1846* (Chambersburg PA: German Reformed Church Publishing House, 1847) 10. See idem, "Brownson Again," 309-10, 317-18. Natural laws are not only objective ideal realities, but constitute the source of natural phenomena.

"inward supremacy" mediated through the human spirit that comprises the self-consciousness of the world. The "ideal" rules the "actual," the absolute (which he defines as "universal reason and universal will") reigns over "the force of all that is simply empirical and particular." "Away with the heresy, dishonorable to man and God alike, that this world is ruled supremely by material forces, or simply sensuous interests of any kind."[34]

The empirical bias of the Common Sense philosophy made itself felt in religion as well as metaphysics. The inductive method became the yardstick of both religious and philosophical inquiry. "The general character of this bastard philosophy," protests Nevin, "is, that it affects to measure all things, both on earth and in heaven, by the categories of the common abstract understanding, as it stands related simply to the world of time and sense." But as Kant has demonstrated, these categories are only the "forms or types" of sensible reality and represent "the conditions merely of existence in space and time. . . . " Nevin believed that Kant struck the fatal blow against the pretensions of Locke who aspired to build a metaphysic of the "absolute and infinite upon deductions from the simply relative and finite." The empirical tradition is powerless to construct such a metaphysic because its ideas are nothing but "intellectual abstractions" without "universal force."[35]

Nevin appealed to the French Revolution for historical vindication of his view. The French Enlightenment was heavily influenced by Locke. From the perspective of idealists and Romantics like Nevin, eighteenth-century French philosophers such as Voltaire, Montesquieu, D'Holbach, La Mettrie, and Cabanis were only carrying Locke's empirical program to its logical completion. Their skeptical philosophy showed beyond doubt that the whole tendency of empirical philosophy is "towards materialism and infidelity." Nevin looked askance on the attempts of American Baconians to forge a connection between empirical philosophy, and

---

[34]Nevin, "A Plea for Philosophy" in *Human Freedom and A Plea for Philosophy: Two Essays* (Mercersburg: P. A. Rice, 1850) 35-36; hereafter PFP. Cf. Schaff, *Principle of Protestantism*, 199: "it is not gold or steam, but ideas that rule the world and constitute the soul, the heart's blood of history, producing all that is either true or abiding." See also Appel, "Atomology," *MR* 23 (1876): 244-47.

[35]Nevin, PFP, 42-44; see Schaff, *Principle of Protestantism*, 19, 206.

the spiritual and supernatural. Since the philosophy itself has no power to transcend to limits of time and space, such a connection can only be "outward" and "traditional" at best rather than "inward and real."[36]

Nevin had little difficulty in overcoming the limits imposed on the Scottish philosophy by Cartesian dualism. Baconians were hard pressed to maintain the connection between Newtonian physics and Christianity, the physical and the spiritual, mind and matter. Nevin's incarnational philosophy rose to the occasion. Christianity, as truly human and divine, says Nevin, raises human nature to its true consummation. It must sanctify the mind as well as the will, transforming the entire organism of the world's life and every human production into its own image.

Contrary to dualism, the contents of faith are not simply an external or foreign element appended to the believer's life; rather they enter into the inner life of humanity itself so that Christianity becomes the absolute truth and inmost substance of the race. Christianity, then, constitutes the self-consciousness of the world in its deepest sense. Though philosophy is not the actual power of this divine life, it reflects the interior *form* of the world's life on which the divine power makes itself felt. It represents the self-consciousness of the world itself at any given time and the medium by which faith comes to reflection in an intelligible form. Only through philosophy, therefore, can the power of Christ take hold of the universal life of humanity in its actual forms, namely, art, science, and social life.[37]

With the restoration of the Union after the Civil War, Nevin's rather dim view of the nation's future seemed to take on a brighter aspect. Nevertheless, his tirade against materialism continued unabated. His criticism in these later writings is no longer directed against Baconianism alone. Not only was the system losing its grip on American institutions of higher learning, but new forms of materialism and skepticism were gradually gaining ground. Humanism, utilitarianism, and positivism all threatened to overthrow the supernatural character of Christianity. These developments did not

---

[36]Nevin, PFP, 43.
[37]Ibid., 37-40.

take Nevin or his colleagues by surprise. The new philosophies were only the natural outgrowth of the sensationalism and metaphysical skepticism fostered by Common Sense.

In a commencement address, given at Franklin and Marshall College in 1867, Nevin spoke in glowing terms about national rebirth, the success of democracy, and the nation's vast resources. His speech was pervaded by an apocalyptic tone, however. The world, in his view, was entering its final chapter in anticipation of Christ's Second Coming. As the momentum of the church moved westward from Europe, the final battle between Christ and Antichrist (that is, between the belief and denial of the true incarnation of the Son of God) would take place in America.[38]

As Nevin saw it, those who repudiated the supernatural reality of the Incarnation resolved divine grace into the forces of nature. This form of materialism was what Nevin called "Humanitarianism." It is similar, perhaps even identical, to what modern evangelicals and conservatives call "secular humanism." Nevin defines it as "the idea of a full completion of the world, morally and physically, in man (who is in fact the immediate completion of nature), without the necessary complement of a higher spiritual life descending into him from the Lord."[39]

American society was rife with this materialistic spirit. As a striking example, Nevin pointed to the Smithsonian Institution. Though, according to the original terms of the endowment (1826), it was founded for the *"Increase and Diffusion of Knowledge among Men,"* its sole focus was the physical sciences. Morality, literature, metaphysics, and philosophy were ignored. The implications were clear: knowledge consists in what can be known only through

---

[38]Appel, *LW*, 634-45 (from Nevin, "Commencement Address," *MR* 14 [1867]: 485-508). The westward progress of church history was a common idea shared by a number of idealist historians. Perhaps no one articulated it better than Nevin's Mercersburg colleague, Philip Schaff; see Klaus Penzel, "The Reformation Goes West: The Notion of Historical Development in the Thought of Philip Schaff," *Journal of Religion* 62 (July 1982): 219-41.

[39]Nevin, "Christianity and Humanity," 484. This paper was delivered before the sixth conference of the World Evangelical Alliance, 6 October 1873. Nevin's implicit censure of materialism (472-74) before this international audience suggests that he regarded the problem as being systemic to modern philosophy in general. See also, Nevin, "Cyprian," *MR* 4 (1852): 547.

these sciences.[40] Materialism, therefore, by denying the reality of the spiritual, resolves the ideal and supernatural into the natural. In the end it destroys the whole idea of revelation as an efflux of divine life and power historically present in the world, reducing Christianity to a form of rationalism.[41]

Recently, we have witnessed a greater awareness and recognition of religion and its role in public life. The advent of conservative politics with its emphasis on traditional values, interest in worship renewal, and even the rise of neopaganism, Eastern religions, native spirituality, and the New Age movement point to a growing spiritual hunger which the husks of materialism cannot satisfy. Nevertheless, for many, religion is still a matter of private taste and individual opinion. The real world is the world we see, touch, hear, and smell. By contrast, the spiritual is felt to be something shadowy and unreal. It is an ornament, a feeling, and an afterthought which has no power to change the course of culture and history.

It is the bane of modern thinking (and most modern theology as well) to turn the world upside down and move from lower to higher, bottom to top. Human experience is thus made the measure and archetype of the divine and heavenly. Religion is reduced to a metaphor of the earthly and the supernatural is displaced by ethics and social justice. This, it seems to me, was the burden of Nevin's warning. And, while there is certainly common ground between Mercersburg's incarnational theology, with its emphasis on history and experience, and recent currents in contemporary religion, the first principles and ultimate objectives of these contrasting systems are virtually irreconcilable.

---

[40]Appel, *LW*, 651.
[41]See Nevin, "Christianity and Humanity," 475-85.

Chapter 5
Religious Skepticism and Uncertainty

One of the most conspicuous marks of the modern and post-modern mind is the reduction of religion to a matter of personal and community taste, or, at best, morality. From the standpoint of modernity, knowledge is equated primarily with science. Consequently religious knowledge is not true knowledge at all, but only opinion. This is the legacy of the Enlightenment. And while most of academe has long since departed these shores, it is nothing less than amazing to see how firmly ensconced this notion is among the general public and some segments of the scientific community.

Postmodernism, on the other hand, reduces *all* knowledge to interpretation. Even empirical "facts" are said to be theory-laden. All analytical methods—including those of science—are conditioned, if not determined, by presuppositions. In this respect, religion and science are both alike, and under postmodernism we have seen a renewed interest in the spiritual and mystical dimension of existence.

Nevertheless, postmodernism ultimately reduces religious knowledge to a matter of opinion; or worse, to a self-serving and even sinister means of exercising political or psychological control over others (hermeneutics of suspicion). Combine these ideas with individualism and a radically pluralistic concept of reality, and religion becomes a matter of *individual* taste. Like one's preference for Italian dressing rather than ranch, or spinach rather than peas, religion is a private affair of the heart in which there is no right or wrong. For, in the sphere of religion especially, there can be no certainty.

Nevin addressed the challenge of modernity by demonstrating the limitations of science. One cannot use the scientific method to scale the invisible and transcendent. Religious knowledge does not come by way of dispassionate observation (though this is not wholly excluded), but by intuition, existential participation, and communion. Nevin's epistemology intersects postmodernism by recognizing that when it comes to religious and metaphysical knowledge, science knows no position of privilege from which to articulate truth. (In postmodernism, of course, the very idea of truth is problematic.)

But, Nevin's critique of Common Sense theology and its empirical approach to religion is much more than a critique of modernity. It confronts the philosophical roots of postmodernism as well by addressing nominalism. The denial of universals in favor of "family resemblances" (Wittgenstein), the idea that all language is in some sense metaphorical, ambiguous, and multivalent, the belief that all knowledge is perspectival, that reality is a mental construct which, at bottom, is radically individual, local, and pluralistic, are all logical concomitants of nominalism. By addressing the problem of nominalism, then, Nevin challenged the very foundation of the postmodern world.

Nominalism and empiricism, as we have already seen, shifts the center of reality away from the universals of Aristotelian and Platonic philosophy to sensible particulars. The impact on epistemology is to elevate the perception of *res corporales* at the expense of *res incorporales*. The actual becomes everything, the ideal nothing. Objectivity comes to be identified with the empirical and the particular while revelation is reduced to a form of information.

The error is one of *misplaced* concretion or objectivity—what Nevin, Samuel Taylor Coleridge, and others regarded as the tyranny of the senses: *The finite and the sensible alone are considered self-evidencing, while the reality or veracity of the ideal and the spiritual are only derivative.* The consequence of this error is, in short, epistemological *dualism.* By elevating the senses at the expense of intuition and faith, Common Sense, as we will see, all but severs the ideal from human intelligence, the supernatural from the natural, and revelation from the inward life of humanity.

In Nevin's view, the solution to this problem is not to eliminate the authority of empirical knowledge which operates in the sphere of the *actual*, but, following the paradigm of the Incarnation itself, to bring the actual into a synthetic but subordinate relationship with the *ideal* by demonstrating the self-authenticating character of "Reason"[1] (which grasps the infinite and eternal) and faith (which lays hold of the supernatural). In so doing, revelation is transformed from information *about* God to the historical disclosure of God Himself.

Scottish Realism:
The Power of Evidences and Ratiocination

The principle deficiency of Baconianism, as I have pointed out, was its tendency toward *misplaced concretion*. Objectivity was equated with the realm of sense and time. This is the realm of concrete certainty. The spiritual, on the other hand, is subjective and elusive. Not surprisingly, this error made itself felt in two primary areas of Baconian religion: Evidentialism and Scripture. In the first, it was supposed that the conclusions of empirical science could establish the truth and authority of revelation (namely, of Scripture). In the second, objective revelation was identified with information. "Objectively considered," says Hodge, Christianity is the "testimony of God concerning his Son, it is the whole revelation of truth contained in the Scriptures." "Subjectively considered, it is the life of Christ in the soul" which is determined by this objective revelation.[2] Hence the objective side of Christianity is equated only with the doctrines of Scripture while any relationship to the spiritual world is relegated to subjectivity.

Though Presbyterians like Hodge believed that the knowledge of God disclosed in Scripture was not simply subjective or

---

[1]Where appropriate, "Reason" and "Understanding" are capitalized throughout this chapter to designate technical terms which differ in content from the commonly used definitions. On this point, Nevin followed Coleridge's widely received distinction which is discussed later.

[2]Hodge, "What Is Christianity?" *PR* 32 (1860): 119; quoted in Charles A. Jones, "Charles Hodge, the Keeper of Orthodoxy: The Method, Purpose and Meaning of his Apologetic" (Ph.D. diss., Drew University, 1989) 208-209.

regulative, but objective and constitutive, this identification between revelation and information was, at bottom, a move away from the ideal and universal toward the particularity of nominalism. By identifying the propositions of Scripture with the objective side of Christianity, Baconian theologians equated objectivity with *discursive* knowledge. Such knowledge, as Nevin and Coleridge suggest, moves only within the categories of space and time which is the realm of Understanding.[3] Beyond this lies the sphere of the universal, eternal, and necessary which can only be grasped *intuitively* by the power of faith and Reason. This dimension was signally lacking in the Baconian ideal of revelation. As with Ockham, there was no intuition of being, no sense of a divine reality lying back of the words of Scripture. So, in the end the Presbyterian doctrine of Scripture was really another example of misplaced concretion.

Presbyterians such as James W. Alexander attempted to defend the Baconian position against Coleridge and others who claimed that an immediate, intuitive knowledge of God and revelation was possible without appealing first to external evidences in order to establish certainty. Alexander rejected Coleridge's distinction between Understanding and Reason. Truths concluded from *intermediate* propositions by "ratiocination" become self-evident and therefore immediate, he contended.[4] The Scottish Realist, then, is at no disadvantage when compared to the transcendentalist.

This view of the Bible and revelation has other consequences as well. In the first place, without an intuitive sense of being, the object of theology is no longer God Himself, but the concept of God—that is, a nominal *representation*. Instead of viewing the language of Scripture as the medium through which we enter into communion with the divine, it becomes an end in itself. Secondly, as Nevin points out, such a detached and representational view of the supernatural results in a false view of authority. The super-

---

[3]As Gerhart said, "the mind thinks of the Absolute in the forms of the Relative, of the Infinite in the forms of the Finite, of the Divine in the Forms of the human." Gerhart, "Mansel's Limits of Religious Thought," 315.

[4]Alexander, "The Doctrine of Perception, as held by Doctor Arnauld, Doctor Reid, and Sir William Hamilton," *PR* 31 (1859): 204; Skinner, "The Bible Its Own Witness and Interpreter," 397.

natural never enters into spontaneous union with the constitution of the believer. Its presence, authority, and power, always stand outside and against the subject. Its authority, therefore, is always heteronomous.

One of the most extreme examples of this abstract, representational approach to revelation is Samuel Tyler's definition of faith. Tyler was a well-known proponent of Baconianism and a disciple of Sir William Hamilton. Hamilton taught that thought operates only in the realm of the conditioned (that is, finite). It stands between unconditioned opposites (e.g., absolute beginning vs. infinite nonbeginning), one of which must be true according to the law of the excluded middle. Faith, on the other hand, though it cannot cognize these unconditioned opposites, can *believe* that one or the other is true based on analogy (e.g., causality leads us to believe in an absolute beginning though we cannot comprehend it). Faith, therefore, is transcendent in nature, having to do with the unconditioned, while knowledge, on the other hand, is conditioned.[5] It would be hard to imagine a more rationalistic and detached concept of religion than this. All that is left for faith is the idea of God as an "unconditioned opposite." The believer is entirely severed from communion with the supernatural.

But, Hamilton's views came under fire from Charles Hodge. With his usual piety and erudition, Hodge criticized Hamilton for his skeptical rationalism. Hamilton had attempted to synthesize Kant's philosophy with Reid's Common Sense. In so doing, however, he followed Kant by reducing faith to regulative (that is, heuristic) knowledge by making the unthinkable or the impossible an object of faith. Hamilton's "unconditioned opposites," according to Hodge, force us to believe what the laws of reason regard as self-contradictory. Relegating faith to mere regulative knowledge, amounts to a denial that God can be known. Indeed, "Hamilton teaches not merely that God may not be what we think Him to be, but that He cannot so be; that we are ignorant [of] what He is; that He is to us an unknown God."[6]

---

[5]Tyler, "Sir William Hamilton and his Philosophy," *PR* 27 (1855): 580-82.
[6]Hodge, *ST*, 1:353, 356; addition in brackets is mine.

It was not the principles of Common Sense which Hodge objected to here, but Hamilton's departure from them. This, according to the Princeton professor, was what lead to Hamilton's (and Henry Mansel's) erroneous and dangerous doctrines of faith. After laying down four cardinal doctrines of Common Sense, Hodge concludes:

> Hamilton and Mansel therefore teach that the veracity of consciousness is the foundation of all knowledge, and that the denial of that veracity inevitably leads to absolute scepticism. Nevertheless they teach . . . that our sensuous, rational, and moral consciousness are alike deceptive and unreliable.[7]

Hodge's attack on Hamilton brought the Princeton theologian to a fork in the road: As a corrective measure, he could either appeal to Scripture as a source of constitutive and authoritative information *about* God, or he could appeal to the self-evidencing revelation of God which is disclosed to faith *through* the Scriptures. His predicament typified the crisis of Baconian religion.

Despite its empirical and rationalistic approach to religion, historically speaking, Scottish philosophy did not preempt the possibility of an immediate, transcendental encounter with the spiritual. Common Sense was nurtured within the womb of Presbyterianism. As such, it was in contact with a tradition of confessionalism and pietism that prevented the system from drifting too far afield. As Christians, Baconians maintained their belief in the reality of the spiritual, but avoided connecting it with the ideal as Nevin had done. The door was always open to the influence of Reformed and evangelical pietism. As a result, they continued to affirm their belief in a personal encounter with Christ through the indwelling of the Holy Spirit.

Generally speaking, Hodge placed a greater emphasis in his theology on this internal, self-authenticating evidence of religious affections or sentiments than some his contemporaries. Like Nevin and Schleiermacher, he believed that the human constitution possessed an intuitive or innate "knowledge" of God which exists universally and necessarily. By innate he meant "the general sense

---

[7]Ibid., 1:361-62.

of a Being on whom we are dependent, and to whom we are responsible." But the "sublime idea of God" held by Christianity "no human mind ever attained either intuitively or discursively, except under the light of supernatural revelation."[8]

Hodge also regarded internal testimony as the most convincing evidence that the Scriptures contain authentic revelation. This emphasis on internal evidence was a combined product of Reformed confessionalism and pietism on the one side (see Westminster Confession I.v.), and the Baconian belief in the veracity of "consciousness" on the other. The utility of external evidences was not denied, but merely relegated to second importance.[9] One of the boldest affirmations of this belief in internal evidence was made by Hodge in 1845:

> We believe in Christ for the same reason that we believe in God. His character and claims have been exhibited to us, and we assent to them; we see his glory and we recognize it as the glory of God. This exhibition is made in the gospel; it is made to every reader of the word. . . . Such a man believes the gospel on the highest possible evidence; the testimony of God himself with and by the truth to his own heart; making him see and feel that it is the truth.[10]

Yet, despite such definitive declarations, Hodge was a prisoner of Baconian presuppositions. In confronting Hamilton's philosophy, which regarded revelation as a form of regulative knowledge, he made no attempt to invoke either the self-authenticating power of faith, or the glory of Christ revealed in the Scriptures. Instead, he appealed exclusively to "divine supernatural revelation" in the form of "real" or constitutive ideas. The abstract and representative nature of these ideas is all too apparent. According to Hamilton, Hodge tells us, there are two kinds of experiential knowledge. One is derived from our own experience, the other is derived "from the experience of others, authenticated to us by adequate testimony." In Hodge's view, revelation is of the latter type. It consists of facts

[8]Ibid., 1:194-95; see also 192, 200.
[9]Ibid., 1:635-36.
[10]Hodge, "Thornwell on the Apocrypha," 274.

which lie beyond our experience. Faith, then, rests in "the divine testimony" and its doctrinal content rather than in the actual revelation of the person of Christ.[11]

Hodge's answer to Hamilton exemplified an understanding of religion and revelation which confirmed all of Nevin's worst fears regarding Baconianism: Divine revelation is essentially a communication of information (that is, constitutive ideas) about God and His works; it is given by God through inspiration and authenticated by miraculous evidences. Nevin believed that in a representational concept of revelation such as this, the supernatural stands outside of the believer. The presence and reality of Christ is known only by intermediate testimony rather than immediate experience. So long as the supernatural is unable to unite spontaneously and organically with the human constitution, its authority will remain heteronomous and despotic instead of being the fountain of human freedom.

The Shadow of Skepticism

Despite the epistemological optimism and certainty historically associated with Common Sense, Nevin believed that it was, in fact, a doorway to both metaphysical and religious skepticism. Just as Common Sense, when severed from Presbyterian influence, ultimately tended toward materialism, so it would, under the same conditions, end in epistemological skepticism.

On the metaphysical side, Baconian theologians had fallen into the error of *misplaced concretion* by regarding the finite and the sensible alone as self-evidencing while the reality or veracity of the ideal was considered only derivative. Nevin challenged this erroneous epistemology not only by demonstrating that the ideal and spiritual are as immediate and self-authenticating as the world of sense, but also by showing that the only possible *basis* of every *individual* percept and concept is an intuition of universal being. The actual or phenomenal world, as we have already seen, derives its reality from the ideal as fully as the ideal is made real by being reified in time and space. The reality and perception of individual

---

[11]See Hodge, *ST*, 1:364.

things—a distinguishing characteristic of nominalism—was never in doubt. What Nevin sought to establish was the corresponding reality of the ideal and its organic relationship to the actual—a relationship governed ultimately by the Incarnation.

Accordingly, Nevin, like Rauch and Samuel Taylor Coleridge, believed that there is a perfect symmetry between the powers of sense on the one side and the powers of the soul on the other. Both are said to operate at an intuitive level prior to reflection and discursive thought; and both have the power to bring the subject into immediate contact with its objects. Reason is said to "feel" ideas as much as sense feels the outer world. This analogy serves both to perpetuate *and* synthesize the distinction between the two worlds—sensible and supersensible—so essential to post-Kantian Platonism.[12]

This restoration of metaphysical optimism was accompanied by the corresponding recovery of a Platonic-Augustinian epistemology in religion. The Cartesian dualism of mind and matter, appropriated by the Scottish philosophy, was discarded like an obsolete hypothesis. Participation, communion, and immediacy took precedence over detachment, observation, and objectivity. The cold and sterile methods of the Enlightenment (that is, evidences and outward authority) and the ecclesiastical authoritarianism found in some forms of Roman Catholicism, were subordinated to intuition and religious feeling. This was not, of course, a total rejection of evidences or authority, but an attempt to show that by themselves such objective methods can never unite nature and supernature, subject and object, the ideal and the actual.

On the religious side, it is not difficult to see how the metaphysical skepticism of Common Sense passed naturally over to religious skepticism. When the intelligibility of universal ideas is challenged, we are only a short step away from religious skepticism or, at the very least, some form of agnosticism. This was the

---

[12]Considered from a structural standpoint, Kant's philosophy invited comparisons to Platonism in three fundamental areas: (1) The dichotomy between the world of appearance (phenomenal) and the world of reality (noumenal); (2) the distinction between Reason and Understanding; and (3) the existence and function of a priori knowledge. On the synthesis of empiricism and post-Kantian Platonism see DiPuccio, "Dynamic Realism," 62-124.

and humanity. Drawing from these resources, Rauch, Gerhart, Nevin, and Schaff overcame the empirical limitations imposed by Kant and Baconian religion by restoring a sense of immediacy and participation to religious epistemology. Faith is not merely an assent to propositions or authority, but an intuitive capacity by which the soul communes with the supernatural. This capacity for faith stands in direct relation to the supernatural just as the human intellect is directly related to the ideal.

Restoring Epistemological Optimism

Having considered the potential threat which Scottish philosophy posed to both metaphysics and religion, it is time to unfold Nevin's epistemology in greater detail. Despite his strenuous opposition to Common Sense and his extensive use of German idealism, he never wandered far from his Baconian roots. His approach to both metaphysical and religious epistemology relies heavily on a form of intuition, which, like Common Sense, offered the possibility of immediate perception accompanied by veridical certainty. Indeed, one might almost say that Nevin's religious epistemology, with its exalted view of faith, is simply the systematic explication of his profound Presbyterian piety using the first principles of Common Sense. However, Nevin's debt to Platonism and idealism (especially Rauch's Hegelianism) is unmistakable and may even account for his continued appropriation of Common Sense. After all, German idealists, such as Hegel, consciously attempted to reconcile and synthesize both rationalism and empiricism, the ideal and the actual.

Knowledge as Intuition

Nevin maintains that the ideal could be realized only *through* the operation of the senses. This is evident in Rauch's *Psychology* (on which Nevin relied) where nascent reason emerges through feeling and sensation. Nevin said it best in his lectures on aesthetics: The idea shines through the form. We look "through the visible to the invisible." "The outward becomes a sacrament of the inward."[14] The sensible object, then, is "not merely an aid, or a bridge," which enables the mind to reach the idea, rather, "it is the middle ground on which the two, the mind and the idea, meet."[15]

The goal of this intuitive process is to "see" the "fundamental Being" of an object. All objects have a spiritual or ideal substance. That substance is the universal idea or prototype which lies behind the image (e.g., humanity is the essence of individual humans). The human spirit or mind can penetrate to the very being of reality because it "is fundamentally one with the universal constitution of things around us."[16] In short, it possesses an intuitive knowledge of the whole. For both Nevin and Rauch, then, *intuition is the process by which knowledge is educed from an apprehension of the whole.*[17] It stands in marked contrast to the inductive method of Common Sense which builds knowledge by observing particulars. The final results are likewise different: While induction yields only generalizations about individual phenomena, intuition apprehends the law or ground of these individual instances.

But intuition, in the sense in which it is used by Mercersburg theology, should not be confused with either a lucid and intellectual realization of something (such as the sudden discovery or discernment of an elusive idea), or a feeling which only reflects the internal state of the subject, but has no basis in the actual constitution of the object. These *subjective* forms of intuitionalism, which find a certain affinity with postmodern thought, were rejected by Nevin. Instead, an intuition is *the immediate communion of the affections, will, and intellect with the whole of any object.* Such intuition, dimly felt at first, has the potential of rising to the level of reflection and discursive knowledge. For, all things, whether sensible or spiritual, are imbued with rationality. This form of intuitionism is objective and ontological.

For Nevin and Rauch, the capacity for noumenal knowledge implies a correlation between feeling and knowing which is fundamental to Mercersburg's intuitive epistemology. Rauch views

---

[14]Nevin, "Lectures on Aesthetics," 32, 39.

[15]Appel, *LW,* 678 (from student notes of Nevin's lectures on aesthetics, ca. 1866–1876).

[16]Nevin, "Lectures on Aesthetics," 343-44.

[17]Cf. Hegel, *Encyclopedia,* §§445 (Zusatz), 446, 449 (with Zusatz).

nature as a system of confluent energies wholly pervaded by ideal law. These powers and laws are coextensive and mutually affective.[18] Knowledge, therefore, entails an actual conjunction between subject and object—a mutually affective relation. To know, then, involves "feeling" an object, whether it is an idea, an object in time and space, or God.

Consequently, thinking, "is as simple an activity as feeling." But, whereas feeling is indistinct and reflexive, thinking is lucid and perfectly free. Thinking begins as sensual feeling, though it does not originate *from* feeling. As the growth of fruit is conditional upon the buds and blossoms, so thinking is conditional upon feeling. Yet, the fruit, in its latency, is actually the origin of the buds and blossoms as thinking is the origin of feeling in humans. Hence, feeling, in Rauch's view, is implicit thought.[19]

Faith as Supernatural Vision

Rauch's intuitive epistemology prepared the way for a theological response to the problem of misplaced concretion which, as we have seen, passed over into the sphere of religion. Evidentialism and biblical rationalism concluded upon the reality of the supernatural only after demonstrating its veracity by miraculous proofs. As Nevin complained, the presence and reality of Christ is thus known only by intermediate testimony rather than immediate experience. The supernatural stands outside of the believer. Nevin encountered a similar problem when he confronted the Roman Catholic propensity toward authority. In both cases a heteronomous or false form of authority is interposed between the natural and the supernatural, God and humanity.

Nevin met the difficulty by contending that faith, by its very nature, is immediate and self-authenticating in the realm of the spiritual, just as pure Reason is immediate and self-authenticating

---

[18]Appel, *Recollections*, 276; Rauch, *Psy* 289, 43, 183.
[19]Ibid., 289-90. On Coleridge's striking comparisons between sense and Reason, see Coleridge, *Aids*, 246; Owen Barfield, *What Coleridge Thought* (Middletown CT: Wesleyan University Press, 1971) 54-55, 128; G. N. G. Orsini, *Coleridge and German Idealism: A Study in the History of Philosophy with Unpublished Materials from Coleridge's Manuscripts* (Carbondale: Southern Illinois University Press, 1969) 252-53.

in the realm of the ideal. In both cases there is an intuitive sense of being or reality which lies at the root of every individual percept and concept whether it is metaphysical or religious.

Nevin's concept of faith is the capstone of his epistemology and embraces both metaphysics and religion, the natural intellect and the spirit. Drawing on the Incarnation, Nevin believes that the reality and presence of the supernatural world are inwardly united with the life of humanity through faith in the same way that the two natures of Christ are joined without confusion or separation. As a result, the final object of faith is not the letter of Scripture or the authority of the church (these are mediate objects), but the God who reveals Himself to us in Christ—the Word made flesh.

Historically, his view of faith was indebted to his "Puritan" piety, the influence of Coleridge, and the writings of German church historian, J. A. W. Neander (1789–1850). One of his favorite authors, Henry Scougal (an Anglican minister), wrote, "true religion is a union of the soul with God, a real participation of the Divine Nature, the very image of God drawn upon the soul, or in the apostle's phrase, 'it is Christ formed within us.'"[20]

As a Christian Platonist Nevin adopted Coleridge's sharp distinction between "Understanding" and "Reason" which is founded on Plato's analogy of the divided line. This distinction became part of his theological prolegomena. He sided with the British poet's interpretation of F. H. Jacobi by attributing to the soul, the innate capacity for beholding "the eternal, the necessary, the universal" with the same immediacy as corporeal vision.[21] According to

---

[20]Scougal, *The Life of God in the Soul of Man* (n.p., 1739; repr.: Harrisonburg VA: Sprinkle, 1986) 34. These sentiments are echoed throughout Nevin's favorite work, *Of the Imitation of Christ*, by Thomas á Kempis. See also, Nevin, *Seal*, 5.

[21]See Erb, *NT*, 13, 66-67; idem, *Party Spirit: An Address Delivered before the Literary Societies of Washington College, Washington Pa. on the Evening of September 24th 1839* (Chambersburg: Publication Office of the German Reformed Church, 1840) 13. On Nevin's relation to Coleridge, see David Layman, "Was Nevin influenced by S. T. Coleridge?" *The New Mercersburg Review* 17 (Spring 1995): 54-58; and the rejoinder, William DiPuccio, "Nevin & Coleridge," *The New Mercersburg Review* 17 (Spring, 1995): 59-63. According to Plato (*Republic* VI.508-10 f), NOESIS, or direct intuition (i.e., NOUS, Reason), stands in relation to the ideal forms and the Good on the one side, while DIANOIA, or discursive reasoning (i.e., Understanding), relates to images, mathematics, etc., on the other. Kant and Hegel made a similar distinction in their systems, though with some important differences. See

Coleridge, "Reason" is "an organ bearing the same relation to spiritual objects, the Universal, the Eternal, and the Necessary, as the eye bears to material and contingent phaenomena." When united with will it becomes faith—"the organ of theology and philosophy." So, faith unites Speculative and Practical Reason. As Coleridge indicates, the apprehension of truth involves both action and reflection.[22]

Nevin defines faith as an actual communion with the spiritual world. It is a "deep feeling of the reality of eternal things, overpowering the impressions of sense. . . . "[23] It is "the power of the soul by which it lays hold of invisible and eternal realities, and causes them to be apprehended and rested in as most certainly true. . . . [It is] the faculty of holding immediate and direct correspondence with the spiritual world."[24] Faith is the "medium" for apprehending God's grace and the "organ by which we perceive and apprehend the spiritual and eternal . . . the very eye itself, rather, that enables us to 'look at things unseen,' and causes their presence to surround us as part of our own life." "Faith, is of the nature of life; it implies an actual contact."[25]

This capacity for religious faith is connatural to the human constitution. Nevertheless, it has been damaged (not destroyed) by sin. The "organ of spiritual vision" slumbers unconsciously but is not extinguished. It operates in degrees ranging from natural revelation to the full light of the gospel by which it is brought to its highest form of existence. But the light of nature, that is to say the light by which God reveals Himself as Creator to fallen humanity, can never kindle a saving faith in Jesus Christ. For, God does not historically objectify Himself in creation. To the fallen mass of humanity, spiritual things are but "dim notions" and "nebulous abstractions" in a distant "land of shadows and dreams."[26]

DiPuccio, "Dynamic Realism," 101-105.

[22]Coleridge, *The Friend*, 155-56, 501; idem, *Aids*, 117, 252-53n., 241-42, 247.

[23]Nevin, "The Active Christian," *The Friend*, 22 Aug. 1833.

[24]Nevin, *Seal*, 6.

[25]Nevin, "Apostles' Creed," 208; Erb, *NT*, 301.

[26]Nevin, "Worldly Mindedness," *WM*, 1 July 1840. See also "Faith," *WM*, 11 March 1840, 925. The existence of God is not simply a logical conclusion from nature. By faith we know that God created the world (Heb. 11:3). See Nevin, "Brownson's Quarterly Review," 68; Erb, *NT*, 165; Nevin, *Seal*, 6.

Even natural reason, according to Nevin, is blind without the clear revelation of God in Jesus Christ. It can only operate properly when God becomes its absolute referent through the power of faith. Consequently, faith elevates the soul above sense and Reason. As Nevin says, faith "constitutes the very highest form of intellect. It is the mind, rising far above the sphere of the speculative reason, and embracing truths which no logical forms can fully measure." It "constitutes the very perfection of rationality, the clearest and most active exercise of intellect."[27]

This elevation of the intellect should not be confused with discursive reasoning. Faith, like Reason, is an intuitive activity which must be distinguished from reflective ratiocination. Because faith brings the spiritual world into immediate conjunction with the human soul, it is prior to reflection just as vision or sensation is prior to understanding. Reflection is a mediate process by which the mind objectifies its own contents by separating itself from them.[28] Faith, on the other hand, "is a direct and immediate act, more of the nature of feeling."[29]

Reception of Christ, therefore, involves a spontaneous and inward sympathy with His person. In Nevin's view, this does not imply full intelligibility of the object any more than sensation implies a full comprehension of physical nature. There is a difference between assurance of faith and assurance of understanding. The latter involves reflection, the former is an immediate act like feeling. Faith does not simply provide new "data" for the mind says Nevin. It does, however, include in itself (potentially at least) reason and knowledge for its own apprehension. The life communicated in the process of regeneration is more than simply an

---

[27]Nevin, *Seal*, 6; idem, "Worldly Mindedness," *WM*, 1 July 1840; idem, "Faith," *WM*, 18 Mar. 1840; Erb, *NT*, 12-17, 222-23; Nevin, "Apostles' Creed," 208, 211; idem, "Faith, Reverence and Freedom," *MR* 2 (1850): 99; idem, "Man's True Destiny," 509; idem, *Heidelberg Catechism*, 134-35; idem, *My Own Life*, 66-69. Cf. idem, *Personal Holiness. A Lecture Delivered, June, 1837, at the Opening of the Summer Term in the Western Theological Seminary* (Pittsburgh: William Allinder, 1837) 6: "Faith, in the sense of the Scriptures, is the most active and comprehensive of all the faculties that enter into the structure of the understanding. It is the crowning power of intelligence."

[28]Nevin, "Apostles' Creed," 204-207.

[29]Erb, *NT*, 301.

unmodulated energy. It is the power of a rational life because it is the life of Christ Himself who is Truth. It unfolds according to the laws of human development filling the entire compass of the personality. So, faith stands in *rational* correspondence to its contents. Justifying faith may begin without a conscious affirmation of Christ. But it carries in itself a reference to Christ as its center which will eventually be made evident.[30]

Saving faith, then, is the beginning of evangelical knowledge. "Subject and object are inseparably conjoined," observes Nevin, "where such faith becomes for the soul the germinant power of a true Christian life." Consequently, following Christ does not depend on "knowing *how* He is the Saviour of the world, or on being assured that He is so by any evidence or argument from beyond Himself." Rather, it results from an actual efflux of power that proceeds directly from Christ Himself. This power "draws the soul towards Him, and binds it more and more to Him, with the intuitional conviction that He is its only proper life and its absolutely supreme good."[31]

In Nevin's view, this *transition* from intuitive faith to understanding, from being to knowledge, is embodied in the Apostles' Creed. The Creed, as we saw in chapter 3, occupies a central position in his religious epistemology. It stands in continuity with the life-power of the Incarnation as it takes form in Peter's confession: "You are the Christ, the Son of the Living God." (see Matt. 16:13-20).[32] That confession, Nevin tells us, was not a product of reflection, but proceeded *directly* from the power of Christ's person operating on the inmost core of Peter's life—back of all thought, volition, or feeling. It was the primitive and spontaneous utterance of undivided faith that can come only by actually being transplanted into the new sphere of life. "Flesh and blood have not revealed this to you," Christ told Peter, "but my Father who is in heaven."[33]

The Creed, then, is not the product of individual or synodical reflection designed to summarize Scripture. It does not bear the

---

[30]Nevin, *MP*, 168-69; idem, "Brownson's Review," 67-70, 322-23; idem, "Apostles' Creed," 204; Erb, *NT*, 37, 301.
[31]Nevin, "Answer to Professor Dorner," *MR* 15 (1868): 567, 605.
[32]Nevin did not believe that the Creed was actually written by the apostles.
[33]Nevin, "Apostles' Creed," 212-14.

marks of a catechism or a confession. These are *mediate* forms of truth in which the mind is forced to objectify its own content. The Creed differs from all of these. "Its object," says Nevin, "is, not to lodge its articles as so many points of Christian orthodoxy in the mind; but so to bring this [the mind] rather into the consciousness of what they affirm, that they may be appropriated by it, and made one with it, as part of its own life."[34] The Creed, then, is "the substance of Christianity in the form of faith"—the church's spontaneous utterance of what is immediately at hand in the Christian consciousness.[35] It represents the system of *life* out of which the Bible (and the other creeds of the church) spring.

Nevin overcame the error of misplaced concretion by appealing to the objective and self-evidencing power of faith as it is found in the Creed. Peter's confession, as Nevin remarks, demonstrates the "boundless difference there is between knowing and being, between thinking and actual life, in the kingdom of God." In our natural life the senses tell us that such a difference exists, for sensation is prior to reflection in the order of time. But because of the fall, our spiritual life is deranged and we often place knowing before being.[36] However, neither a knowledge of Bible doctrines, nor empirical evidences, nor blind assent to any outward authority can unite us to the supernatural realities revealed through Christ in Christianity. Only through faith can we behold the spiritual world in its own self-authenticating light. "Our nature," as Nevin says, "is formed for such direct communion with the world of the spirit."[37]

Mysticism, Pantheism, and Revelation

Nevin's subjective and even mystical concept of faith overcame the limitations posed by Baconian religion and external authority by organically uniting the supernatural to the inward life of humanity. In so doing, however, did he obliterate the possibility of objective revelation by confusing subject and object? In other

---

[34]Ibid., 215; brackets mine.
[35]Ibid., 201-15; Nevin, *Antichrist*, 23-29.
[36]Nevin, "The Supreme Epiphany; God's Voice Out of the Cloud," 218.
[37]Nevin, "Apostles' Creed," 208.

words, given Nevin's emphasis on the inward and participatory nature of faith, can we still distinguish between supernatural revelation and self-consciousness? If not, then revelation ceases to be transcendent and objective. Since everything emanates from the subject, our knowledge of God is no longer constitutive of an objective being, but merely describes the content of our own consciousness.

This question echoes the dilemma of postmodern religion in Western culture. Following Kant, it is believed that reality comes into being only through the creative action of the mind. The thing-in-itself cannot be known except as it is interpreted and mediated through the existential situation of the subject. Consequently, our understanding of God, is essentially a reflection of our own encounter with the transcendent. Our language about God consists in *metaphors* which attempt to grasp the transcendent and the unknown by comparing them with our own experience. It is no longer possible, given these presuppositions, to clearly distinguish subject and object, God and humanity. The notion of an objective, supernatural revelation which originates outside the subject is all but obliterated. In existential theology, liberation theology, and social justice theology, for example, revelation is often collapsed into human experience. It is no wonder that there has been an increasing tendency toward monism and naturalism among some Christian theologians. Many feminists and ecotheologians are especially enamored with the idea that the world is God's body (panentheism) or that God gave birth to the world (emanationism). Nevin's approach, which avoids both dualism and monism, is particularly relevant to today's theology.

Despite its appearance, Nevin's view of faith is not a transcendental lapse into mysticism or postmodern existentialism. The immediacy of faith does not occur without instrumentality. That would entail a denial of the historical Incarnation. The supernatural is revealed *in and through* the natural in the same way that the ideal is made known only in and through the actual. As the intellect ascends through the senses to take hold of the ideal, so faith always depends on an external *means* of grace (that is, word, sacraments, and church) to lay hold of the supernatural.

Apart from such historical mediation, religion turns inward. Nevin vehemently opposed this type of subjective piety which, in his view, formed the heart and soul of revivalism, Methodism, sectarianism, and Transcendentalism. As a German Reformed theologian, he held fast to the belief that the powers of the world to come are "mediated for the apprehension of faith by the power of the Holy Ghost through the word and sacraments."[38]

Nevin did not oppose all forms of mediation, then. His struggle was against those forms which, when all is said and done, are unable to organically unite divine revelation with the life of humanity. In other words, the medium becomes a barrier to true faith or even an end in itself. For Nevin a medium must be *self-effacing, transparent*, and *iconic*, rather than opaque and representational. Nevin's remarks on the nature of aesthetics, which we considered above, apply with equal force to the question of faith and immediacy: We look "through the visible to the invisible." "The outward becomes a sacrament of the inward."[39] As a result, Nevin looks upon miracles, the Bible, and the church as the necessary outflowing of divine revelation. Without them revelation would be "gnostically unreal and inconceivable." Yet, these mediums should not be confused with the revelation itself.[40]

Consequently, Nevin was not opposed to "Christian evidences" in *principle*, but only to their elevation above true faith. Christ first authenticates Himself to us by the power of His person which, in turn, serves as the spontaneous source of His miracles. These are the necessary seal of His mission and the reflected radiance of His glory.[41] Word and miracle are inseparably wedded like soul and body. "The internal evidence embodies in itself the external, and the external is animated by the internal."[42] In summarizing two works by R. C. Trench (1807—1886), Nevin concurred with the conclusion of the British author, saying that if outward evidence alone were sufficient to establish faith, then "Christianity is not the deep-

---

[38]Nevin, "Nature and Grace," 503.

[39]Nevin, "Lectures on Aesthetics," 32, 39.

[40]Nevin, "Christ and His Spirit," 373.

[41]Erb, *NT*, 24-25; Nevin, "Apostles' Creed," 328. Apologetics is properly illustrative says Nevin; Erb, *NT*, 64-67; Nevin, *My Own Life*, 69.

[42]Erb, *NT*, 24.

est and most comprehensive form of truth for the human mind."[43] There would be a truth beyond it which is more certain, or at least more immediately evident and complete without Christianity. This truth would then be the necessary condition and measure of the Christian religion subordinating the truth of Christ to human reason instead of making Christ the inmost soul and life reason. This is rationalism.[44] As Trench said, *"we believe in the miracles for Christ's sake*, [rather] than Christ for the miracles sake."[45]

Not only did Nevin recognize the value of evidences and the means of grace, but he and his colleagues were fully aware of the danger of collapsing religion into self-consciousness and responded accordingly. Indeed, Mercersburg's attempt to synthesize the theology of Schleiermacher with Reformed theology, along with their adaption of German idealism (which tended to collapse Kant's noumenon and phenomenon into human consciousness) became a primary point of contention.[46]

Though Nevin admired Schleiermacher's Christocentric theology, he clearly rejected the German thinker's subjectivity and intuitionalism in the same way he rejected Horace Bushnell's resistance to dogma. Christianity must take full possession of our being including the intellect. This is involved in the very definition of life as being more than feeling or will.[47] Nevin insists "that the authority of Christ's presence and person (objective Christianity exhibited to us in Christ,) is the ground of all subjective Christiani-

---

[43]Nevin, "Trench's Lectures," 606; idem, "Christ and His Spirit," 386.

[44]Nevin, "Brownson's Review," 68-70; idem, "The New Testament Miracles," *MR* 2 (1850): 576-77, 580-81; idem, "Trench's Lectures," 606-607; idem, *My Own Life*, 69. Miracles are not a violation of natural law but are above and beyond it as it is known to us; idem, "Trench's Lectures," 576; Erb, *NT*, 25-27. It is evident from what has been said here that Nevin rejected philosophical foundationalism.

[45]R. C. Trench, *Notes on the Miracles of Our Lord* (New York: D. Appleton & Co., 1850) 81 (repr.: Grand Rapids MI: Baker, 1949, p. 60); quoted in Nevin, "New Testament Miracles," 584 (brackets mine). See Erb, *NT*, 39-41.

[46]Nevin's most brilliant critic, in this respect, was the American Roman Catholic theologian and philosopher, Orestes Brownson. For the primary literature associated with this exchange, see the bibliography. For a complete analysis of the controversy, see DiPuccio, "Dynamic Realism," 257-76.

[47]Erb, *NT*,11-20; Nevin, "Publications," *MR* 1 (1849): 312; idem, "The Anti-Creed Heresy," 607-608; Moses Kieffer, "Dogmatic Theology," 454-62. See also Schaff, *Principle of Protestantism*, 198-99.

ty. Faith, in its last and deepest sense, is simply submission (free, but yet unseeing also, and implicit) to such objective authority."[48] Revelation, therefore, is first objective and historical, then subjective and experiential.

Like Rudolf Otto Nevin maintained that the intuitional sense of the numinous, which he called faith, has, in Otto's words, "immediate and primary reference to an object outside itself." The numen is actually and objectively present to consciousness.[49] Revelation, therefore, originates beyond the subject, but enters into the subject. In joining itself to the subject, however, it does not become *identical* to self-consciousness. Christ's "*Person* is always thus the actual bearer of *our* persons. And yet there is no mixture or flowing of one into the other as individually viewed." Indeed, we achieve a higher sense of individuality and a *new* consciousness in Christ (who is the ground of all personality), than we possess in our natural state. If this is pantheism, quips Nevin, then Puritans like Howe, Baxter, and Owen were also guilty of teaching Buddhism.[50] Nevin taught a union of *life* between Christ and believers, not a union of *substances*.

As if this were not enough, he also argues that our "constitutional fittingness and capability" for receiving revelation is purely passive. This belief is in keeping not only with his Reformed confessionalism, but with his Platonism as well. Like knows like: The means of perception is suited (that is, connatural) to its object. The ear is for hearing, the eye is for seeing, Understanding is for the senses, Reason is for ideas, and faith is for God.[51] Yet faith, like

---

[48]Nevin, "Answer to Professor Dorner," 643, 641.

[49]Rudolf Otto, *The Idea of the Holy* (New York: Oxford University Press, 1950) 10-11.

[50]Nevin, *MP*, 173-74, 169n. Faith entails a movement whereby the totality of one's being swings "from the center of self" on which the "consciousness has been poised, over upon Christ, now revealed to his view, as another centre altogether" (ibid., 176, see also 168).

[51]In the *Timaeus* (45), Plato attributes the capacity of vision to the innate similarity between the luminous substance of the eye and the light which is outside the body. This ancient principle was also held by the Pythagoreans, the Stoics, the Neoplatonists, Augustine, and others. "Only the *like* can enter into the nature of the *like*," says Rauch speaking on love, "the spiritual that of spirit, the sensual that of sensation." Rauch, *Psy*, 318.

the eye, is awakened only in the presence of a power beyond itself. As the eye cannot create or determine the world it sees, so faith cannot create or determine the truth which moves it. Hence it is moved to assent not by its own power, but by the *self-evidencing* power of the *object* itself. We cannot be saved apart from a communication of Christ's power through faith; "but the power that saves, is not, for this reason, in our experience or faith; it is wholly in the object with which our faith is concerned." Faith is the *form and condition* of the justified state but not its content and principle.[52] As he later explained it, faith

> is the subjective and objective sides of divine revelation mysteriously blended into one. Faith as the act of the believer, is subjective; but drawing as it does, its whole existence and force at the same time from the supernatural realities that call it into exercise, it has part also in their objectivity, and is at once thus the certification of their truth as well as its own.[53]

From his days at Western Seminary (1830–1840) to his last article in the *Mercersburg Review* (1883), Nevin never lost sight of the distinction between subject and object, the natural and the supernatural. In keeping with the genius of his Christian Platonism and his incarnational theology, he regarded the two spheres as organically united yet essentially distinct. As he said in 1838, "There must be a subjective revelation, as well as one which is objective and outward. This revelation is effected by the Spirit, through the organ of faith."[54]

The Incarnation as the Archetype of Epistemology

Mercersburg's epistemology, as we have seen, was dependent ultimately on the Incarnation. Nevin's attempt to correct the error of misplaced concretion is unintelligible apart from understanding the hypostatic union between the divine and human natures of Christ. The two natures retain their essential distinctions, being

---

[52]Nevin "Brownson Again," 321-23; idem., "Answer to Professor Dorner," 592; Erb, *NT*, 305.
[53]Nevin, "Christ and His Spirit," 385. See also idem, *Seal*, 15.
[54]Nevin, *Seal*, 6.

joined without confusion or transmutation as Chalcedon affirmed. Therefore, Nevin could not have confused God and creation, the natural and the supernatural, subject and object, or faith and revelation without abandoning the very foundations of his system.

The degree to which this theanthropic union regulated his epistemology can only be fully appreciated when we consider the markedly asymmetrical relation between the metaphysical and religious sides of Mercersburg's epistemology. On the metaphysical side, Nevin regards the human mind as being *super*ordinate to the outer world. Standing at the apex of the sensible order, human intelligence assumes its objects and raises them to a higher level of existence in the same way that the Logos assumed and ennobled human nature.

The object as it is in the mind, then, is not simply a reflection of reality, but a "new creation." Human intelligence, says Nevin, is the full perfection of creation: "the world itself is made for this mode of existence . . . so that, short of this, it must ever be a rude and unformed mass, carrying in it no right sense, and representing no proper reality whatever."[55] Like Kant and Gerhart (Nevin's colleague), Nevin believed that the matter or content of our perceptions is supplied by the object, while the form is furnished by the subject. The "latent life of the soul," its "inward form," takes "hold of the *rudis indigestaque moles*" of the sensations and reduces them to "order and shape" for the intelligence.[56]

Similarities to Kant notwithstanding, Rauch, Nevin, and Gerhart all insisted that true knowledge necessitates an objective correspondence or concurrence between mind and the outer world. According to Gerhart, the *content* of knowledge is determined by the object, yet the mind is harmoniously "adjusted" to receive it. The *form* of knowledge is determined by the categories of thought, yet the object is "preadapted" to such conformity. Gerhart draws

---

[55]Appel, *LW*, 520 (from Nevin's 1859 address to Marshall College, "The Wonderful Nature of Man").

[56]Nevin, "Sacred Hermeneutics," 25-26. Cf. this description of postmodernism by Richard Tarnas, *Passion of the Western Mind*, 397: "The mind is not the passive reflector of an external world and its intrinsic order, but is active and creative in the process of perception and cognition. Reality is in some sense constructed by the mind, not simply perceived by it. . . . "

an analogy from natural vision in order to illustrate this: The "construction and capacities" of the eye are adjusted to the light just as the "constitution and laws" of mind "correspond" to the world. Likewise, the "nature of light" is adapted to "the receptivity and form of the eye" in the same way that the sensible world is adapted to the "intuitions and laws" of the mind. The eye cannot see without light and light cannot be seen without the eye. So too, the mind can have no knowledge without an object and the object could not be known apart from mind.[57]

The system of nature, as Nevin tells us, "has a being of its own" apart from human intelligence. But detached from intelligence it is no better than "thick, impenetrable darkness. In such view, it is for us as though it did not exist at all." To become real *for us* it "must not only *be*," it must also conform to the categories of human intelligence endowed by the creator.[58] Consequently, our inner reason recognizes the reason impressed upon nature by the Divine Mind. "The spirit or mind in us is fundamentally one with the universal constitution of things around us."[59]

So, though Nevin acknowledges that *a priori* principles and categories have a formative role in the construction of knowledge, unlike postmodernism, he maintains that the mind does not impose an *alien* structure upon the outer world. Rather, (to elaborate on his model) it functions like a prism by revealing the world's actual color and constitution. The idea of an intelligent Creator entails an implicit assumption of epistemological harmony between reality and the human mind.[60] There is, then, even as Common Sense Realism maintains, an objective correspondence

---

[57]Gerhart, *IP*, 134, 50. See also Gerhart's extended treatment of the epistemological problem in *IP*, 101-40. Schaff called Gerhart's work "a legitimate application" of Mercersburg theology "to metaphysical speculation." Schaff, "Recent Publications," *MR* 10 (1858): 161.

[58]Appel, *LW*, 520 (from "The Wonderful Nature of Man"). See also Erb, *NT*, 78. On Rauch's view, see *Psy*, 212-15.

[59]Nevin, "Lectures on Aesthetics," 344. See idem, "Philosophy of History. XIII. Historical Science—Inward Qualifications," *College Days*, May 1874; idem, HF, 6; Rauch, *Psy*, 189.

[60]As Rauch observes, the laws of human reason, given by the Divine Being, are "one and the same substance or being" with the laws of nature (Rauch, *Psy*, 256-57).

between reality and mind—something that both Kant and post-modernism would question or even deny.

The religious side of Mercersburg's epistemology is, as I have suggested, decidedly different from the metaphysical side. Though the human mind is said to be *super*ordinate to the outer world in the same way that the Logos is superordinate to the human nature of Jesus, in the universal order of being the human mind is strictly *sub*ordinate to the divine. After all, the initiative in the Incarnation belongs to the divine will. As John Meyendorff has said, commenting on the patristic concept of humanity, "*theocentricity* is a *natural* character of humanity; thus asymmetry does not prevent the fact that Christ was fully and 'actively' man."[61] Humanity is, therefore, apprehended and sanctified by God in the same way that human intelligence assumes and ennobles the created order. So whatever coefficiency or connaturality there may be between God and the human spirit in the process of religious epistemology, the human element is decidedly *passive*.[62] Faith, then, does not denominate the form of revelation in the same way that human reason actively elicits order out of the chaos of the outer world. Both faith and reason, however, presuppose the object for which they are formed.

This epistemological asymmetry should not be pressed too far, for even our knowledge of the outer world is in some sense dependent upon God. Nevin's metaphysical epistemology was rooted in an Augustinian dependence on the Logos as the ultimate source of all intellectual light and truth. Christ is the "*absolute fountain of all truth and reason for men*." He is the source "of all the power of thinking in a created form."[63] In Nevin's scheme, therefore, the

---

[61]John Meyendorff, *Byzantine Theology* (New York: Fordham University Press, 1979) 154.

[62]Passivity should not be equated with unresponsiveness. Faith is active and responsive, but its activity is dependent upon the divine initiative. Nevin draws an analogy between the inward, germinal power of the seed (as found in Christ's parables) and the word of God. In both cases the outward form is the medium of the inner life. This analogy, according to Nevin, demonstrates that in the process of regeneration, all human "co-efficiency" is "mere passive reception." See Nevin, "The Pope's Encyclical," 44.

[63]Appel, *LW*, 619 (from "Undying Life in Christ," an address delivered at the Convention of the Third Centennial of the Heidelberg Catechism, January 19, 1863, Race Street Reformed Church, Philadelphia).

order of nature, which centers in humanity, gives way to a universal order of being which centers in Christ. Christ is the fountain of a new creation and the perfection of the old. On this ground "we ascribe to Christianity, as compared with the world in any other view, the character of *absolute* reality and truth," says Nevin. "Nature itself is only relatively true and real. It finds its actual sense, as we have seen, only in the idea of humanity; and in this idea at last, only as actualized in the mystery of the Incarnation."[64]

Conclusion

Nevin's confrontation with Common Sense theology contains a number of implications for religious epistemology. At the risk of overgeneralizing, we might almost say that any system of philosophy or hermeneutics which begins by assuming that only individual things are real, or that universal ideas are only linguistic conventions rather than ontic realities, is destined to end in religious skepticism and uncertainty, or to reduce Christianity to a form of ethical, political, economic, or social salvation. As we have seen, Presbyterian attempts to fuse Common Sense Realism with Christian piety were largely inconsistent and unsuccessful. The two systems were held together more by the force of authority and tradition than by logical affinity. In the end, our view of reality and our understanding of Christianity will either begin with the actual and existential (accompanied by a corresponding emphasis on human experience) or with the ideal and universal (accompanied by a corresponding emphasis on supernatural revelation).

Nevertheless, Mercersburg theology did not repudiate contemporary thought, nor did it attempt to circumvent the problems and questions posed by Kant and others. To a large degree it did affirm Descartes' so-called turn to the subject by insisting on the epistemological primacy of the human mind and the necessity of a subjective faith. (Though admittedly this turn inward was probably rooted more in Augustinianism than Cartesian subjectivism.) But this tradition of anthropocentrism need not terminate, as it has often done, in religious and metaphysical uncertainty. As we have

---

[64]Nevin, *MP*, 207.

seen from the asymmetrical character of Nevin's epistemology, this is a false dilemma. Though the created order is, in some sense, centered in humanity, this order gives way to a higher center, namely, Jesus Christ. Humanity is, by design, fundamentally theocentric, not egocentric. The very logic of Christianity as it is unfolded in the Incarnation, therefore, argues for two foci: the first centered upon God, the second upon humanity. This insight comprises the essence of Nevin's unique epistemology.

.

Chapter 6
Individualism and Sectarianism

Nevin's society, like ours, was overrun by individualism and sectarianism. What he sought was not merely a theoretical answer to these problems, but a remedy which could be applied to the structures of society and institutions, especially the church. He was not, however, insensitive to both sides of the issue. In fact, he insisted on a concept of human freedom which fully acknowledged individuality, but only as this is viewed from the whole. "The whole bears the parts, not the parts the whole."[1]

Nominalism, on the other hand, begins by assuming that only individual things are real. Accordingly, American Common Sense theology, regarded humanity, society and the church more as a collection of individuals than an organic whole.[2] Mercersburg considered this error as the root of radical individualism and sectarianism which would eventually destroy the unity of church and society. In response, Nevin affirmed the organic unity of humanity, society, and the church by demonstrating the priority of the universal over the particular, the ideal over the actual.

One of the greatest questions facing nineteenth-century philosophy and theology was the perennial problem of the one and the many. This was especially evident in German idealism which sought to synthesize universality (that is, the ideal) with particularity (that is, the actual). In concrete terms, the issue was one of *relationality*: How does the part relate to the whole? For

---

[1]Nevin, "Educational Religion," *WM*, 30 June 1847.

[2]While English philosopher Thomas Reid (the father of Common Sense) subscribed to the social contract theory, his disdain for private property (which he nonetheless tolerated) coupled with his belief in the common good distinguished him from his American counterparts. See Ellingsen, *A Common Sense Theology*, 96-101.

Mercersburg the battle was fought primarily over issues of anthropology: In what sense can we call humanity, society, and the church a corporate whole while yet acknowledging the individuality of each member? Realists and nominalists gave very different answers to these questions. Far from being abstract, however, their philosophy was translated directly into institutional and political structures. Indeed, their entire outlook and approach to issues in society and church was, in a sense, driven by their philosophical assumptions.

Nevin regarded universals (such as "humanity") as the common nature which unites each individual member of a species together. But, in nominalism, as we have seen, only the individual is real. Indeed, the cornerstone of nominalism is the belief that our primary cognition is of individual things rather than universals (Ockham). This principle is derived from our common experience. We move in a world of individually existing things, not in a world of universals. Consequently, it is similarity and universality that need to be explained, not individuation.[3]

Each philosophy, as one would expect, commences with a different theology of creation. For Mercersburg, God, the Absolute Ground of reality, provides the basis of ultimate *unity*. By analogy, the ideal *in* creation (that is, the seminal or genetic idea which gives rise to the cosmos) imparts unity by bringing together the multiplicity of natural phenomena under a single law. Natural law, then, constitutes the ground of all phenomena. So, for example, all trees are in fact manifestations (that is, "instantiations") of one archetypal law or idea we call "tree." This, in turn, is part of the vegetable kingdom, which is subsumed under the idea of organic matter, etc. Natural laws, therefore, are not only objective realities, but the unified source of natural phenomena. The unity implicit in the ideal is bodied forth by a corresponding unity in nature. There is a difference between the ideal and nature, however: Whereas the ideal includes all *potential* phenomena, nature includes only *actual* phenomena.

A creation rooted in nominalistic assumptions looks very different. The emphasis is upon the Divine word (Ockham and

---

[3]See the introduction for a discussion of these issues.

Calvinistic predestination) or covenant (Federal theology) accomplishing by *fiat* what might otherwise be attributed to the divinely ordained laws of nature. Whereas Nevin's theology moves toward affirming the integrity and enduring constitution of the created order, the goal of this system is to uphold the utter contingency of all things upon God. We see this tendency in Ockham who, for the sake of divine transcendence, was willing to dispense with physical and moral laws, and even epistemological certainty.[4] We see it also in Hodge who, despite his "moderate realism," believed that the laws and primordial forms of nature reside not in creation, but only in the mind of God. In anthropology (the focus of this chapter) Hodge imputes the *guilt* of Adam's sin to the human race not because of any seminal (that is, real or natural) connection between Adam and his offspring, but because Adam was *appointed* the Federal head of the race by divine fiat.[5]

These principles, when applied to humanity, society, or the church yield very different results. For realists, universality has priority; the whole is antecedent to its parts. Individuality is derived from participation in an essential nature. That nature may be humanity (derived from one head, Adam), when the race is taken as a whole, or a national *Volksgeist* (sometimes concentrated in a world-historical personality as Hegel believed), or the incarnate life of Christ in the church (sometimes thought to be focussed in an ecclesiastical hierarchy). In any case, the lines of organization and authority flow from a single center to the periphery.

The quintessential model of this philosophy is the organism. The constituent parts are energized by one life-principle which pervades the whole and takes its direction from the head. Medieval

---

[4]Gordon Leff, *The Dissolution of the Medieval Outlook* (New York: Harper & Row, 1976) 65. Thus Ockham asserted the intuitive cognition of nonexistents by direct divine causality; see Leff, *William of Ockham: The Metamorphosis of Scholastic Discourse* (Totowa NJ: Rowman and Littlefield, 1975) 14-30; Copleston, *Philosophy*, 3:64-74.

[5]Hodge readily admits that the *effects* of Adam's sin hold in the seminal relationship between Adam and his offspring. But this relationship is no different than what we find between any parent or child. See below and Hodge, *ST*, 2:196-97.

church and society, with their monolithic structures and central authorities, are preeminent historical examples of this. Better still, however, is the family where organic unity, individuality, authority, and love coalesce to reflect their Trinitarian archetype. The potential danger of this philosophy, of course, is the temptation to elevate the whole at the expense of the individual, leading to authoritarianism and abuse of power.

For nominalists, individuality has priority; the parts are antecedent to the whole. The whole therefore is simply a composite. Humanity, society, and church are terms used to categorize individuals with similar attributes, beliefs, or affiliations. They do not, however, share in a single (metaphysical) nature or essence. Hence, the lines of organization and authority flow from the periphery to the center. The best example of this is the voluntary society. Here, the necessity of political organization is viewed as *conventional* rather than natural. As articulated first by Hobbes (an ardent nominalist), then by Locke and Rousseau, humans begin as independent and free beings in a state of nature, governed only by the laws of nature. They enter into social contract (forming a government) only as a means of preserving this freedom and independence, and promoting general harmony.[6]

This, of course, is the very philosophy which underlies American government and even American religion. Its adaptation to theology is exemplified in congregationalism, voluntary para-

---

[6]Nevin calls this a "monstrous fallacy"; see Nevin, "Philosophy of History. III. History as Particular," *College Days*, March 1873. See also Thomas Hobbes, *Leviathan, or the Matter, Form, and Power of a Commonwealth Ecclesiastical and Civil*, ed. Michael Oakeshott (New York: Collier, 1962); the critical edition of John Locke's second treatise on government in, *Two Treatises of Government* (Cambridge: Cambridge University Press, 1960; repr. with amendments: New York: New American Library, 1965); Jean Jacques Rousseau, *On the Social Contract: With Geneva Manuscript and Political Economy*, ed. Roger D. Masters, trans. Judith R. Masters (New York: St. Martin's Press, 1978). The tendency toward voluntarism is also evident in Ockham's nominalism; see Paul Foriers and Chaim Perelman, "Natural Law and Natural Rights," in *Dictionary of the History of Ideas*, 3:19: In Ockham "there arises the tendency to think of law chiefly as starting from the individual and not by virtue of relationships among individuals, which tendency will lead ultimately to formulating individual prerogatives and to setting down exactly the rights of individuals. The very idea of natural order appeared to Ockham contrary to divine omnipotence."

church organizations, independent benevolent associations, and the general tenor of American religion which values private opinion and individual experience above all else. The danger of this philosophy, addressed by Nevin and others, is a radical individualism which results in the general dissolution of social and ecclesiastical unity.[7]

Individualism and Common Sense Theology

It is not too much to say that Charles Hodge and John Nevin, despite their many confrontations, shared some of the same theological concerns. Like Nevin, Hodge was concerned about maintaining a balance between objective and subjective Christianity. Doctrine and life are two sides of the same coin. Both men, therefore opposed the extreme subjectivity of New England Transcendentalism on the one side, and the authoritative objectivity of Roman Catholicism on the other. Both also recognized and opposed the dangers of self-autonomy and individualism represented by Charles Finney and his brand of eruptive revivalism. Moreover, both agreed that the remedy for such subjectivism lies

---

[7]On the adaptation of empirical philosophy (i.e., Locke and Common Sense), voluntarism, and individualism to religion and American government see Ahlstrom, *Religious History*, 362-63; Noll, *A History of Christianity in the United States and Canada* (Grand Rapids MI: Eerdmans, 1992) 148-62; idem, Nathan O. Hatch, George M. Marsden, David F. Wells, and John D. Woodbridge, ed., *Eerdman's Handbook to Christianity in America* (Grand Rapids MI: Eerdmans, 1983) 184. There are a number of informative articles in Daniel G. Reid, ed., *Dictionary of Christianity in America*, s.v. "Democracy and Christianity in America" by D. S. Armentrout, "Enlightenment Catholicism" by P. W. Carey, "Enlightenment Protestantism" by W. L. Pitts, "Individualism" by E. B. Holifield, "Revivalism, Catholic" by J. P. Dolan, "Revivalism, German-American" by J. S. O'Malley, "Revivalism, Protestant" by W. G. Travis, and "Voluntaryism; Voluntarism" by the editors. See also Nathan O. Hatch, *The Democratization of American Christianity* (New Haven CT: Yale University Press, 1989); Noll, *Princeton and the Republic, 1768–1822: The Search for a Christian Enlightenment in the Era of Samuel Stanhope Smith* (Princeton NJ: Princeton University Press, 1989); Henry F. May, *The Enlightenment in America* (New York: Oxford University Press, 1976); R. N. Bellah et al. *Habits of the Heart: Individualism and Commitment in American Life* (Berkeley: University of California Press, 1985); Alexis de Tocqueville, *Democracy in America*, trans. Henry Reeve (New York: Adlard and Saunders, 1838).

in an organic, orderly, and confessional orthodoxy coupled with Augustinian piety[8]

Yet there were major philosophical and even theological differences between Hodge and Nevin in regards to anthropology, the church, and the Eucharist. Most, if not all of these differences, can be traced to the distinction between realism and nominalism. Hodge was aware of the significance of these opposing philosophies for theology. He even identified himself with realists "of one class" who taught that "the attributes of God are objectively true as revealed" over and against those nominalists who held that God's attributes are only different names for the same thing. (He considered the latter view to be essentially pantheistic or, at least, agnostic.) On the other hand, Hodge sought to avoid any form of extreme realism that would destroy the simplicity of the divine nature by hypostatizing each divine attribute.[9]

But, Hodge could not escape the nominalism inherent in his own presuppositions. As Bozeman has observed, though the Presbyterians equated truth with "the general structure of the material world, it rested upon a radically nominalist vision of singular material objects. Hence individual entities were to be grasped in truthful clarity of detail."[10] So, in his attempt to avoid the errors of Nevin's "ultrarealism," Hodge unwittingly rejected moderate realism as well. Consequently, his anthropology, ecclesiology, and sacramental theology had, from Nevin's point of view, more affinity with the revivalism and voluntarism he sought to avoid, than with the confessional orthodoxy and Augustinian piety he sought to affirm.

It is important to note the connections which subsisted between Hodge's anthropology and ecclesiology. Careful examination reveals that his entire system was informed and pervaded by the same nominalistic presuppositions. Hodge did not, of course, regard philosophy as determinative for theology. In his view, the authority of Scripture and theological considerations always took

---

[8]On Hodge's pietism, see Noll's biographical essay in *Charles Hodge: The Way of Life*, 32-42.
[9]Hodge, *ST*, 1:368-72.
[10]Bozeman, *Protestants*, 57.

precedent. He was, however, aware that all theological beliefs entail some sort of philosophical assumption. But, owing to his Common Sense worldview, he often operated as if the Bible and theology could be understood apart from any philosophical context. The beguiling simplicity fostered by the Scottish school made him more a slave than a master to his own philosophy.

The Priority of the Individual

Hodge spent considerable time and effort in his *Systematic Theology* analyzing and disproving what he considered to be a pantheistic form of realism espoused by the German idealists and Mercersburg theology. His ongoing critique of Mercersburg and German idealism was an attempt to maintain the first principles of Common Sense philosophy against monism and Romantic subjectivism. He considered his "moderate realism" to be wholly different from the extreme realism of the pantheistic school. In that theory the universal is said to be *ante rem*. The individual is simply a manifestation of "the general principle of humanity in union with a given corporeal organization." A person, therefore, is nothing more than an accident or modification—the *modus existendi*—of the generic substance humanity. Each soul is not an individual essence, but one essence "acting in many separate organisms." Thus, German theologians, especially the followers of Schleiermacher (among whom he ranked Nevin), use the terms "life, law, and organic law" to describe the organic unity of all the individuals within a genus. Substance is transmitted by propagation from one generation to the next in opposition to the doctrine of individual creation which regards each soul as a newly created being.[11]

Hodge systematically carries out his view of creationism by espousing a nominalistic concept of imputation and racial unity. He begins by attacking the realistic theory of imputation which teaches that guilt is attributed to the individual by virtue of his or her *seminal* or genetic participation in fallen humanity. Thus, when

---

[11]Hodge, *ST*, 2:51-55. These accusations were rooted in Baconianism's utter distaste for Spinoza.

Adam sinned, the whole race fell in him. After recapitulating his general objections to this form of philosophical realism, the Princeton theologian proceeded to demonstrate the impossibility of ascribing personal guilt to an act that is not properly our own. "We had no being before our existence in this world; and that we should have acted before we existed is an absolute impossibility." If Adam's first sin is imputed to us because of our common humanity, why not his other sins as well? "Besides, why is it the sin of Adam rather than, or more than the sin of Eve, for which we are responsible?" After all, Eve sinned before Adam.[12]

The only solution to these problems, according to Hodge, is to be found in the theory of Federal headship. Through natural headship Adam's posterity is *affected* by his sin in the same manner that any offspring suffer because of the sins of their parents. Through Federal headship, however, Adam becomes the *representative* of the entire race and his *guilt* is imputed to us personally by divine fiat.[13] Though Hodge acknowledges that seminal headship is important in establishing a connection between Adam and his posterity, it plays no role in the imputation of Adam's guilt to his posterity. This is carried over to the individual legally and forensically, but not ontologically.[14] In other words, his sin is ours only because it is imputed to us, but it is not imputed to us because it is properly ours. Hence our condemnation in Adam is rooted in a nominal rather than a real concept of humanity. For, our union with him rests primarily upon this legal arrangement rather than his seminal headship.

---

[12]Hodge, *ST*, 2:222-25. Responding to the same argument put forward in the *Princeton Review*, Apple says, "the first act of disobedience on the part of our first parents was a determining act, and in this respect unlike other acts." All subsequent acts follow upon this as the fruits of that first act. See Apple, "The True Doctrine of Realism in its Bearing on Theology" *MR* 17 (1870): 587.

[13]Hodge, *ST*, 2:196-97, 216-27. For historical background on this issue, see David A. Weir, *The Origins of Federal Theology in Sixteenth Century Reformation Thought* (Oxford: Clarendon Press, 1990).

[14]This is admitted in the anonymous article, "The Relation of Adam's First Sin to the Fall of the Race," *PR* 42 (1870): 248: "The federal or representative school have almost universally found the reason of God's constituting a federal headship, in a prior natural headship . . . but they have maintained that the ground of the imputation of his first sin to his posterity is that therein Adam acted in his federal or representative capacity."

The same is true of our redemption in Christ: According to Hodge, "There is a federal union with Christ which is antecedent to all actual union, and is the source of it."[15] By contrast, the Westminster Confession (VI.iii)—the confessional foundation of Hodge's theology—asserted that our first parents "being the root of all mankind, the guilt of this sin was imputed, and the same death in sin and corrupted nature conveyed to all their posterity descending from them by ordinary generation."[16]

Philip Schaff (Nevin's colleague at Mercersburg) attributed Hodge's Federalism and its "nominalistic premises" to the Protestant scholastic, Francis Turretin (1623-87), who was held in high esteem by Princeton. Though maintaining his belief in both the natural and federal headship of Adam, Turretin, says Schaff, "evidently lays the chief stress upon the latter, and prepares the way for giving up the former." Hodge's error, according to Schaff is in his failure to distinguish "between a virtual or potential, and a personal or individual coëxistence and coägency of the race in Adam." Augustine held only the former. The latter is "impossible and absurd" unless one assumes the preexistence of souls.[17]

Hodge's theology of imputation, then, begins with Adam and Christ in their individuality. Subsequently, they are made to assume a representative role by divine fiat. As a result, the individual is said to be prior to the general or universal life of the race. A similar pattern is evident in Hodge's view of the church. The individual believer comes before the general life of the church; this is the essence of the voluntary principle. As Hodge once observed in his dispute with Nevin over the Eucharist, "The main question [is] whether we come to Christ, and then to the church; whether we by a personal act of faith receive him, and by union with him become a member of his mystical body; or whether all

---

[15]Charles Hodge, *A Commentary on the Epistle to the Ephesians* (New York: Robert Carter & Bros., 1856) 30-31; quoted in Nevin, "Hodge on the Ephesians," 215.

[16]However, every effort was made to demonstrate that the Confession favored Federalism. See "The Relation of Adam's First Sin to the Fall of the Race," 251.

[17]Schaff et al., *Romans,* in *A Commentary on the Holy Scripture by John Peter Lange* by J. P. Lange, Philip Schaff, et al. (New York: Charles Scribner's Sons, 1869; repr.: Grand Rapids MI: Zondervan, 1960) 193-94.

access to Christ is through a mediating church, Dr. Nevin decides against the evangelical system."[18]

The Princeton professor employed the same critique against Nevin's Christology believing that it was essentially one with Schleiermacher's theology and Romantic idealism. Again, he recognized in Mercersburg theology the overwhelming presence of a realist theory of human nature which, in his view, is simply pantheistic. The life of humanity, he complains, is nothing more than the development of "an infinite, absolute, and universal something, spirit, life, life-power, substance, God, Urwesen, or whatever it may be called. . . . " Likewise, Christ, the "archetypal man," was united to this generic humanity and so perfected and glorified human nature. Hodge objects to this scheme because it "perverts" the plan of salvation by teaching that "Christ saves us not by what He teaches, or by what He does, but by what He is. He infuses a new principle of life into the Church and the world. . . . All is natural. There is nothing supernatural but the initial point" after which all proceeds by the laws of historical development. The final result, concludes Hodge, is nothing less than the rejection of the Catholic doctrines of the atonement, regeneration, sanctification, forensic justification, and faith in Christ's *work*.[19]

The "All" and the "Whole": Nevin's Organic Holism

Mercersburg responded to Baconian nominalism and individualism by demonstrating the priority of the universal over the particular, and the ideal over the actual. The whole is prior to its parts while the parts subsist as individuals only *in* the whole. This subordination of the individual is grounded in an ontology which regards the ideal and universal as the *fundamentum* of reality. The ideal/universal, in turn, is manifested in creation only as it is embodied in *individual* things. It is this law of reification, therefore, which recognizes *both* the priority of the ideal/universal and the

---

[18]Charles Hodge, "Doctrine of the Reformed Church on the Lord's Supper," 273; see also [Hodge], "Bushnell on Christian Nurture," *PR* 19 (1847): 538. Schleiermacher used this same distinction to differentiate between Protestantism and Catholicism (*The Christian Faith*, §24).

[19]Hodge, *ST*, 2:448-49, 450-51; see also 3:19-22.

dignity of individuality. The archetype for this ontology is, of course, the Incarnation: Christ's divine nature, though superordinate and foundational to His humanity, was organically united to His human nature without eclipsing or destroying its created integrity and individuality.

Mercersburg addressed the problem of individualism by appealing to an organic model of reality. Organic wholeness was contrasted to the idea of mechanism which was rejected as incomplete and atomistic. In the early nineteenth century, such organic models were prevalent in Romanticism and idealism. They affected nearly every discipline, not the least of which was historiography (that is, the theory of historical development) and theology. By mid-century, of course, organicism became a force in science by virtue of Darwin's theory of development.

In his early work, *The Anxious Bench*, Nevin critiqued the individualism and sensationalism associated with revivalism, arguing that true religious conversion takes place only as the particular becomes a "tributary to the tendencies and purposes" of the general. In contrast to revivalism, the traditional catechetical system maintains that "the general must go before the particular and support it as its proper ground." Thus sin is not simply the "offspring of a particular will," but "a general and universal force, which includes and rules the entire existence of the individual man. . . . " Likewise, salvation begins beyond the individual. Fallen humanity is raised in Christ. The individual is saved by a "living union with Christ" through the medium of the church, not unlike the bond by which he has been joined to Adam. The system of "new measures," on the other hand, is based on a scheme of sin and salvation which is strictly individual.[20]

Nowhere is this contrast more apparent than in Nevin's distinction between the two kinds of generality or universality, "All" and

---

[20]Nevin, *The Anxious Bench*, 123-30. This organic model of relationality was first set forth by Rauch (Nevin's early colleague) in the first two chapters of his book, *Psychology*. While the body of Rauch's work reflects the general outline of Hegel's philosophy of spirit as found in the third division of his *Encyclopedia* (1830 ed., §§377-577), the first two chapters recapitulate portions of Hegel's philosophy of nature—particularly the third section on organics (§§337-76). Thus a number of Mercersburg's philosophical principles were adapted from Hegelianism.

"Whole."[21] Throughout his writings, he applies this distinction not only to the church and humanity, but also to the organism of the cosmos itself which is unfolded from one, genetic idea. As Gerhart has said, there is a "generality of being," a "common principle," which underlies and identifies all phenomena and embodies the wisdom, power, and goodness of God the Creator.[22] "The whole constitution of the world," Nevin once remarked, "contradicts the unit or atom theory of religion."[23]

The *all*, says Nevin, is merely an abstract collection of individuals grouped according to their common properties. It is strictly a finite quantity—limited by the "empirical aggregation" of individuals which comprise it. The individual, therefore, is primary, universality is secondary. The concept is reached by a process of induction and comparison beginning with single units and ending in generality. The unity in such a case is mechanical and outward. It is an arbitrary product of the mind. The individual components exist separately and independently of the totality. They lack an internal ground or power to unite them together.[24]

The *whole*, by contrast, is a concrete reality. "It is wrought", says Nevin, "into the very nature of the things themselves, and they grow forth from it as the necessary and perpetual ground of their own being and life." It is not, then, the product of individuals, but neither can it exist without them. Nevertheless, in the order of being it is the individual which depends on and subsists in the whole as its "proper original." This mode of generality, unlike the other, is *infinite* because it is has no empirical limits. It is not "the creature of mere experience." Rather, as an idea it is

---

[21]Rauch makes a similar distinction in his philosophy, see Rauch, *Psy*, 277; Hegel, *Encyclopedia*, §175 (Addition), §§135-36. Like many of Nevin's ideas, this distinction originates in Plato (*Theatetus* 204a,b).

[22]Gerhart, *IP*, 76-77.

[23]Nevin, "Educational Religion," *WM*, 23, 30 June 1847.

[24]Nevin, "Catholicism," 2-5; see also Nevin, "Philosophy of History. IV. History as General or Universal," *College Days*, Apr. 1873; Appel, *LW*, 592. Some may argue that since this process of classification is based on actual properties it is not merely notional, but real. However, what is to prevent us, under this scheme, from making *arbitrary* classifications? Why not include birds and humans under the same division since both have two legs? or construct a single category for all people and pets named "William"?!

always more than the actual totality of things in the world at a given moment. It includes all potential as well as all actual phenomena.[25]

The *whole*, unlike the *all*, is an organic unity. The parts do not exist independently or apart from the totality (as they might in a machine). Instead, they "draw their being from the universal unity itself in which they are comprehended, while they serve at the same time to bring it into view." This concept of totality, unlike the other, therefore, is both intensive and extensive. Considered intensively, the whole always possesses the same genetic characteristics (that is, idea) regardless of its volume, just as the character of the seed remains essentially unchanged throughout the entire course of its development. Considered extensively, the whole is enlarged not by the mechanical addition of parts, but by concrescence and intussusception. That is to say, the new life unfolds from within by the convergence of internal forces. Foreign material is assimilated and transformed by being permeated with the life-law which pervades the whole.[26]

The application of this organic paradigm to theology was a watershed in Nevin's thinking. It became the basis upon which he distinguished his views of creation, predestination, humanity, freedom, church, and society, from those of the prevailing American culture. The former are organic, objective, holistic, *a priori*, and deductive; the latter are atomistic, subjective, partial, empirical, and inductive.

Nevin's understanding of the church, the world, and the cosmos as an organic rather than a mechanical entity anticipated twentieth-century process thought which maintains that reality is a purposeful community of "actual entities" organically related and mutually affecting one another. These atomic entities are said to "concresce" or grow together into organized structures or "societies" through the influence of divine causation. This divine causation, which is persuasive rather than coercive, provides the impetus by which such entities reach satisfaction or creative actualization and interrelatedness.

---

[25]Nevin, "Catholicism," 5.
[26]Ibid., 3-6, 19-20.

Nevin's view of divine predestination bears a striking resemblance to this theory of divine causation. Unlike many of his peers, he preferred to speak of unconditional, individual election (that is, Calvinism) as "an impenetrable mystery." At the same time, he believed that the divine decree is also immanent and conditional in its movement: "eyeing all existences from eternity as they actually are in time; seeing the whole always in the parts, and parts in their whole, as well as in the relations they bear mutually among themselves; determining and fixing things concretely; the only way that can be said to answer truly at last to their being; the only way, indeed, in which they can be ever really and truly the object of either purpose or thought at all."[27]

The Church: One, Holy, Catholic, and Apostolic[28]

Nevin, as we have seen, distinguishes between two fundamentally different orders of existence based on the Incarnation: ideal and actual. The ideal is the sphere of the universal and supersensible. The actual is the sphere of the particular and sensible. These two orders are organically united, however, in one cosmic system. The church is no exception to this principle. Like every other genus, it is both ideal and actual at the same time. The ideal church is universal, the actual church is empirical. The first is embodied or reified in the second. Unlike a genus in nature, though, the ideal church is a supernatural revelation. It is thus an object of faith rather than natural intelligence.

Aware of the importance of philosophical realism for ecclesiology, one writer in the *Mercersburg Review* noted that the apostolic writers made use of Platonic forms of thought in their consider-

---

[27]Nevin, "Hodge on the Ephesians," 221; see also Erb, *NT*, 138-48. There is also an epistemological similarity. Like Alfred North Whitehead, Rauch and Nevin believed that thought begins *in* feeling. Consequently, Whitehead's concept of "causal efficacy," which he calls the "withness of the body," is nearly identical to Rauch's concept of "feeling". See Rauch, *Psy*, 176, 289.

[28]The immediate historical derivation of Nevin's ecclesiology is to be found in the writings of Schleiermacher, Neander, Carl Ullmann, Richard Rothe, et al. Despite these Germanic roots, Nevin once conceded that his use of creeds and his doctrine of the church is more Anglican than German; Appel, *LW*, 730, 732 (repr. from Nevin, "Our Relations to Germany," *MR* 14 [1867]: 627-33).

ation of the church. The generic unity of Christ's body presupposes that universal ideas are real and objective, rather than the subjective creatures of the mind which nominalism assumes them to be.[29]

The origin of the *ideal* church is Christ. Like Schleiermacher, Nevin regarded Christ as the *"Urbild"*—the ideal or archetypal man—whose life is realized in the Incarnation and subsequently through the historical church.[30] According to Mercersburg theology, the ideal church is an organic system of life centered upon Christ—a new order of humanity bearing the same constitution as the first humanity under Adam. It is a true body, a unified "Whole" rather than an atomistic "All." The life of this body is diffused throughout the entire organism. The parts share in the life of the whole and find their identity only in reference to the whole. The general, in other words, is prior to the particular.[31]

In accordance with the law of reification, the ideal character of the church necessitates its visible manifestation. As Nevin explains it, "it is a fixed law in life, that every spiritual force which it comprehends must take some outward form, in order to become complete." Moreover, the more spiritual a force is, "the more urgent and irresistible" is its tendency to corporealize itself. Since the church comprehends in itself the "deepest life of humanity," its existence could never be simply inward and invisible. Just as the idea of humanity supposes a body, so the idea of the church includes visibility as an organic body "in whose presence alone all individual Christianity becomes real."[32]

The Incarnation would be "shorn of its meaning" if Christ did not exercise His saving presence through the church. His universal life can come to expression only through a universal, organic,

---

[29]Dubbs, "Nominalism and Realism," 171-72.

[30]See Nevin, *MP*, 229-30; Schleiermacher, *The Christian Faith*, §93. The *Urbild*, as Nevin explains, stands in contrast to the *Abbild* which is an image or copy of the heavenly.

[31]Nevin, "Catholic Unity," 40-41; idem, *The Church: a sermon preached at the opening of the Synod of the German Reformed Church at Carlisle, October 1846* (Chambersburg PA: German Reformed Church Publishing House, 1847) 8-9; idem, "Answer to Professor Dorner," 577. See also Schaff, *Principle of Protestantism*, 36-40; idem, *What Is Church History*, 30-37, 118.

[32]Nevin, *The Church*, 10-11; idem, "Catholic Unity," in *The Mercersburg Theology*, ed. James H. Nichols (New York: Oxford University Press, 1966) 41.

human medium in the same way that the life of the head requires the body as its medium. Apart from a "supernatural constitution in the world as the idea of the church implies" the Incarnation becomes an isolated, evanescent theophany and the gospel is subverted.[33]

The *actual* church is the historical church which extends from the Incarnation to the present. In its ideal aspect it remains unchanged throughout the vicissitudes of history because it is grounded in the power Christ's theanthropic life. But as a truly historical organization it is always in the process of actualizing its ideal potential (this is the basis of historical development). Like a leaven, the church is transfusing the life of the world with its own divine character—a process that will never cease until the ideal and the actual church become one at the Second Coming of Christ.[34]

This incarnational model of the church provided Mercersburg theology with a platform for critiquing other models of the church. Failure to recognize both the *union* and *distinction* of the ideal and the actual results in a false ecclesiology and even a false Christology. The error of Roman Catholicism, according to Schaff and Nevin, is that it identifies the ideal church in Christ with the empirical church. The perfection of the church is thus fully and always realized in history from the beginning. Accordingly, there is no room for true historical development and actualization. The church along with her traditions and structures bear the same authority and infallibility as Christ Himself.[35]

---

[33]Nevin, *The Church*, 16-17. See also Erb, *NT*, 271: "As without Christ there could be no Church, so without the Church there could be no Christ. What we mean by this is that the Church is Christ's body, the completion of Himself as the new creation." In other words, the church is a necessary concomitant of the Incarnation. This remark, of course, bears only on the Incarnation and not on the existence of the eternal Logos or Son.

[34]Nevin, *The Church*, 11-12.

[35]Schaff, *Principle of Protestantism*, 101-104, 160; Nevin, *The Church*, 13; idem, "Reply to an Anglican Catholic," 424; Theodore Apple, "The Objective in Christianity," *MR* 33 (1886): 430-31. Hodge accused Nevin of Romanizing by confusing the mystical body with the historical church; see Hodge, "Doctrine of the Reformed Church on the Lord's Supper," 273.

The opposing error is to so sever the ideal and actual church that they become two entirely separate orders (that is, dualism). The ideal church becomes a gnostic abstraction. Its order and structure bear little or no resemblance to the empirical church. The idea of development is thus negated. Catholicity and unity are only spiritual and invisible ideals. The actual church may be fragmented into a million pieces, but all this is of no account so long as one recognizes her heavenly unity. This is the philosophy of voluntarism and sectarianism against which Schaff, and especially Nevin, expended so much labor.[36]

The Sect System

The first half of the nineteenth century saw an eruption of sectarianism—what Sydney Ahlstrom has called the "Sectarian Heyday."[37] This phenomena, which continues even to the present, was usually associated with revivalism. Its proclivity was rooted in the democratic ethos and bears all the marks of a nominalist philosophy. Society and church are not organic wholes, but are formed from an aggregate of individuals. Conspicuously absent is any *a priori* sense of unity or life which goes before the individual. Everything is made to depend on the voluntary association of wills—a veritable Rousseauian "social contract," formed around a particular set of beliefs. Though the shibboleth of every sect is "the Bible alone," in reality, as Nevin complained, it is private judgment that reigns supreme and becomes the measure of truth and biblical interpretation.[38]

According to Mercersburg theology, however, the church, can never be complete, without a *visible* unity of organization and worship. The American sect system, which Nevin regarded as an "abomination," must pass away before such visible unity can become a reality. The sectarian impulse is the part usurping the powers and prerogatives of the whole. By denying the unity of Christ's body it turns the Incarnation into a gnostic unreality,

---

[36]Nevin, "Hodge on the Ephesians," 224-26; Erb, *NT*, 426-27.
[37]See Ahlstrom, *A Religious History of the American People*, 472-90. For other works and articles see n. 7, above.
[38]See his article on "The Sect System" *MR* 1 (1849): 482-507, 521-39.

effectively denying that Christ has come in the flesh. This, says Nevin, is the spirit of antichrist.[39]

The sect system is the embodiment of nominalism. It begins in subjective rationalism which, as Nevin defines it, denies the objective reality of the universal and reduces the ideal to mere abstraction. By nullifying the law of reification, rationalism disposes of external forms of religion. "All must be resolved into the exercise of the worshipper's own mind. The subjective is everything; the objective next to nothing."[40] Rationalism has its practical counterpart, then, in sectarianism:

> Both systems are antagonistic to the idea of the *Church*. Both are disposed to trample under foot the authority of *history*. Both make the *objective* to be nothing, and the *subjective* to be all in all. Both undervalue the *outward*, in favor of what they conceive to be the *inward*. Both despise *forms*, under pretense of exalting the *spirit*. Both of course sink the sacraments to the character of mere outward rites. . . . Both affect to make much of the *bible*; at least in the beginning; [but in the end] it is forced to submit, to the tyranny of mere private interpretation, as the only proper measure of its sense. [The sect principle] begins in the spirit, only to end the more certainly in the flesh.[41]

In keeping with its nominalistic presuppositions, sectarianism is inherently atomistic, individualistic, divisive, and unspiritual. Hence it disowns the catholic (that is, whole) church as an article of faith set forth in the Apostles' Creed. The sect mind repudiates the organic unity between the ideal and the actual, the supernatural and the natural. It is, therefore, dualistic and eruptive. It knows of no mediation between God and humanity through the Incarnation, and no supernatural Christian economy in the present world. It thus holds the historical church in contempt and denies that there is real divine power in the ministry, sacraments, or in worship.[42]

---

[39]Nevin, *Antichrist*, 47, 76-78; idem, "Catholicism," 23.
[40]Nevin, *MP*, 142.
[41]Nevin, *MP*, 148; see Schaff, *Principle of Protestantism*, 140-55.
[42]See Nevin, *Antichrist*, 48-68.

Variations of the Sect System. But the sect system was not the only example of nominalistic Christianity in Nevin's view. The "sect mind" had become an integral dimension of democratic voluntarism. An entire host of like errors populated the landscape of American religion at every level. Not the least among these was the ecclesiology of "Puritanism" which, in Nevin's view, continued to dominate all aspects of American Christianity. The Puritan mind-set can be found in most denominations. It denies the supernatural constitution of the church by reducing it to a voluntary organization—that is, an institution formed from the bottom-up instead of from the top-down. The church is not a living constitution but a school. Its divinity resides in the Scriptures. Its mystery is reduced to the level of a social institution on a par with all other human organizations. Its power rests in the people. The church, under this view, is a glorified democracy where divinity is transmuted into common sense and popular vote.[43]

A more sophisticated form of this nominalistic ecclesiology is put forward by Calvinism and may be found in the writings of Charles Hodge. The true church is regarded as a hyperspiritual idea in the Divine Mind. In this dualistic economy, the *objective* order of grace never enters into a living union with its historical *subject*. Salvation history (including the Incarnation) is simply a mechanism designed to bring God's eternal decrees to fruition—an epiphenomenon at best. The church, therefore, is not a visible organization, but the elect individuals known only by God.

This scheme, says Nevin, empties the exhortations in Scripture of all force. If the elect cannot fall away from the faith, what need is there to make their calling and election sure? Shall we adopt the transparent evasion that the apostolic authors were addressing the nonelect?! Calvinistic predestination, therefore, does an injustice to the idea of the church as a *historical* economy of redemption in which believers actually participate in the powers of the world to come.[44]

---

[43]Nevin, "Early Christianity," 538-39; idem, "Cyprian," 361; idem, "Hodge on the Ephesians," 240-45; Erb, *NT*, 450. On Puritanism and Congregationalism etc., see Schaff, *Principle of Protestantism*, 144-55, 171.

[44]Nevin, "Hodge on the Ephesians," 50-83, 225-29. Resolve the economy of redemption into "an abstraction, a mere Gnostic philosophem," says Nevin else-

Proposed Solutions. Though Nevin believed that the unity of the church could not be reduced to an invisible unity without turning the church into an abstraction, he was also aware that unity could not be accomplished in a single stroke by obliterating every existing sect. This would not eradicate the life-principle which gives birth to sects. On the other hand, a catholicity that is indifferent to sectarianism surrenders the substance of Christianity. True Catholicity is *exclusive* according to Nevin. It comprehends the whole of the new creation in Jesus Christ while at the same time expelling all that is foreign to its genetic make-up.

For this reason, Nevin believed that a federal union of churches could never be a church. Like the sectarianism it seeks to address, a federal union is only a voluntary association.[45] In the same vein, church unity could never be brought about by external organizations such as the papacy, the episcopacy, or the state. It must emerge spontaneously and organically out of the life of the church.

Unlike Schaff, Nevin showed no particular affection toward the American system of government. "The entire separation of Church and state is a contradiction," he complained, "and can never be enforced in all details." It will result in tyranny from one side or the other. One may be independent of the other, but "Christianity cannot permit any form of life to lie entirely beyond its jurisdiction"[46] Consequently, the state can never be the ultimate and normal order of human existence. The economy of nature does not contain the elements necessary for the perfection of humanity. This requires a translation into a higher, supernatural order of being. The church, therefore is not accidental to the religious life of the world.[47]

---

where, and the fall also becomes "a philosophical myth . . . a Calvinistic or Hegelian *necessity*" in our natural life; Nevin, "Cyprian," 547.

[45]Nevin, *Antichrist*, 76-83. At first, Nevin and Schaff opposed the formation of the World Evangelical Alliance (1846) and its American division (1847). However, with time they became more irenic.

[46]Erb, *NT*, 456.

[47]This was Nevin's critique of Richard Rothe's *Theologische Ethik* (Wittenberg: Zimmermann, 1845–1848). See Nevin, "Early Christianity," *MR* 4 (1852): 39-43; idem, "Answer to Professor Dorner," 642; Appel, *LW*, 632 (repr. from "Our Relations to Germany").

The mechanism of the episcopacy does not have the power to unite Christianity or restore continuity with the apostolic church either. Though in form it may bear a greater resemblance to the ancient church, it may still be void of that life which originally animated the church. As Nevin would have it, the outward form of the church's life (that is, its government) is neither an external arrangement appointed by Christ for all time, nor a human device, nor an arbitrary agreement; it is a spontaneous outgrowth of the church's life. It is possible, therefore, to conceive of this life as existing under different forms.[48]

Hence, the divine life of the church, especially since the time of the Reformation, has been extended to many different and divided communions. "We must believe," remarks Nevin, "that under all this division is working continually a deeper force, by which even now the apparently sundered sections of the Church are bound together as a single visible reality in the world, and that will not rest till its own unity shall be fully and forever impressed upon the whole."[49] This is an evil that it tolerates in anticipation of a true future union. The actual church, says Nevin, though "defective and abnormal, in the midst of all excrescences and disproportions, it represents always notwithstanding the life and power of the ideal Church, in the stage of development it has reached at the time."[50]

---

[48]Nevin, "Cyprian," 386-87, 418-19; Erb, *NT*, 437; idem, "The Anglican Crisis," *MR* 3 (1851): 376-78; idem, "Brownson's Review," 61-62, 319-22; idem, "Apollos: or the Way of God," *MR* 21 (1874): 5-41; idem, "Reply to an Anglican Catholic," 406-22; Schaff, *Principle of Protestantism*, 161-64, 210.

[49]Nevin, *The Church*, 21-22; see Schaff, *What Is Church History*, 81-83.

[50]Nevin, *The Church*, 15; see idem, *Antichrist*, 82; idem, "Cyprian," 418-19; idem, "Catholic Unity," 45-55; idem, "The Sect System," 501, 538; Erb, *NT*, 437; Schaff, *Principle of Protestantism*, 168. On a more positive note, Schaff acknowledged a "divine significance" and historical value to sects. They are a "disciplinary scourge, a voice of awakening and admonition by which the church is urged to new life. . . . " They have no right to exist, therefore, once the fault they are protesting is corrected by the body from which they have seceded; Schaff, *Principle of Protestantism*, 171-72.

Human Freedom and Divine Law

The question of human freedom is foundational to Mercersburg's critique of American individualism. Here, more than any place else perhaps, Nevin demonstrates his sympathy with the ideals of the Enlightenment, Romanticism, and American democracy. Yet, freedom, in his view, is defined simply by applying the concept of the *whole* to human volition. It is the relation between universal law (that is, the whole) and individual will (that is the part). The domination of the latter is the source of sectarianism, fanaticism, and individualism. These he regards as false forms of freedom and authority—the tyranny of private conscience. Law is thus reduced to a mere abstraction. Liberty is converted into licentiousness. Unfortunately, these errors had come to characterize much of American Protestantism. Though the Reformation opened up a new fountain of civil and religious liberties, the tendency toward private independence was being carried to its extreme.[51]

Conversely, Nevin looks upon the elevation of universal law, to the virtual exclusion of the individual, as a form of heteronomy. The law stands over and against the individual in an outward way and is never able to unite itself with his or her inward life. Authority is turned into despotism. This form of heteronomy characterized the church and state before the Reformation. In his view, the Pope's declaration of infallibility (*Pastor aeternus*, Pius IX, 18 July 1870) was the culmination of this Roman tendency toward heteronomy.[52]

In both of the cases outlined above, authority and freedom are made to contradict one another. As Nevin later observed, however, authority and freedom are not contradictory, "their opposition is polar; antithetic in order that it may become synthetic." This synthesis "cannot be by any outward conjunction or juxtaposition, but only through inward concretion. If the one is not thus concretely and livingly in the other, their relation ceases to be

---

[51]Nevin, HF, 14, 18-21. This perspective echoes Schaff's general view of history found in *The Principle of Protestantism* and *What Is Church History*.

[52]Nevin, HF, 14, 18-19; idem, "The Old Catholic Movement," 240-94, see esp. 269-77.

normal; and both become in fact formal abstractions, void of their own proper sense and power."[53] It was Nevin's object, therefore, to organically unite universal authority with individual autonomy.

Freedom involves a *consubstantiality* between will and law. The constitution or essential properties of the will must become one with the constitution of the law in order to be free. This is precisely what Nevin asserts in his essay on "Human Freedom" (1848). The autonomous and self-conscious action of the will moving *voluntarily* in the orbit of the law "implies, of course, that the will is of the same nature with the law." So, in obeying the law it is obeying its own constitution. This same view was repeated many years later in his lectures on ethics (1866-76).[54]

Nevin regards the autonomy of the will to be a necessary component of human freedom. On this point he aligns himself with Kant despite the "great abuse" which the idea had suffered in his school. "The will," he insists, "can endure no heteronomy. It must be autonomic, subjectively independent, the fountain of its own activity, wherever it is found in its true and proper exercise."[55] Nevin believes that such autonomy raises the subject above natural causality. The rational will "is not under the law of cause and effect in the manner of the simply physical world, but carries in itself the power of acting on the course of this law from without, in a free self-determining way."[56] The determinate nature of freedom, therefore, is not a product of natural forces. Yet, it is certainly adumbrated by these forces.[57] It is not mere arbitrariness. Rather, as the apostle Paul taught, it is the power to choose what is right. We are either slaves of sin or slaves of Christ.

---

[53]Nevin, "The Old Catholic Movement," 270.

[54]Nevin, HF, 17; see Appel, *LW*, 692-95, for a synopsis of Nevin's ethical lectures on freedom. See also Nevin, "Man's True Destiny," 504-6; idem, "The Inspiration of the Bible," 38.

[55]Nevin, HF, 9-10. Nevin apparently felt that Kant's ethical theory was unable to spontaneously unite objective law with the autonomy of the individual subject. He speaks disparagingly of the "terrible categoric imperative, *Thou shalt*, crushing his liberty completely to the earth" (ibid., 14).

[56]Nevin, "Natural and Supernatural," 196; see also Appel, *LW*, 692.

[57]Appel, *LW*, 526 (from Nevin's 1859 address to Marshall College, "The Wonderful Nature of Man").

However, autonomy also involves the power of contrary choice. Without this there could be no true freedom or culpability; human action would simply be the result of instinct or blind causation. Though the human mind is conditioned to a great extent by natural forces and other external influences, it possesses an "independent causation" which can "overthrow all previous calculations and determinations, and can set itself up even against the will of God." (Nevin espouses a form of *scientia media* by which God's knowledge is conditioned by the free agency of individuals and not simply by His own will.)[58]

The perfect objectivity of Divine law stands in polar relation to subjective autonomy. As Nevin later remarked, "There is absolutely but one Reason, but one Will, but one Intelligence. Individual Reason implies the possibility of divergence from the true Reason, that is the conception of error."[59] Nevin holds that God's justice is an absolute expression of His nature, "a fixed immutable principle of His nature, necessary and universal." Consequently, he rejects the nominalistic notion of divine law (held by Ockham) which maintains that what is morally right now could be morally wrong in another creation. In the universe divine law is not merely an "abstraction," but it is "concretely real."[60] It is the essence and life of reality manifesting its power in the particular, first through the medium of the species, then descending organically to the individual. Thus the particular has meaning only insofar as it is united with this universal.[61]

These polar distinctions (that is, individual autonomy and universal divine law) must finally concresce into one organic life without overwhelming or excluding each other. Such polar opposition is a constituent dimension of all concrete existence (physical or spiritual). It is emphatically "conservative and not destructional." Indeed, without distinction in the first place how

---

[58]Erb, *NT*, 214, 138-40; see also 144, 193; Nevin, HF, 9. The depth and breadth of Nevin's conviction regarding individual autonomy may be gaged by his early opposition to slavery. See his biographical account with excerpts from his early articles (written for *The Friend*) in Nevin, *My Own Life*, 89-95; Appel, *LW*, 72-73.
[59]Nevin, "Lectures on Aesthetics," 13.
[60]Erb, *NT*, 91-92; Nevin, HF, 11-12.
[61]Nevin, HF, 11-14.

can we speak of "concretion"? Without distinction, all that remains is abstraction or, at best, an ideal potential which has "not yet become real."[62] As a result, all life subsists under these forms and is at once both universal and particular. But, whereas in nature this union goes forward by blind necessity, in humanity it is formed through the spontaneity of the individual will. *Moral freedom, then, is the individual will voluntarily (that is, spontaneously) moving in the orbit of the general will.*[63]

There is no room here for either radical individualism or heteronomous rule. When the individual will is bonded to the Divine will by faith, it unfolds "organically in and through the law itself, as its own element and sphere" so that the divine law becomes the inner form of the subject's existence. This is freedom. Christians, as Nevin said in an earlier article, "enter into the idea of his [Christ's] life, as a free inward evolution, falling in harmoniously with the will of God."[64] Whereas sin is the separation of independence and law, true freedom unites these spheres so that, in their polarity, they hold together by mutual attraction. Thus, there is freedom in the necessity of the divine law. "Freedom, in order that it may be free, *must* be bound."[65]

Nevin's ethical theory is cut from the same cloth as his piety: both hang on the concept of inner communion or participation. The reconciliation of individual freedom and universal law is accomplished by love. Love operating through faith is the magnetic force which binds the human and divine wills together. It is the deep between the determinism of Calvinism and the arbitrariness of Pelagianism, for love is neither arbitrary nor coercive. As Rauch once said, in love "we surrender the independence of our existence, and desire to become self-conscious, not in ourselves only, but especially in the consciousness of another. . . . Then the other

---

[62]Ibid., 15.
[63]Ibid., 1-7, 11-13, 15-16.
[64]John W. Nevin, "Worldly Mindedness," *WM*, 15 July 1840.
[65]Nevin, HF, 3-11, 14-15, 17. See also Appel, *Recollections*, 250-55, 269-72; Nevin, "Brownson's Review," 33-80, 111, 307-24; Schaff, *Principle of Protestantism*, 169.

lives only in us, as we live in him. Thus both are identical, and each lays his whole soul into his identity."[66]

Nevin's later writings (after 1870) reinforce Rauch's notion. Love and its corresponding reality, the good, is said to be the "very life of the will" just as wisdom and truth are said to be "the very life of the understanding." But love is the "first essence or substance" of human life, while wisdom is derivative and dependent. Freedom is "simply the will's love determining itself toward its own end." That end, indeed the only true end for human willing and understanding, is God.[67] In Nevin's view, true freedom overcomes the opposition between individual autonomy and universal law. It is the only remedy to the error of individualism in American culture and religion.

Conclusion

Hodge did not fully grasp the wider ramifications of the nominalistic tradition in which he stood (namely, Scottish Realism). He was more aware of the dangers which German idealism posed to theology and philosophy than the dangers of his own philosophical tradition. He did not systematically trace the roots of individualism to a particular philosophy as Nevin had done. As a consequence of these two factors, Hodge and Nevin pursued divergent paths in their struggle with revivalism and individualistic religion. While Nevin's path ran through German idealism and Romanticism, Hodge's path ran through Scottish Realism and American Presbyterianism.

Whatever differences there were between Hodge and Nevin, it is clear that they also represented two divergent aspects of American culture and religion. Mercersburg's polemic with Princeton was a critique of the prevailing American ethos. Nevin believed that the incipient materialism, skepticism, and individualism overrunning the land were not simply contemporary trends. They were part of the general fabric of American life. The nominal-

---

[66]Rauch, *Psy*, 349; see also 317-19.
[67]Nevin, "Bible Anthropology," 342-43, 350, 364. This article is the fullest articulation of Nevin's later position. See also Nevin, "The Bread of Life," 29, 37, 39-40.

ism of the empirical tradition, which magnified the actual at the expense of the ideal, was now running its course. Princeton was also disturbed by these developments and attempted to address them in its own way. So far as Mercersburg was concerned, however, Princeton was part of the problem not the solution.

The organic unity of church and society depend, at least in part, upon our perception of the whole and its relation to the parts. To the degree that we regard ourselves primarily as individuals, or even groups (placing the part before the whole), our ecclesiastical and political structures will never rise above the level of a voluntary association. Here, unity and organic wholeness are nothing more than nominalistic abstractions. Only the individual is real and enduring. The organization is, by comparison, an arbitrary convention. This inherently unstable structure will, in the end, give way to self-interest, chaos, and secession.

Historically, however, the tendency toward democracy, voluntarism, and decentralization in our society is a legitimate reaction against top-heavy organic structures (political and ecclesiastical) that have become too powerful and bureaucratic. It is essential, therefore, that the rights and freedoms of the individual be preserved while, at the same time, avoiding the error of radical individualism and balkanization. In Nevin's view such a balance cannot be achieved simply by legislation, reorganization, or even education—though these are necessary. Rather, these external arrangements must be the spontaneous outgrowth of a deeper sentiment which originates not in politics or business, but in the transforming and leavening power of religion in society.

Unity and freedom begin with the love of God. Not, however, by way of natural religion or even individual Christianity (these are dim and fragmentary at best), but through the mediatorial life of Christ supernaturally present in the church and its ministry. "The soul," says Nevin, "takes its quality and complexion always from the objects with which it is accustomed most intimately and habitually to converse." Participation in this spiritual world of powers leads to a kind of apotheosis, so that by beholding the glory of Christ the inner person is changed into His likeness. "This spiritual vision imparts a heavenly complexion to his soul, answerable to its own object."[68] In the end, it is only as we are taken up into the transcendental reality of this Trinitarian communion, through the ministry of the word and sacrament, that we come to realize the archetype of organic unity and individual freedom. This realization is the only passage that leads finally from the "all" to the "whole."

---

[68]Nevin, *Party Spirit*, 12; idem, *Seal*, 8.

Conclusion

John W. Nevin's transcendental hermeneutics is, perhaps, one of the most penetrating and sophisticated theological systems to emerge from American soil. Such a comment, of course, immediately invites comparisons to other luminaries of the past such as Jonathan Edwards. Though Nevin lacked the historical impact of Edwards, his thought was, in many respects, equally profound. Both shared a kind of Platonic view of reality by which they discerned "images of divine things" throughout creation. Both addressed the revivalism of their day. Both were philosophically minded.

But the most important similarity between the New England divine and the Mercersburg doctor was an interest in synthesizing contemporary Anglo-American philosophy with idealism. For Edwards this synthesis primarily involved a combination of Lockean empiricism with Puritan Platonism. For Nevin it entailed a hybrid of Common Sense Realism, Puritan and post-Kantian Platonism, and German idealism.

Despite Nevin's scathing criticisms of Common Sense, he never intended to abandon it altogether. As we have seen, his emphasis on the ideal and the spiritual is balanced by a historical and sacramental (that is, empirical) emphasis rooted in the Incarnation of Christ. The ideal and the spiritual must, in his view, actualize themselves in time and space in the same way the Son of God revealed Himself to us in human flesh. Even Nevin's realism, which was pivotal to his theology and hermeneutics, was tempered by Common Sense nominalism. As his biographer observed, though "some generalities, such as the State, the Church, the race, humanity, the law of life, life itself, corporeity and others" possessed a "concrete existence" for Nevin, "as a general thing he regarded the mass of our conceptions and ideas as mere abstractions formed by the human mind, or as he was accustomed to call them, 'abstract generalities.'"[1]

Though Nevin is often looked upon as a stranger among his own countrymen, in many ways this synthetic approach reflects the tapestry of nineteenth-century American life with its spectrum of immigrant communities and its practical tendency to borrow, adapt, and even improve European technology and ideas. Despite his love for German thought and his severe criticism of American culture and religion, Nevin's system was in many respects an American theology.

It would, however, be too much to call Mercersburg a "Common Sense theology." Nevertheless, approaches to Nevin's thought may be found in some forms of contemporary American theology. In *A Common Sense Theology*, Mark Ellingsen argues that postliberal and biblical narrative theologies possess a certain affinity for the American tradition of Common Sense. Though there are important methodological differences, narrative theology is, in many respects, the closest contemporary counterpart to Mercersburg. In Nevin's view, the Incarnation is the story which, to use the words of Eric Auerbach, "is not satisfied with claiming to be a historically true reality—it insists that it is the only real world, is destined for autocracy. All other scenes, issues, and ordinances . . . will be given their due place within its frame. . . . Far from seeking like Homer, merely to make us forget our reality for a few hours, it seeks to overcome our reality; we are to fit our own life into its world, feel ourselves to be elements in its structure of universal history."[2]

For Nevin, Christianity is not primarily a feeling or a set of propositions (though it includes both), but "a Life"—a system of life rooted in the incarnation of Christ.[3] Like a narrative it infolds a praxis, a faith, indeed, an entire reality into its expansive context. It is not simply an *aspect* of our life in this world, but an order of existence in its own right. The new creation in Christ, as he so

---

[1]Appel, *LW*, 294.

[2]Eric Auerbach, *Mimesis*, trans. Willard Trask (Princeton NJ: Princeton University Press, 1953) 14-15; cited in Mark Ellingsen, *A Common Sense Theology. The Bible, Faith, and American Society*, StABH 9 (Macon: Mercer University Press, 1995) 27. Auerbach was referring to the narrative world of Scripture in general.

[3]See Nevin, *MP*, 213.

aptly remarked, "comprehends in itself a world of laws, actions, powers, results, etc.,—all comprehended in the mediatorial work, which flows from His person."[4]

The similarities between narrative theology and Mercersburg theology do not end with hermeneutics. The narrative significance of the Incarnation event, according to Alister McGrath, is "that God really became involved in our world of space and time, that God really entered into history, that God really came to meet us where we are."[5] Likewise, Nevin regarded the Incarnation as an actual *historical* entrance of the Divine life into the world. Here is where narrative theology and Mercersburg theology part company with Transcendentalism, pantheism, rationalism, and mysticism. Christian revelation is not a subjective impulse, a universal law of reason, or a form of natural theology. The Incarnation is supremely *historical*. Through it, the supernatural becomes natural not by putting off its own distinctive character, but, in Nevin's words, "by falling into the regular process of the world's history, so as to form to the end of time indeed its true central stream."[6]

Philosophically, Nevin's epistemology shares common ground with the religious epistemology of Karl Barth, the grandfather of narrative theology. For Mercersburg, as for Barth, Christ is the foundational, epistemic norm for all theology and knowledge. Reason and experience are meaningful only insofar as they find their center in Christ. Indeed, for Nevin, Gerhart tells us, "Jesus, the Word made flesh, the Christ of God, became with him the principle of theology, and of all sound philosophic thought."[7] As with Barth, the Incarnation provides the context by which we interpret not only *our* world, but all of reality as well. It is the

---

[4]Erb, *NT,* 244. As he wrote in 1840, "The principles, views, sentiments and affections, by which this life works, are peculiar, proceeding from God and always flowing toward Him. Together they make up a complete organic existence, symmetrical, self-consistent, and altogether distinct from the experience of life under any other view." Nevin, "Worldly Mindedness," *WM,* 24 June 1840.

[5]Alister McGrath, *Christian Theology: An Introduction* (Cambridge: Blackwell, 1994) 173.

[6]Nevin, *MP,* 246.

[7]Gerhart, "John Williamson Nevin: His Godliness," in "A Memorial Service," *MR* 34 (1887): 15.

cosmic metanarrative in which all other narratives must find their place.[8]

Consequently, Nevin's transcendental hermeneutics is a clarion call not only to abandon the materialism, skepticism, and radical individualism of American society, but to end our methodological infatuation (obsession? pathology?) with human experience and subjectivity which dominates so much of our theology and church life today. At the same time, it confronts our continuing preoccupation with the Enlightenment, and its naive assumptions about scientific objectivity, by challenging us to recognize the inherent limitations and hermeneutical bias of the historical-critical method.

Though theologians and church leaders have often decried the vagaries of American society, many continue to espouse a bottom-up theology rooted in human experience and/or historical criticism. However, all of these elements are logically interconnected. To affirm the theological priority of human experience (postmodernism) or the autonomy of human reason (modernism) entails an implicit affirmation of the very elements of western culture which many contemporary theologians and churches find so distasteful.

It is disingenuous to scorn American materialism and religious skepticism, on the one hand, while implicitly affirming the naturalistic presuppositions that make it possible on the other. Nevertheless, this is precisely what we find in many quarters of the religious academy and the church today. The repudiation of supernaturalism (that is, the top-down view of reality), the rejection of Christ's divine sonship, the denial of miracles, and the belief that the Bible is no different than any other book, are conclusions which ultimately rest upon historicism and naturalistic first principles. Yet, it is astounding to see how many otherwise astute thinkers fail to recognize the incongruity between their rejection of cultural materialism and their indebtedness to philosophical materialism.

---

[8]On Nevin's antifoundationalism, his anticipation of postliberalism, and the similarities between Barth's view of revelation and Nevin's belief that revelation is a divine, historical act, see Layman, "Revelation in the Praxis of the Liturgical Community," chaps. 11–12. In many other areas, including "natural theology" and cosmology, Barth and Nevin are poles apart.

The same might be said of individualism. Professors bemoan the religious individualism of their students and their utter disdain for religious community. Clergy deplore the sectarianism and disunity which plague their church and denomination. Yet many of these scholars and ministers also insist upon a radically individual religious hermeneutic. Recent controversies over homosexuality in the Episcopal church (and other mainline denominations) clearly demonstrate this. The interpretation of the Scriptures, the creeds, and the liturgy is largely the prerogative of the individual. Each person is free to practice the Christian faith in accordance with his or her personal experience. Organic unity has little to do with doctrine and practice (issues of social justice being the exception). Rather, it consists in our willingness to worship Christ together. Here again, those who condemn the self-styled individualism of American society apparently see no contradiction in promoting "designer" religion—so long as we do it together.

At every turn, then, sections of the religious academy and the church, have indiscriminately adopted (in whole or in part) the very elements of American society of which they so strongly disapprove. The church's hermeneutical tradition has been rejected in favor of naturalism, historicism, and individualism. Truth, salvation, and holiness have been replaced by inclusivity, tolerance, and free speech.[9] But, such inclusivity and tolerance come at a high price. For, if we listen closely to the rhetoric of inclusivity and social justice advocated by some church leaders, feminists, and liberation theologians, it is, at bottom, a form of humanism rather than theism.[10] In other words, our humanity, according to this

---

[9]Within the church, an appeal to free speech is sometimes made by clergy and laypeople against the "intolerance" of traditional theology. However, this again confuses the church with society. Even in a constitutional democracy, private institutions (such as the church) may place limitations on free speech as a condition of membership. Indeed, one would be hard pressed to find an organization which does not exercise such restrictions. Could a lawyer or representative of the ACLU be a vocal advocate for racism or neo-Nazism? Even the most tolerant church would be strained to make room for such an individual. The appeal to free speech is not only spurious, therefore, but inconsistent and selective as well.

[10]See the introduction. This is not to discount the valuable insights that these theologies have provided. They have opened our eyes to the plight of the poor, women, and other oppressed groups, and to the systemic injustices they have

view, is more fundamental than our faith. What binds us together as humans matters more than our belief in Christ. Consequently, "purely" theological issues are of little importance when compared to issues dealing directly with *human* justice and freedom. To expect conformity in matters purely theological is considered intolerant, but to expect conformity and compliance in matters of social justice is considered virtuous.

The growth of religious pluralism in the church and academy completes the cycle of cultural conformity, mirroring a similar trend in the society at large. The reduction of religion to social ethics represents the common denominator which unites the world's religions, enabling them to finally work together for justice and peace. Significantly, this is also an argument from natural law, since these ethical principles are derived primarily from an analysis of human needs and human nature, rather than revelation.[11] It is no coincidence that natural law (primarily by way of deism) also provided the historical basis of American constitutional democracy. As a result, even the first principles of what we have called "bottom-up" theology are a reflection of American culture.

The story of the Incarnation, on the other hand, entails an entirely different vision of reality. Here, we come face to face with a supernatural order of existence and a transcendental hermeneutic. This hermeneutic, which is embodied by the Catholic tradition, is not the product of white Europeans, political oppressors, or affluent elitists (so the hermeneutics of suspicion). Instead, it was born in the midst of the suffering, poverty, and persecution of the early

---

suffered at the hands of religious, political, and social institutions down through history. As I have pointed out, Nevin's emphasis on the Incarnation and the historical immanence of revelation shares some common ground with liberation theology and other praxis oriented systems.

[11]Pluralists may find support for the principles of social justice in the Scriptures. But, since they reject the revelatory nature of the Bible (as traditionally defined), the veracity of these principles is not *dependant* upon Scripture (as it would be for orthodoxy).

church.[12] For that reason it is eminently qualified to address the economic, political, and ethical concerns raised by social justice.[13]

Such issues find their proper context only within the sacramental reality of the new creation where the presence of Christ is felt, above all else, through His word. This is more than an aesthetic appreciation for the text, or an invitation to enter the literary world generated by the text (Ricoeur). It is an encounter with the supernatural substance of the text (what Nevin called the "theopneustic sense"), which carries with it all the power and authority of the risen Christ.

In his review of *The Literary Guide to the Bible* (ed. Robert Alter and Frank Kermode; Harvard, 1988), George Steiner criticizes the failure of literary hermeneutics to discern this sense of the numinous in Scripture. Instead, we are led into an aesthetic experience of the text which omits that which is essential. As Steiner explains, "the plain question of divine inspiration—of orders of imagining and composition signally different from almost anything we have known since—must be posed, must be faced squarely and unflinchingly. . . . "[14]

As Nevin maintained, the meaning of Scripture can only be grasped when we hear it speak from its own element which is the life and power of Christ. Even more fundamental than an understanding of the Bible's grammar and history (though these are

---

[12]As Thomas Oden points out, "The classic ecumenical consensus was maturely formed well before the formation of Europe. . . . It is implausible to think of the martyrs of the Decian persecution as winners, or Athanasius, who was exiled a half-dozen times and chased all over the Mediterranean world as a winner. . . . " Oden goes on to mention John Chrysostom, Jerome, and a dozen other prominent names in this context. See Thomas C. Oden, *Life in the Spirit: Systematic Theology: Volume Three* (San Francisco: Harper, 1992) 488-91.

[13]Like all good things, this tradition has been misinterpreted and exploited by tyrants and oppressors in the past. However, to conclude from this that it is inherently oppressive is to ignore its historical and theological derivation.

[14]George Steiner, "Books," *The New Yorker*, 11 Jan. 1988, 97; see also Krister Stendahl, "The Bible as a Classic and the Bible as Holy Scripture," *JBL* 103/1 (1984): 3-10. As Rudolph Otto has shown, there is a qualitative difference between an aesthetic experience and a numinous encounter. The two are not, of course, mutually exclusive. A numinous encounter can be an aesthetic experience, but every aesthetic experience is not a numinous encounter. See *The Idea of the Holy*, 41-49, 147-49, 160-61.

necessary) is a true faith which holds directly to Christ in and through the apostolic life and teachings of the church. This is the only proper context for Scripture. Like all literature the Bible can never be rightly interpreted when it is severed from the life out of which it springs. Apart from the spiritual order revealed in Jesus Christ, the Bible is only a composite of commands, stories, poems, letters, etc., thrown together willy-nilly. It is a body without a soul.

The apostolic or Catholic tradition (what Thomas Oden calls, "Proximate Consensus"), then, provides the hermeneutical lens through which Scripture is correctly understood.[15] However, this tradition is not simply an object of historical curiosity or reflection. It is the narrative community in which we live, move, and have our very being. We must, as Nevin said, stand in the truth, have sympathy with it, and feel the authority that belongs to it in order to do justice to its presence. In short, we must consciously plant ourselves within the horizon of the new supernatural creation we are called to contemplate.

Lex orandi, lex credendi.[16]

---

[15]See Oden, *Life in the Spirit*, 473-501; DiPuccio, "Hermeneutics and the Rule of Faith: An Ancient Key to Biblical Interpretation," *Premise* 2/9 (October 1995): http://capo.org/premise/95/oct/p950905.html (021298). Following Walter Bauer, some scholars still insist that heresy actually predates orthodoxy. On the logical and chronological priority of orthodoxy, and the notion of a guarded tradition, see Vittorino Grossi, "Heresy—Heretic," in *Encyclopedia of the Early Church*.

[16]A hermeneutical translation: "The way of prayer is the context of belief."

Bibliography

I. Primary Works

Unpublished

Nevin, John Williamson. "Ethics." Lectures transcribed by J. A. Huber, 1873–1874. AMsS. Archives of the United Church of Christ and the Evangelical and Reformed Historical Society, Lancaster PA.

_____. "History of Philosophy Lectures." Transcribed by George B. Russel (1850–1851). AMsS. Archives of the United Church of Christ and the Evangelical and Reformed Historical Society, Lancaster PA.

_____. "Lectures on Aesthetics." Transcribed by George D. Gurley, 1870–1871. AMsS. Archives of Franklin and Marshall College. Uncatalogued.

_____. "Moral Philosophy." Lectures transcribed by E. K. Eshbach, 1868. AMsS. Archives of the United Church of Christ and the Evangelical and Reformed Historical Society, Lancaster PA.

_____. "Moral Philosophy." Lectures transcribed by J. Conrad Hauler, 1861. AMsS. Archives of the United Church of Christ and the Evangelical and Reformed Historical Society, Lancaster PA.

Published

Alexander, James W. "The Doctrine of Perception, as held by Doctor Arnauld, Doctor Reid, and Sir William Hamilton." _Princeton Review_ 31 (1859): 177-206.

_____. Review of _Psychology: or a View of the Human Soul_, by Frederick A. Rauch. In _Princeton Review_ 12 (1840): 393-410.

Appel, Theodore. "Atomology." _Mercersburg Review_ 23 (1876): 227-47.

_____. _The Life and Work of John Williamson Nevin_. Philadelphia: Reformed Church Publishing House, 1889.

_____. _Recollections of College Life at Marshall College_. Reading PA: Daniel Miller, 1886.

_____. "A Sketch of Marshall College, Mercersburg, Pa. from 1836–1841. Under the Presidency of Dr. Rauch." *Reformed Quarterly Review* 34 (1887): 518-47.

Apple, Thomas G. "Christian Life Deeper Than Conscious Experience." *Reformed Quarterly Review* (January 1883): 40-64.

_____. "The True Doctrine of Realism in its Bearing on Theology." *Mercersburg Review* 17 (1870): 571-92.

Bomberger, J. H. A. "The Rule of Faith." *Mercersburg Review* 1 (1849): 44-68, 347-71.

Brownson, Orestes A. "The Mercersburg Hypothesis." *Brownson's Quarterly Review* 16 (April 1854): 253-65.

_____. "The Mercersburg Theology." *Brownson's Quarterly Review* 12 (July 1850): 353-78.

_____. "Reply to the Mercersburg Review." *Brownson's Quarterly Review* 12 (April 1850): 191-228.

Calvin, John. *Institutes of the Christian Religion*. Two volumes. Edited by John T. McNeill. Translated by Ford Lewis Battles. Library of Christian Classics 20. Philadelphia: Westminster Press, 1960.

Coleridge, Samuel Taylor. *The Collected Works of Samuel Taylor Coleridge*. Edited by Barbara E. Rooke. Volume 1, *The Friend*. Princeton NJ: Routledge & Kegan Paul, 1969.

_____. *The Complete Works of Samuel Taylor Coleridge*. Edited by W. G. T Shedd. Volume 1, *Aids to Reflection*. New York: Harper & Brothers, 1858.

Dubbs, J. H. "Nominalism and Realism." *Mercersburg Review* 16 (1869): 165-79.

"Emanuel Swedenborg." *Mercersburg Review* 23 (1876): 120-57.

Erb, William H., ed. *Dr. Nevin's Theology, Based on Manuscript Class Room Lectures*. Reading PA: I. M. Beaver, 1913.

Gerhart, Emanuel V. "The Fall and the Natural World." *Mercersburg Review* 12 (1860): 505-24.

_____. "The German Reformed Church." *Bibliotheca Sacra* 20 (1863): 1-78.

_____. "The Interpretation of the Parable." *Mercersburg Review* 10 (1858): 578-99.

_____. *An Introduction to the Study of Philosophy with an Outline Treatise on Logic*. Philadelphia: Reformed Church Publishing Board, 1857.

_____. "John Williamson Nevin: His Godliness." In "A Memorial Service." *Reformed Quarterly Review* 34 (1887): 13-19.

_____. "Man: His Relation to Nature and to God." *Mercersburg Review* 21 (1874): 624-638.

_____. "Mansel's Limits of Religious Thought." *Mercersburg Review* 12 (1860): 294-318.

_____. *Prolegomena to Christian Dogmatics.* Lancaster PA: Lecture Printing Society of the Theological Seminary of the Reformed Church, 1891.

_____. "Religion and Christianity." *Mercersburg Review* 11 (1859): 483-505; 12 (1860): 251-68.

Hegel, G. W. F. *The Encyclopaedia Logic (with the Zusätze).* Third edition (1830). Translated with Introduction and notes by T. F. Geraets, W. A. Suchting, and H. S. Harris. Indianapolis: Hackett Publishing, 1991.

Henry, Matthew. *Matthew Henry's Commentary on the Whole Bible.* Six volumes. Repr.: Peabody MA: Hendrickson Publishers, 1991.

Hodge, Charles. "Doctrine of the Reformed Church on the Lord's Supper." *Princeton Review* 20 (1848): 227-78.

_____. "Nature of Man." *Princeton Review* 37 (1865): 111-35.

_____. *Systematic Theology.* Three volumes. New York: Scribner, 1872–1873; repr.: Grand Rapids MI: Wm. B. Eerdmans Publishing Co., 1981.

_____. "Thornwell on the Apocrypha." *Princeton Review* 17 (1845): 268-282.

_____. "The Unity of the Church Based on Personal Union with Christ." In *History, Essays, Orations, and Other Documents of the Sixth General Conference of the Evangelical Alliance,* ed. Philip Schaff and S. Irenaeus Prime, 139-44. New York: Harper & Brothers, 1874.

_____. "What Is Christianity?" *Princeton Review* 32 (1860): 119.

Hume, David. *An Enquiry Concerning Human Understanding.* In *English Philosophers of the Seventeenth and Eighteenth Centuries,* 305-445. Harvard Classics, ed. Charles W. Eliot, no. 37. New York: P. F. Collier & Son Company, 1910.

Kant, Immanuel. *Religion Within the Limits of Reason Alone.* Translated with an introduction and notes by Theodore M. Greene and Hoyt H. Hudson, and an essay by John R. Silber. New York: Harper & Row, 1960.

Kieffer, Moses. "Dogmatic Theology. Its Conception, Sources, and Method." *Mercersburg Review* 12 (1860): 451-78.

King, Hiram. "The Mission of Philosophy." *Mercersburg Review* 23 (1876): 211-26.

Locke, John. *An Essay Concerning Human Understanding.* Critical edition. Edited with an introduction by Peter H. Nidditch. Oxford: Clarendon Press, 1975.

_____. *The Works of John Locke. A New Edition, Corrected.* Volume 2, *An Essay Concerning Human Understanding.* Fifth edition (1706). London: Thomas Tegg et al., 1823; repr.: Darmstadt: Scientia Verlag Aalen, 1963.

Nevin, John Williamson. "The Active Christian." *The Friend,* 22 August 1833.

_____. "Aesthetics: I. The Idea of Beauty." In Theodore Appel. *The Life and Work of John Williamson Nevin,* 667-85. Philadelphia: Reformed Church Publishing House, 1889.

_____. "Allegoric Vision." *The Friend,* 18 July 1833.

_____. "The Anglican Crisis." *Mercersburg Review* 3 (1851): 359-97.

_____. "Answer to Professor Dorner." *Mercersburg Review* 15 (1868): 534-646.

_____. "The Anti-Creed Heresy." *Mercersburg Review* 4 (1852): 606-19.

_____. *Antichrist, or the Spirit of Sect and Schism.* New York: John S. Taylor, 1848.

_____. *The Anxious Bench.* 2nd ed. Chambersburg: M. Kieffer & Co., 1846.

_____. "Apollos: or the Way of God." *Mercersburg Review* 21 (1874): 5-41.

_____. "The Apostles' Creed." *Mercersburg Review* 1 (1849): 105-26, 201-21, 313-46.

_____. ed. "An attempt to explain the Laws of Nature, in a series of letters, addressed to Louis Marchand, M.D., of Uniontown, Pa., by his friend and former pupil, David Porter, M.D. LETTER II." *The Friend,* 9 May 1833–11 July 1833; 18 December 1834–12 March 1835.

_____. "Arianism." *Mercersburg Review* 14 (1867): 426-44.

_____. "Athanasius." *Mercersburg Review* 14 (1867): 445-57.

_____. "Athanasian Creed." *Mercersburg Review* 14 (1867): 624-27.

_____. "Bible Anthropology." *Mercersburg Review* 24 (1877): 329-65.

_____. "Bible Christianity." *Mercersburg Review* 2 (1850): 353-68.

_____. *Biblical Antiquities.* Two volumes. Philadelphia: American Sunday School Union, 1829, 1830.

_____. "The Bread of Life: A Communion Sermon." *Reformed Quarterly Review* 26 (1879): 14-47.

_____. "Brownson's Quarterly Review." *Mercersburg Review* 2 (1850): 33-80.

_____. "Brownson's Review Again." *Mercersburg Review* 2 (1850): 307-24.

_____. *Catholic and Reformed : Selected Theological Writings of John Williamson Nevin.* Edited by Charles Yrigoyen, Jr. and George H.

Bricker. Pittsburgh Original Texts and Translations, ed. Dikran Y. Hadidian, no. 3. Pittsburgh: Pickwick Press, 1978.

_____. "Catholic Unity." In *The Mercersburg Theology*, ed. James H. Nichols, 35-55. New York: Oxford University Press, 1966. Originally published in Philip Schaff, *The Principle of Protestantism*, 193-215. Chambersburg PA: Publication Office of the German Reformed Church, 1845.

_____. "Catholicism." *Mercersburg Review* 3 (1851): 1-26.

_____. *Christ, and Him Crucified. A Concio ad Clerum, Preached in Grace Church, Pittsburgh, November 18, 1863, at the opening of the First General Synod of the German Reformed Church in America.* Pittsburgh: Synod of the German Reformed Church in America, 1863.

_____. "Christ and His Spirit." *Mercersburg Review* 19 (1872): 353-93.

_____. "Christ the Inspiration of His Own Word." *Reformed Quarterly Review* 29 (1882): 5-45.

_____. "Christian Hymnology." *Mercersburg Review* 8 (1856): 549-87.

_____. "The Christian Ministry." *The Weekly Messenger of the German Reformed Church*, 27 May 1840.

_____. "Christianity and Humanity." *Mercersburg Review* 20 (1873): 469-86.

_____. "Christianity and Humanity." In *History, Essays, Orations, and Other Documents of the Sixth General Conference of the Evangelical Alliance*, ed. Philip Schaff and S. Irenaeus Prime, 302-308. New York: Harper & Brothers, 1874.

_____. *The Church: a sermon preached at the opening of the Synod of the German Reformed Church at Carlisle, October 1846.* Chambersburg: German Reformed Church Publishing House, 1847.

_____. "The Church Year." *Mercersburg Review* 8 (1856): 456-478. In Theodore Appel, *The Life and Work of John Williamson Nevin*, 462-80. Philadelphia: Reformed Church Publishing House, 1889.

_____. *The Claims of the Bible Urged upon the Attention of Students of Theology. A Lecture, Delivered November 8, 1831, at the Opening of the Winter Session of the Western Theological Seminary of the Presbyterian Church.* Pittsburgh: D. & M. Maclean, 1831.

_____. "The Classis of Mercersburg." *Mercersburg Review* 1 (1849): 379-88.

_____. "Closing Notice." *Mercersburg Review* 4 (1852): 620.

_____. ed. "Coleridge and German Philosophy." *The Friend*, 27 June 1833.

_____. ed. "The Coleridge Philosophy," *The Friend*, 4 July 1833.

_____. "Commencement Address." *Mercersburg Review* 14 (1867): 485-508. In Theodore Appel, *The Life and Work of John Williamson Nevin*, 634-54. Philadelphia: Reformed Church Publishing House, 1889.

_____. "Cur Deus Homo?" *Mercersburg Review* 3 (1851): 220-38.

_____. "Cyprian." *Mercersburg Review* 4 (1852): 259-77, 335-87, 417-52, 513-63.

_____. "Doctrine of the Reformed Church on the Lord's Supper." *Mercersburg Review* 2 (1850): 421-548. Reprinted and enlarged from "Review and Criticism of Hodge on the *Mystical Presence.*" *The Weekly Messenger of the German Reformed Church*, 24 May–9 August 1848.

_____. "Dr. Berg's Last Words." *Mercersburg Review* 4 (1852): 283-304.

_____. "The Dutch Crusade." *Mercersburg Review* 6 (1854): 67-116.

_____. "Dorner's History of Protestant Theology." *Mercersburg Review* 15 (1868): 260-90, 325-66.

_____. "Early Christianity." *Mercersburg Review* 3 (1851): 461-89, 513-62; 4 (1852): 1-54.

_____. "Education." *Mercersburg Review* 18 (1871): 5-19.

_____. "Educational Religion." *The Weekly Messenger of the German Reformed Church*, 23, 30 June 1847; 7, 14 July 1847.

_____. "Election Not Contrary to a Free Gospel." *The Presbyterian Preacher* 2 (1833): 209-24.

_____. "The Elements of Christian Science." *Mercersburg Review* 3 (1851): 285-95.

_____. "Essay on the Interpretation of the Bible." *The Friend*, 10 April; 9, 16, 30 May; 6, 13 June; 11, 18, 25 July; 1, 22 August 1833.

_____. "Ethics: I. Lemmata; II. Virtue; III. The Good." In Theodore Appel. *The Life and Work of John Williamson Nevin*, 687-97. Philadelphia: Reformed Church Publishing House, 1889.

_____. "Eulogy on the Rev. Dr. Rauch." *Mercersburg Review* 11 (1859): 442-66.

_____. "Evangelical Radicalism." *Mercersburg Review* 4 (1852): 508-12.

_____. ed. "Evidences of Christianity." *The Friend*, 16 January 1834.

_____. "Faith." *The Weekly Messenger of the German Reformed Church*, 12, 19, 23 February; 4, 11, 18 March 1840.

_____. "Faith, Reverence and Freedom." *Mercersburg Review* 2 (1850): 97-116.

_____. "Fairbairn's Typology." *Mercersburg Review* 4 (1852): 76-80.

_____. "False Protestantism." *Mercersburg Review* 1 (1849): 194-97.

_____. *Fancy Fairs*. N.p., 1843.

_____. "Franklin and Marshall College." *Mercersburg Review* 5 (1853): 395-419. In Theodore Appel, *The Life and Work of John Williamson Nevin*, 445-54. Philadelphia: Reformed Church Publishing House, 1889. This address was delivered at the formal opening of Marshall College in Lancaster PA, 7 June 1853, Fulton Hall.

_____. *The German Language. An Address Delivered before the Goethean Literary Society of Marshall College, at Its Anniversary, August, 29 1842.* Chambersburg PA: Publication Office of the German Reformed Church, 1842. Reprinted from *The Weekly Messenger of the German Reformed Church*, 21 September 1842.

_____. ed. "German Philosophy in America." *The Friend*, 11 September 1834.

_____. "The German Professorship." *The Weekly Messenger of the German Reformed Church*, 8 March 1843.

_____. *The Goethean Hall; or the Anniversary of Goethe's Birth-Day, August 28, A. D. 1846, in Mercersburg.* Chambersburg PA: Goethean Literary Society of Marshall College, 1846.

_____. "The Grand Heresy." *The Friend*, 5 February 1835.

_____. "The Heidelberg Catechism." *Mercersburg Review* 4 (1852): 155-86.

_____. "The Heidelberg Catechism." *The Weekly Messenger of the German Reformed Church*, 9 December 1840–14 April 1841; 27 April–24 August 1842.

_____. "Historical Development." *Mercersburg Review* 1 (1849): 512-14.

_____. *History and Genius of the Heidelberg Catechism.* Chambersburg PA: Publication Office of the German Reformed Church, 1847.

_____. "Hodge on the Ephesians." *Mercersburg Review* 9 (1857): 46-82, 192-245.

_____, trans. "The Holy Eucharist: An Extract from Theirsch's Lectures." *Mercersburg Review* 3 (1851): 446-60.

_____. *Human Freedom and A Plea for Philosophy: Two Essays.* Mercersburg: P. A. Rice, 1850. Reprinted from "Human Freedom," *The American Review: a Whig journal devoted to politics and literature* 7 (April 1848): 406-18; "A Plea for Philosophy." *The American Review: a Whig journal devoted to politics and literature* 7 (February 1848): 143-55.

_____. "The Idea of God." *The Friend*, 5 February 1835.

_____. "Inaugural Exercises: 'The Christian Ministry.'" *Mercersburg Review* 7 (1855): 68-115.

_____. "The Inspiration of the Bible: The Internal Sense of Holy Scripture." *Reformed Quarterly Review* (1883): 5-39.

_____. "Is the Bible of God?" *The Friend*, 23 January; 13 March 1834.

_____. "Jesus and the Resurrection." *Mercersburg Review* 13 (1861): 169-90.

_____. "Kirwan's Letters." *Mercersburg Review* 1 (1849): 229-62.

_____. Letter to Henry Harbaugh, ca. 1860–1867. In *Catholic and Reformed : Selected Theological Writings of John Williamson Nevin*, 407-11. Edited by Charles Yrigoyen Jr. and George H. Bricker. Pittsburgh Original Texts and Translations, ed. Dikran Y. Hadidian, no. 3. Pittsburgh: Pickwick Press, 1978.

_____. "The Letters of John W. Nevin to William R. Wittingham." Edited by David Hein. *Anglican and Episcopal History* 60 (June 1991): 197-211.

_____. "Liebner's Christology." *Mercersburg Review* 3 (1851): 55-72.

_____. "The Liturgical Movement." *Mercersburg Review* 1 (1849): 608-12. In Theodore Appel. *The Life and Work of John Williamson Nevin*, 482-85. Philadelphia: Reformed Church Publishing House, 1889.

_____. *The Liturgical Question with Reference to the Provisional Liturgy of the German Reformed Church.* Philadelphia: Lindsay and Blakiston, 1862.

_____. "The Lutheran Confession." *Mercersburg Review* 1 (1849): 468-77.

_____. "Man's True Destiny." *Mercersburg Review* 5 (1853): 492-520.

_____. "Modern Civilization." *Mercersburg Review* 3 (1851): 165-208.

_____. "The Moral Order of Sex." *Mercersburg Review* 2 (1850): 549-72.

_____. "Morell's Philosophy of Religion." *Mercersburg Review* 1 (1849): 400-406.

_____. *My Own Life: The Early Years.* Papers of the Eastern Chapter, Historical Society of the Evangelical and Reformed Church, no. 1. Lancaster: Historical Society of the Reformed Church, 1964. Originally published in seventeen articles in *The Weekly Messenger of the German Reformed Church*, 2 March–22 June 1870.

_____. *The Mystical Presence. A Vindication of the Reformed or Calvinistic Doctrine of the Holy Eucharist.* Philadelphia: J. B. Lippincott & Co., 1846.

_____. *The Mystical Presence and Other Writings on the Eucharist.* Edited by Bard Thompson and George Bricker. Philadelphia: United Church Press, 1966.

_____. "Natural and Supernatural." *Mercersburg Review* 11 (1850): 176-210.

_____. "Nature and Grace." *Mercersburg Review* 19 (1872): 485-509.

_____. "The New Creation." *Mercersburg Review* 2 (1850): 1-11.

_____. "The New Testament Miracles." *Mercersburg Review* 2 (1850): 573-84.

_____. "Noel on Baptism." *Mercersburg Review* 2 (1850): 231-64.

_____. "The Old Catholic Movement." *Mercersburg Review* 20 (1873): 240-94.

_____. "The Old Doctrine of Christian Baptism." *Mercersburg Review* 12 (1860): 190-215.

_____. "Once for All." *Mercersburg Review* 17 (1870): 100-24.

_____. "Origin and Structure of the Apostles' Creed." *Mercersburg Review* 16 (1869): 148-56.

_____. "Our Relations to Germany." *Mercersburg Review* 14 (1867): 627-33. In Theodore Appel, *The Life and Work of John Williamson Nevin*, 728-33. Philadelphia: Reformed Church Publishing House, 1889.

_____. *Party Spirit: An Address Delivered Before the Literary Societies of Washington College, Washington Pa. on the Evening of September 24th 1839.* Chambersburg PA: Publication Office of the German Reformed Church, 1840.

_____. *Personal Holiness. A Lecture Delivered, June, 1837, at the Opening of the Summer Term in the Western Theological Seminary.* Pittsburgh: William Allinder, 1837.

_____. "Philosophy of Dr. Rauch." *The American Biblical Repository*, 2nd ser. 10 (1843): 418-31.

_____. "Philosophy of History." *College Days* (Lancaster), January, February, March, April, May, June, November, December, 1873; January, February, March, April, May, October, November, 1874.

_____. "Philosophy of History." In Theodore Appel, *The Life and Work of John Williamson Nevin*, 591-601. Philadelphia: Reformed Church Publishing House, 1889.

_____. "The Pope's Encyclical." *Reformed Quarterly Review* 27 (1880): 5-50.

_____, trans. "Practical Exegesis: From an Article by *Neander* in the *Deutsche Zeitschrift* of Berlin, for February, 1850." *Mercersburg Review* 3 (1851): 152-65.

_____. "Preliminary Statement." *Mercersburg Review* 1 (1849): 1-9.

_____. "Presbyterian Union Convention." *Mercersburg Review* 14 (1868): 73-109.

_____. *The Presbytery of Ohio on the Claims of the Christian Sabbath; A Report Read and Adopted April 21, 1836, at a Meeting of the Presbytery held at Raccoon Church* . Pittsburgh: William Allinder, 1836.

_____, ed. "Professor Tholuck of Germany." *The Friend*, 3 July 1834.

_____. "The Psalms." *The Friend*, 11 September 1834.

_____. "Pseudo-protestantism." *Weekly Messenger of the German Reformed Church*, 13, 20, 27 August 1845; 3, 10 September 1845.

_____. "Publications." *Mercersburg Review* 1 (1849): 309-12.

_____. "Puritanism and the Creed." *Mercersburg Review* 1 (1849): 585-607.

_____. "Rauch's Psychology." *Weekly Messenger of the German Reformed Church,* 10 June 1840.

_____. "Religion a Life." *The Friend,* 25 Dec. 1834; 15, 22, 29 January 1835.

_____. "Reply to an Anglican Catholic." *Mercersburg Review* 21 (1874): 397-429.

_____. "The Revelation of God in Christ." *Mercersburg Review* 18 (1871): 325-42.

_____. "Sacred Hermeneutics." *MR* 25 (1878): 5-38.

_____. "Sartorius on the Person and Work of Christ." *Mercersburg Review* 1 (1849): 146-64.

_____. "Schaff's Church History." *Mercersburg Review* 3 (1851): 296-305.

_____. *The Scourge of God, a Sermon preached in the First Presbyterian Church, July 6, 1832, on the Occasion of a City Fast observed in reference to the approach of the Asiatic Cholera.* Pittsburgh: Johnston & Stockton, 1832.

_____. *The Seal of the Spirit: A Sermon, the substance of which was preached in the Presbyterian Church at Uniontown, Pa. January 21, 1838.* Pittsburgh: William Allinder, 1838.

_____. "The Sect System." *Mercersburg Review* 1 (1849): 482-507, 521-38.

_____. ed. "Sound Reasoning." *The Friend,* 29 May 1834.

_____. "The Spirit of Prophecy." *Mercersburg Review* 24 (1877): 180-212.

_____. "The Spiritual World." *Mercersburg Review* 23 (1876): 501-27.

_____. "The Supreme Epiphany; God's Voice Out of the Cloud." *Mercersburg Review* 25 (1878): 211-57.

_____. "The Testimony of Jesus." *Mercersburg Review* 24 (1877): 5-33.

_____. "The Theology of the New Liturgy." *Mercersburg Review* 14 (1867): 23-66.

_____. "Thoughts on the Church." *Mercersburg Review* 10 (1858): 169-98.

_____. "Trench's Lectures." *Mercersburg Review* 2 (1850): 604-19.

_____. "The Trinitarian and Unitarian Doctrines Concerning Jesus Christ." *The Presbyterian Preacher* 1 (1832): 64-80.

_____. "True and False Protestantism." *Mercersburg Review* 1 (1849): 85-104.

_____. "Undying Life in Christ." In Theodore Appel, *The Life and Work of John Williamson Nevin,* 607-27. Philadelphia: Reformed Church Publishing House, 1889.

_____. "The Unity of the Apostles' Creed." *Mercersburg Review* 16 (1869): 313-17.

_____. *Vindication of the Revised Liturgy, Historical and Theological.* Philadelphia: Jas. B. Rodgers, 1867.

_____. "Wilberforce on the Eucharist." *Mercersburg Review* 6 (1854): 161-86.

_____. "Wilberforce on the Incarnation." *Mercersburg Review* 2 (1850): 164-95.

_____. "Woman's Rights," *American Review* 2 (October 1848): 367-81.

_____. "The Wonderful Nature of Man." *Mercersburg Review* 11 (1859): 317-37. In Theodore Appel. *The Life and Work of John Williamson Nevin,* 515-28. Philadelphia: The Reformed Church Publishing House, 1889.

_____. "A Word of Explanation." *Mercersburg Review* 4 (1852): 202-205.

_____. "Worldly Mindedness." *Weekly Messenger of the German Reformed Church,* 24 June; 1, 15, 22, 29 July; 5 August 1840.

_____. "The Year 1848." *Mercersburg Review* 1 (1848): 10-44.

_____. "Zacharias Ursinus." *Mercersburg Review* 3 (1851): 490-512.

_____. "Zwingli No Radical." *Mercersburg Review* 1 (1849): 263-72.

Nichols, James H., ed. *The Mercersburg Theology.* New York: Oxford University Press, 1966.

Plato. *The Dialogues of Plato. Great Dialogues of Plato.* Translated by W. H. D. Rouse. New York: Mentor, 1984.

Rauch, Frederick Augustus. "Faith and Reason." *Mercersburg Review* 8 (1856): 80-93.

_____. "Lectures on Aesthetics." In Theodore Appel, *Recollections of College Life at Marshall College,* 222-49. Reading PA: Daniel Miller, 1886.

_____. *Psychology; or, a View of the Human Soul.* New York: M. W. Dodd, 1840.

_____. *Psychology; or, a View of the Human Soul.* Fourth edition with a notice by John W. Nevin. New York: M. W. Dodd, 1846.

Reid, Thomas. *Thomas Reid's Inquiry and Essays.* Edited by Ronald E. Beanblossom and Keith Lehrer. Indianapolis: Hackett, 1983.

Reily, William M. "John Williamson Nevin, D.D., LL.D." *Magazine of Christian Literature* 2 (Sept. 1890): 324-327.

_____. "Schleiermacher and the Theology of the Mercersburg Review." *Mercersburg Review* 18 (1871): 165-182.

"The Relation of Adam's First Sin to the Fall of the Race." *Princeton Review* 42 (1870): 239-62.

"Rothe and Swedenborg." *Reformed Quarterly Review* 36 (1889): 139-66.

Schaff, David S. *The Life of Philip Schaff.* New York: Charles Scribner's Sons, 1897.

Schaff, Philip. ed. *A Commentary on the Holy Scripture by John Peter Lange. Romans*, by J. P. Lange, Philip Schaff, et al. New York: Charles Scribner's Sons, 1869; repr.: Grand Rapids MI: Zondervan, 1960.

_____. *The Principle of Protestantism.* Edited by Bard Thompson and George H. Bricker. Lancaster Series on the Mercersburg Theology. Philadelphia: United Church Press, 1964.

_____. *Reformed and Catholic: Selected Historical and Theological Writings of Philip Schaff.* Edited by Charles Yrigoyen, Jr. and George H. Bricker. Pittsburgh Original Texts and Translations Series, ed. Dikran Y. Hadidian, no. 4. Pittsburgh: Pickwick Press, 1979.

_____. *What is Church History? A Vindication of the Idea of Historical Development.* Philadelphia: J. B. Lippincott and Co., 1846.

Schleiermacher, Friedrich. *The Christian Faith.* Translated from the second German edition (1830). Edited by H. R. MaCkintosh and J. S. Stewart. Edinburgh: T. & T. Clark, 1928.

_____. *On Religion: Speeches to Its Cultured Despisers.* Translated from the third German edition (1831) by John Oman. New York: Harper & Row, 1958.

Scougal, Henry. *The Life of God in the Soul of Man.* N.p., 1739; repr.: Harrisonburg VA: Sprinkle, 1986.

Starbuck, Charles C. "Richard Rothe." *Reformed Quarterly Review* 34 (1887): 257-65, 393-403.

Swedenborg, Emanuel. *Arcana Coelestia.* Edited by John F. Potts. New York: Swedenborg Foundation, 1915.

_____. *A compendium of the theological writings of Emanuel Swedenborg.* Edited by Samuel M. Warren. New York: Swedenborg Foundation, 1875.

Thomas Aquinas. *Summa Theologica.* Five volumes. New York: Benziger Brothers, 1948; repr.: Westminster MD: Christian Classics, 1981.

Tyler, Samuel. "The Baconian Philosophy." *Princeton Review* 12 (1840): 350-77.

_____. "Connection between Philosophy and Revelation." *Princeton Review.* 18 (1845): 381-408. [Some bibliographies have incorrectly attributed this article to James Alexander. But, both the author and the editor identify it as the fourth in a series of articles written by the same hand. The first three articles have been positively identified as belonging to Tyler.]

_____. "The Influence of the Baconian Philosophy." *Princeton Review* 15 (1843): 481-506.

_____. "Sir William Hamilton and his Philosophy." *Princeton Review* 27 (1855): 553-600.

Ullmann, Karl. "Über den unterscheidenden Charakter des Christenthums mit Beziehung auf neuere Auffassungsweisen." *Theologische Studien und Kritiken* 18 (January 1845): 1-61. Translated and condensed in John W. Nevin, *The Mystical Presence. A Vindication of the Reformed or Calvinistic Doctrine of the Holy Eucharist*, 13-47. Philadelphia: J. B. Lippincott & Co., 1846.

II. Secondary Works

Adler, Mortimer J. *Ten Philosophical Mistakes*. New York: Macmillan, 1985.

Ahlstrom, Sydney E. *A Religious History of the American People*. New Haven CT: Yale University Press, 1972.

_____. "The Scottish Philosophy and American Theology." *Church History* 24 (1955): 257-72.

Angeles, Peter A. *Dictionary of Philosophy*. New York: Barnes and Noble Books, 1981.

Avens, Roberts. *Blake, Swedenborg, and the Neoplatonic Tradition*. New York: Swedenborg Foundation, n.d.

Barfield, Owen. *What Coleridge Thought*. Middletown CT: Wesleyan University Press, 1971.

Bendroth, Margaret Lamberts. "Women in Twentieth-Century Evangelicalism." *Evangelical Studies Bulletin* 13 (Spring 1996): 4-6.

Binkley, Luther J. *The Mercersburg Theology*. Manheim PA: Sentinel Printing House, 1953.

Bozeman, Theodore Dwight. *Protestants in an Age of Science: The Baconian Ideal and Antebellum American Religious Thought*. Chapel Hill: University of North Carolina Press, 1977.

Carey, Patrick. ed. *Orestes A. Brownson: Selected Writings*. New York: Paulist Press, 1990.

Carre, Meyrick H. *Realists and Nominalists*. London: Oxford University Press, 1946.

Conser, Walter H., Jr. *Church and Confession: Conservative Theologians in Germany, England, and America 1815–1866*. Macon GA: Mercer University Press, 1984.

Copleston, Frederick. *A History of Philosophy*. Nine volumes. New York: Image Press, 1946–1974; Westminster MD: Newman Bookshop, 1946–1974.

Courtenay, William J. "Ockham, William of." In *Dictionary of the Middle Ages*. New York: Charles Scribner's Sons, 1987.

DiPuccio, William. "Before Mercersburg: Nevin's Philosophy." *The New Mercersburg Review* 17 (Spring, 1995): 15-24.

_____. "The Dynamic Realism of Mercersburg Theology: The Romantic Pursuit of the Ideal in the Actual." Ph.D. diss., Marquette University, 1994.

_____. "F. A. Rauch." In *The Blackwell Dictionary of Evangelical Biography: 1730–1860*, ed. Donald Lewis. Cambridge: Basil & Blackwell, 1995.

_____. "The Foundations of Christian Theology: A Structural Study of the Philosophy and Prolegomena of the Mercersburg Theology." M.A. thesis, Wheaton College Graduate School, 1988.

_____. "Hermeneutics and the Rule of Faith: An Ancient Key to Biblical Interpretation." *Premise* 2/9 (October 1995): http://capo.org/premise/95/oct/p950905.html.

_____. "John Nevin." In *The Blackwell Dictionary of Evangelical Biography: 1730–1860*, ed. Donald Lewis. Cambridge: Basil & Blackwell, 1995.

_____. "Mercersburg and Contemporary Thought: The Incarnation as Meta-Narrative." *The New Mercersburg Review* 20 (Fall 1996): 29-52.

_____. "Nevin & Coleridge." *The New Mercersburg Review* 17 (Spring 1995): 59-63.

_____. "Nevin, John Williamson." In *Biographical Dictionary of Christian Theologians*, ed. Patrick W. Carey. Westport CT: Greenwood Press, forthcoming.

_____. "Nevin's Idealistic Philosophy." In *Reformed Confessionalism in Nineteenth-Century America: Essays on the Thought of John Williamson Nevin.* ed. Sam Hamstra, Jr. and Arie J. Griffioen. American Theological Library Association Monograph Series. Lanham MD: Scarecrow Press, 1995.

_____. "Philip Schaff: An Evangelical's Non-Evangelical." Review of *Cosmos in the Chaos: Philip Schaff's Interpretation of Nineteenth-Century American Religion* by Stephen R. Graham. In *Evangelical Studies Bulletin* 13 (Summer 1996): 3-4.

_____. "Schaff, Philip." In *Biographical Dictionary of Christian Theologians*, ed. Patrick W. Carey. Westport: Greenwood Press, forthcoming.

Ellingsen, Mark. *A Common Sense Theology: The Bible, Faith, and American Society.* Studies in American Biblical Hermeneutics 9. Macon GA: Mercer University Press, 1995.

Escobar, Samuel. "Liberation Theology." In *The Blackwell Encyclopedia of Modern Christian Thought*, ed. Alister E. McGrath. Cambridge: Basil Blackwell, 1993.

Fletcher, Angus. "Allegory in Literary History." In *Dictionary of the History of Ideas*, ed. Philip Wiener. New York: Charles Scribner's Sons, 1973.

Foriers, Paul, and Chaim Perelman. "Natural Law and Natural Rights." In *Dictionary of the History of Ideas*, ed. Philip Wiener. New York: Charles Scribner's Sons, 1973.

Formigari, Lia. "Chain of Being." In *Dictionary of the History of Ideas*, ed. Philip Wiener. New York: Charles Scribner's Sons, 1973.

Gerrish, B. A. "Friedrich Schleiermacher." In *Nineteenth Century Religious Thought in the West*, ed. Ninian Smart, John Clayton, Steven Katz, and Patrick Sherry, 1:123-56. Cambridge: Cambridge University Press, 1985.

_____. *Tradition and the Modern World: Reformed Theology in the Nineteenth Century*. Chicago: University of Chicago Press, 1978.

Gilson, Etienne. *The Unity of Philosophical Experience*. New York: Charles Scribner's Sons, 1950.

Graham, Stephen R. *Cosmos in the Chaos: Philip Schaff's Interpretation of Nineteenth-Century American Religion*. Grand Rapids: Eerdmans, 1995.

Griffin, Nicholas J. "Possible Theological Perspectives in Thomas Reid's Common Sense Philosophy." *Journal of Theological History* 41 (July 1990): 425-42.

Grossi, Vittorino. "Heresy-Heretic." In *Encyclopedia of the Early Church*, ed. Angelo Di Berardino. New York: Oxford, 1992.

Hagen, Kenneth. "The History of Scripture in the Church." In Kenneth Hagen, Daniel J. Harrington, Grant R. Osborne, and Joseph A. Burgess, *The Bible in the Churches*, 3-34. New York: Paulist, 1985.

Hamstra, Sam Jr., and Arie J. Griffioen, ed. *Reformed Confessionalism in Nineteenth-Century America: Essays on the Thought of John Williamson Nevin*. American Theological Library Association Monograph Series. Lanham MD: Scarecrow Press, 1995.

Henry, Carl F. H. *God, Revelation, and Authority*. Volume 1, *God Who Speaks and Shows: Preliminary Considerations*. Waco TX: Word Books, 1976.

Hill, Brennan R., Paul Knitter, and William Madges. *Faith, Religion, and Theology: A Contemporary Introduction*. Mystic CT: Twenty-Third Publications, 1990.

Hodgson, Peter C. "George Wilhelm Friedrich Hegel." In *Nineteenth Century Religious Thought in the West*, ed. Ninian Smart, John Clayton, Steven Katz, and Patrick Sherry, 1:81-122. Cambridge: Cambridge University Press, 1985.

Holifield, E. Brooks. "Mercersburg, Princeton, and the South: The Sacramental Controversy in the Nineteenth Century." *Journal of Presbyterian History* 54 (Summer 1976): 238-58.

Howe, Daniel Walker. "The Cambridge Platonists of Old England and the Cambridge Platonists of New England." In *American Unitarianism 1805–1865*, ed. Conrad Edick Wright, 87-117. Boston: Massachusetts Historical Society and Northeastern University Press, 1989.

Jones, Charles A. "Charles Hodge, the Keeper of Orthodoxy: The Method, Purpose, and Meaning of His Apologetic." Ph.D. diss., Drew University, 1989.

Jonsson, Inge. "Swedenborg, Emanuel." In *The Encyclopedia of Philosophy*, ed. Paul Edwards et al. New York: Macmillan Publishing Co. and the Free Press, 1967.

Kelly, J. N. D. *Early Christian Doctrines*. San Francisco: Harper & Row, 1978.

Kuklick, Bruce. *Churchmen and Philosophers*. New Haven CT: Yale University Press, 1985.

Layman, David. "Revelation in the Praxis of the Liturgical Community: A Jewish-Christian Dialogue, with Special Reference to the Work of John Williamson Nevin and Franz Rosenzweig." Ph.D. Diss., Temple University, 1994.

_____. "Was Nevin influenced by S. T. Coleridge?" *The New Mercersburg Review* 17 (Spring 1995): 54-58.

Leff, Gordon. *The Dissolution of the Medieval Outlook*. New York: Harper & Row, 1976.

Lovejoy, Arthur, O. *The Great Chain of Being: A Study of the History of an Idea*. Cambridge: Harvard University Press, 1936.

Maurer, Armand A. "Analogy in Patristic and Medieval Thought." In *Dictionary of the History of Ideas*, ed. Philip Wiener. New York: Charles Scribner's Sons, 1973.

McGrath, Alister E., ed. *The Blackwell Encyclopedia of Modern Christian Thought*. Cambridge: Basil Blackwell, 1993.

_____. *Christian Theology: An Introduction*. Cambridge: Blackwell, 1994.

Meyendorff, John. *Byzantine Theology*. New York: Fordham University Press, 1979.

Muller, Richard A. *Dictionary of Latin and Greek Theological Terms*. Grand Rapids MI: Baker, 1985.

Nichols, James H. *Romanticism in American Theology: Nevin and Schaff at Mercersburg*. Chicago: University of Chicago Press, 1961.

Noll, Mark, ed. *Charles Hodge: The Way of Life*. New York: Paulist Press, 1987.

_____. "Common Sense Traditions and American Evangelical Thought." *American Quarterly* 37 (Summer 85): 216-38.

_____. ed. *The Princeton Theology 1812–1921*. Grand Rapids MI: Baker Book House, 1983.

Oden, Thomas C. *Systematic Theology*. Volume 3, *Life in the Spirit*. SanFransico: Harper, 1992.

Orsini, G. N. G. *Coleridge and German Idealism: A Study in the History of Philosophy with Unpublished Materials from Coleridge's Manuscripts*. Carbondale: Southern Illinois University Press, 1969.

Otto, Rudolf. *The Idea of the Holy*. New York: Oxford University Press, 1950.

Patrides, C. A. "Hierarchy and Order." In *Dictionary of the History of Ideas*, ed. Philip Wiener. New York: Charles Scribner's Sons, 1973.

Payne, John B. "Schaff and Nevin, Colleagues at Mercersburg: The Church Question." *Church History* 61 (June 1992): 169-90.

Penzel, Klaus, ed. *Philip Schaff: Historian and Ambassador of the Universal Church. Selected Writings*. Macon GA: Mercer University Press, 1991.

_____. "The Reformation Goes West: The Notion of Historical Development in the Thought of Philip Schaff." *The Journal of Religion* 62 (July 1982): 219-41.

John Polkinghorne, "Physical science and Christian thought." In *The Blackwell Encyclopedia of Modern Christian Thought*, ed. Alister E. McGrath. Cambridge: Basil Blackwell, 1993.

Shriver, George H. "Passages in Friendship: John W. Nevin to Charles Hodge, 1872." *Journal of Presbyterian History* 58 (Summer 1980): 16-122.

_____. *Philip Schaff: Christian Scholar and Ecumenical Prophet*. Macon GA: Mercer University Press, 1987.

M. Simonetti. "Allegory—Typology." In *Encyclopedia of the Early Church*, ed. Angelo Di Berardino. New York: Oxford, 1992.

Skinner, Thomas M. Jr. "The Bible Its Own Witness and Interpreter." *Princeton Review* 32 (1860): 389-427.

Stace, W. T. *The Philosophy of Hegel: A Systematic Exposition*. London: Macmillan and Co., 1924.

Swander, John I. *The Mercersburg Theology*. Philadelphia: Reformed Church Publication Board, 1909.

Tarnas, Richard. *The Passion of the Western Mind*. New York: Ballantine, 1993.

Thiselton, Anthony. *New Horizons in Hermeneutics*. Grand Rapids: Zondervan, 1992.

Von Leyden, W. "What is a nominal essence the essence of?" In *John Locke: Problems and Perspectives,* ed. John W. Yolton, 224-33. Cambridge: Cambridge University Press, 1969.

Weber, T. P. "Bible and Prophetic Conference Movement." In *Dictionary of Christianity in America,* ed. Daniel G. Reid. Downers Grove IL: Intervarsity Press, 1990.

Welch, Claude. *Protestant Thought in the Nineteenth Century.* Two volumes. New Haven CT: Yale University Press, 1972.

_____. "Samuel Taylor Coleridge." In *Nineteenth Century Religious Thought in the West,* ed. Ninian Smart, John Clayton, Steven Katz and Patrick Sherry, 2:1-28. Cambridge: Cambridge University Press, 1985.

Wentz, Richard E. *John Williamson Nevin: American Theologian.* New York: Oxford University Press, 1997.

White, L. Michael. "Real Presence." In *Encyclopedia of Early Christianity,* ed. Everett Ferguson et al. Garland Reference Library of the Humanities volume 846. New York/London: Garland Publishing, 1990. Second edition: GRLH 1839. 1997.

Ziegler, Howard J. B. *Frederick Augustus Rauch: American Hegelian.* Manheim: Sentinel Printing House, 1953.

Index

The Interior Sense of Scripture.
The Sacred Hermeneutics of John W. Nevin.
  by William DiPuccio
Studies in American Biblical Hermeneutics 14 (StABH 14)

Mercer University Press, Macon, Georgia 31210-3960 USA.
Isbn 0-86554-568-5. Catalog and warehouse pick number: MUP/P167.
Text and interior designs, cover design, composition, and layout
  by Edmon L. Rowell, Jr.
Cover illustration: *Jesus with the Doctors* (Luke 2),
  a nineteenth-century woodcut (by A. Bertrano)
    of an illustration by (Paul-) Gustave Doré (1832–1883).
Camera-ready pages composed on a Gateway 2000
  via WordPerfect 5.1/5.2 and printed on a LaserMaster 1000.
Text font: (Adobe) Palatino 11/13 and 10/12.
Display font: (Adobe) Palatino 24-, 12-, and 11-point bf.
Printed and bound by McNaughton & Gunn Inc., Saline, Michigan 48176.
  Printed on web-fed 50# Writers Natural (500ppi).
  Perfectbound in 10-pt. c1s stock, printed one PMS color,
    and lay-flat laminated.

[March 1998]

021698elr